TWO IRELANDS

James MacKillop, *Series Editor*

TWO IRELANDS

LITERARY FEMINISMS NORTH AND SOUTH

Rebecca Pelan

Syracuse University Press

Copyright © 2005 Syracuse University Press
Syracuse, New York 13244-5160

First Edition 2005
05 06 07 08 09 10   6 5 4 3 2 1

The paper use in this publication meets the minimum requirements
of American National Standard for Information Sciences—Permanence
of Paper for Printer Library Materials, ANSI Z39.48-1984∞™

Library of Congress Cataloging-in-Publication Data

Pelan, Rebecca, 1954–
       Two Irelands : literary feminisms north and south / Rebecca Pelan.—1st ed.
          p. cm.—(Irish studies)
       Includes bibliographical references and index.
       ISBN 0-8156-3059-X (alk. paper)
     1. English literature—Irish authors—History and criticism.   2. Feminism and literature—
Ireland—History—20th century.   3. English literature—Women authors—History
and criticism.   4. Women and literature—Ireland—History—20th century.
5. Women—Northern Ireland—Intellectual life.   6. Feminism and literature—Northern
Ireland.   7. Women and literature—Northern Ireland.   8. Women—Ireland—Intellectual
life.   9. Northern Ireland—In literature.   10. Ireland—In literature.   11. Feminism in
literature.   12. Sex role in literature.   I. Title.   II. Series: Irish studies (Syracuse, N.Y.)
PR8733.P45   2005
820.9'9287'0941509045—dc22   2005002600

Manufactured in the United States of America

In memoriam:

To the first and best feminist in my life—

my Mum, Ruby (Blair) Pelan,

1920–2005

REBECCA PELAN is director/senior lecturer in women's studies at the National University of Ireland, Galway, and is general editor of *Irish Feminist Review*. She has held teaching positions at the University of Queensland in Brisbane, Australia, and the University of Ulster, Northern Ireland, and a research associateship at the Women's Research and Resource Centre, University College, Dublin. She has published extensively on the subjects of Irish women's writing, Edna O'Brien's fiction, feminist/literary theory, and women and the Troubles.

Contents

Acknowledgments *ix*

Introduction: "A Proper Object of Study"—Contemporary
  Women's Writing *xi*

1 Undoing That "Other" Conquest: *Women's Writing
  from the Republic of Ireland* *1*

2 The Unfinished Revolution: *Women's Writing
  from Northern Ireland* *52*

3 Surveying the New Minefield *102*

Works Cited *137*

Selected Readings *151*

Index *191*

Acknowledgments

SINCERE THANKS to Carole Ferrier and Barbara Garlick for their friendship and mentoring over many years. Thanks also to the staff—academic and administrative—of the School of English, Media Studies and Art History, the University of Queensland, Brisbane, Australia. In Ireland, I would like to thank Ailbhe Smyth, director of the Women's Education Research and Resource Centre (University College, Dublin), and Kathleen McCracken of the University of Ulster, for their generosity and kindness, and Anne O'Connor for her valued friendship and support in times of need. A very special acknowledgment and thanks to Mary Paul Keane for her editorial advice on an earlier draft and, more importantly, for her crucial contribution in getting so many Irish women writers of the contemporary period into print. I am also very grateful to Robyn Colwell for bringing to my attention the intertextual allusions to a number of Robert Frost's poems in Fiona Barr's story, *Wall Reader*. Finally, thanks to those who give me space as well as a reason for breathing—Trevor, Catherine, Robert, and wee James.

Introduction

"A Proper Object of Study"—Contemporary Women's Writing

> It is rare for historical research to accomplish the task of getting a society to contemplate its own identity without the help of literature. . . . The clues to the position of women in Irish history are invariably present in the literature of a particular phase of Irish history.
>
> —Margaret MacCurtain, "The Historical Image"

TRADITIONALLY, women writers in Ireland,[1] as elsewhere, have had to conform to and write in the permitted literary codes of their particular day; still others had to leave Ireland before they could write anything at all. But from the early 1970s, Irish women writers have needed to use neither code nor exile in order to express themselves but have been involved instead in radical cultural and literary practices that have allowed them to confront issues of gender, sexuality, and national/ethnic identity from within the country itself. Primarily, this shift has been facilitated by the second wave of the women's movement, which created a framework for women's voices to be heard and through which literature (re)gained its place as a key site for the articulation of political issues that directly affect women. As a result, the writing from this period represents an extremely valuable tool in assessing the relationship between a body of written work and the society that produced it.

1. I will be using the terms "women writers in Ireland" and "Irish women writers" interchangeably to identify women writers on the island of Ireland. On those occasions when it is necessary to make a distinction, I shall identify the writers as being from either the Republic of Ireland or Northern Ireland.

In concentrating on writing by Irish women since 1970 I am not, of course, suggesting that writers before the 1970s did not intervene in the political and cultural issues of their day. Rather, I am using this time of intense activity and change to investigate the somewhat obvious, but rarely stated, fact that altered contexts radically affect the content of creative production. But I am also interested in the effect of context on the development of a feminist consciousness. I am not going to claim, for instance, that the women's movement allowed Irish women miraculously to bypass somehow other dominant political movements—far from it, since it is clear in any investigation of the recent period that the contexts of religion, region, class, and national/ethnic identity have been equally crucial factors in shaping vastly different feminist consciousnesses in the north and south.

Nevertheless, as a means of examining the contribution of creative writing in facilitating change, I will concentrate principally on the body of radical fiction produced during the period from 1970 through the mid-1990s, a time when women's writing in Ireland proliferated as a body of work that, even from this short critical distance, appears to have had an unusually cohesive political agenda. I am also limiting myself to this time frame because contexts have changed again in the past few years and I no longer think it is possible to argue for a body of work produced by women in Ireland that represents any kind of collective creativity in the way the earlier writing did. Certainly there are still individual examples of the kind of gendered critique of Irish society found in the work of the earlier period, but, to a large extent, the intense literary activity directly associated with the second wave of the women's movement has passed, in Ireland and elsewhere.

This suggests that Irish women's writing during the period under study, though radical, was not revolutionary in nature since it has, without a great deal of resistance, been overtaken by a model that fits more comfortably with Ireland's substantial contribution to globalization. Recent changes, in fact, have demonstrated a reexploitation of the very stereotypes of Ireland that so much contemporary feminist activity challenged. This reexploitation of an Ireland that is homogeneously "green," indigenous, Catholic, and male continues to be most evident today in the extensive cultural commodification of "Irishness" evidenced through the marketing of multiple *River-*

dance clones and the success of made-to-measure Irish theme pubs that have proliferated even in places not conventionally associated with the Irish diaspora, such as Sweden, the Netherlands, and Japan. And, in keeping with an Ireland that the outside world wants to know (or be sold) rather than one that it perhaps should know, Irish chick lit has become the popular alternative to the bulk of women's radical fiction produced over the last thirty years. Novels such as Marian Keyes's *Watermelon* (1995) and *Lucy Sullivan Is Getting Married* (1996), Anne Dunlop's *Kissing the Frog* (1996), Clare Dowling's *Fast Forward* (2000), Claudine Cullimore's *Lola Comes Home* (2001), Sheila O'Flanagan's *He's Got to Go* (2002), or the collection *Irish Girls about Town* (2002) offer readers an Irish-style *Sex and the City* sassiness, a breezy preoccupation with looks, men, and careers by quirky young women—a considerable shift from the focus of earlier works, which generally concerned issues of family (usually dysfunctional) and religion (together with its impact on sexuality), as well as a variety of societal ills. This change of focus clearly has enormous appeal for young women readers both inside and outside Ireland: inside, perhaps, as a result of Ireland's newfound affluence and sophistication, which no longer sits well with a creative articulation of anger and bitterness about past ills. And outside? Well, outside Ireland the stereotype was never really even dented by the changes that went on within.

In terms of women's writing from the period under study, two anthologies were widely distributed outside Ireland: *Territories of the Voice*, edited by DeSalvo, D'Arcy, and Hogan (1989) and *Stories by Contemporary Irish Women*, edited by Casey and Casey (1990), both of which brought a healthy sampling of women's writing from north and south to audiences far away. To a large extent, however, most of the radical political writing discussed in this book stayed within Ireland, and now exists in Irish libraries or in the private collections of those of us interested in the field of contemporary Irish women's writing. I remember being at a noisy party in Australia, and an acquaintance asking me what I was working on. When I responded "Irish women's writing," he looked surprised and said, "I didn't think they had any." It turned out that, in the noise, he thought I had said "Irish women's rights" but ultimately decided that the same answer applied in both cases. And, so, despite a number of impressive achievements by Irish women of the period—not least the election of two successive women presidents—the period of change in Ireland appears not to have made the impact that once was hoped.

This raises some interesting questions concerning the relationship between the second wave and contemporary feminism in Ireland, as well as definitions of both. What I am examining here is a body of work that not only has clear links to the second wave of the women's movement but is also linked to a feminist agenda at the heart of which are two essential components: a sense of conscious, collective action and a gendered critique of hegemonic ideologies for the purpose of promoting change. This, of course, is not to argue that the writers had any clear or cohesive plan when they sat down to write. But I do suggest that much of that writing so clearly engages with and addresses aspects of postindependence/partitioned Irish society over which women have had little or no control, such as nationalist history, the alliance of church and state in the Irish Republic, and (predominantly male) unionist and nationalist politics in Northern Ireland. The writing of these women is an example of stories that have now been admitted into what Ken Plummer calls, in the context of narrative theory, "communities of memory"—in other words, stories that lie dormant and often never get told because they await "interpretive communities" (1995, 45).[2] The modern women's movement, together with its accompanying interest in women's stories and publishing, represents just such an interpretive community.

Ironically, this diverse set of contexts is perhaps the reason why the writing of modern Irish women has not had a greater long-term influence, given its quantity and singularity of vision. The body of radical fiction produced over the past thirty years cannot be classified, for instance, as a literary movement: certainly it shares an era and a location, and in its preference for realism may even be said to share a style, but in terms of its social and political impact on its societies, it had only a limited, albeit crucial, effect as a direct result of the fact that the writers were facilitated by a political movement rather than by a literary one. What is more, the content of this

2. The concept of "interpretive communities" first appeared in the work of Stanley Fish. See his *Is There a Text in This Class?* (Cambridge, Mass.: Harvard Univ. Press, 1980).

fiction was almost exclusively a response to existing strictures, sociopolitical and literary, that existed in Irish society. And since the effects of such strictures have been most keenly felt within the family in Ireland, it will come as no surprise to discover that the vast majority of contemporary women writers have used that institution to interrogate hegemonic ideologies, primarily through the eyes of a central female character or characters. This is creative writing that foregrounds the complexity of the relationship between women and their wider, political worlds not by juxtaposing ideologies of the family and the state but rather by critiquing the effects of dominant political ideologies *through* their impact on women and, by extension, their worlds, including the family. In doing so, the writers inevitably draw feminist discourses into existing dominant (male) discourses and alter our understanding of both.

The statement that the prolific growth of women's writing in Ireland, as elsewhere, over the past thirty years has had a direct connection to the second wave of the women's movement, whereby women's publishing and a newly aware community of women readers have demanded books that confront and deal with women's lives, is hardly contentious. Certainly, Irish women writers have responded to the enormous changes in their societies by writing and publishing in quantities greater than at any other time, although there remains a vast difference in the volume of women's publishing in the two Irelands. Certainly, too, much of the history of women's publishing in Ireland is similar to many other countries and can be attributed to the same influences. Comparisons, however, suggest that similar influences and conditions found in earlier periods did not bring about the same results.

Laurel Bergmann's study of New Zealand women's fiction throughout the 1970s and 1980s, for instance, offers a useful comparison to developments in the Republic of Ireland. Although Bergmann explicitly compares the situation in New Zealand with that of Australia, demographic statistics for 1994 (when her study was done) reveal that the Republic of Ireland was very similar to New Zealand in terms of population and sex distribution. In that year, the Republic of Ireland had a total population of 3,516,000, of which 49.74 percent were male and 50.26 percent female, while New Zealand had a population of 3,520,000, of which 49.26 percent were male and 50.73 percent female (*Encyclopaedia Britannica Year Book*).

Bergmann asserts that although the 1980s witnessed an explosion of local literary activity generally, there is little doubt that it was the "decade of women's fiction in New Zealand" because "women took advantage of the empowering force of the 'second wave' feminist movement, with renewed confidence in the standpoints from which they wrote, and in their collective ability to take on the entrenched institutions that had orchestrated their exclusion" (1994, 217). As in Ireland, a significant feature of this empowerment for New Zealand women writers was the establishment of women's presses, including university presses and feminist book festivals.

Despite similarities in the development of women's writing in the two countries, though, the major difference seems to be in the long-term state of women's publishing. In New Zealand, according to Bergmann, the health of women's writing and publishing throughout the 1970s and 1980s did not continue, and the future had become quite grim by the early 1990s as a result of what she describes as "intransigent government policies," (222) general economic constraints and the threat of multinational market dominance by Whitcoull's, a chain bookstore:

> Already New Women's Press appears to be defunct, Daphne Brasell has given up publishing fiction for the time being, and Bridget Williams says the future does not look hopeful. Whitcoull's aggressive discount selling is also a serious threat to independent bookstores. If the latter should close, it seems unlikely that Whitcoull's would be interested in promoting serious literature of any kind, particularly that which is challenging and is likely to have a small, select market. (223)

By contrast, and despite similar origins and history to that of New Zealand, women's writing and publishing in the Republic of Ireland continued to flourish during the same period in an economic environment no more favorable than New Zealand's.[3] There was a time between the mid-1980s and

3. The situation changed, of course, with the arrival of the "Celtic Tiger" economy in Ireland. But in 1994, Ireland's gross national product was US$10,780 per capita compared to New Zealand's GNP of US$12,000 per capita (*Encyclopaedia Britannica Year Book* 1994).

mid-1990s when writing by women in the Republic appeared to be everywhere. As readers, we were spoiled for choice, not just in volume but in diversity of genre: short stories, novels, plays, poetry, comics, feminist fairy tales. And all seemed to have one aim: to change the way women had been represented in Ireland in political, social, and literary contexts.

In 1985, for example, the Irish Arts Council estimated that Irish publishing accounted for 33 percent of the total book market in the Republic of Ireland with annual sales amounting to £16.3 million. By 1991, this figure had grown to 41 percent, with sales reaching £27.7 million, and sales rose to £28.6 million in 1993. In 1994, the Irish corner of the market had dropped slightly to 40 percent, with annual sales of £33.2 million. In the most recent survey of 1998, the figures show that Irish publishing has retained 40 percent of the total market in the Republic, with sales of £39.3 million. The number of full-time employees in the Irish book publishing industry in 1994 was 424, but this dropped slightly in 1998 to 396. New publications, however, rose from 790 in 1994 to 841 in 1998 (*Irish Book Publishing Survey* 1998).

What none of the statistical resources show in any detail, however, is the significant contribution made by women writers to the Irish publishing industry during this period. What information is available is sketchy. In 1983, for instance, a WIP (Women in Publishing) survey discovered that 11 percent of all books published in the Republic of Ireland in that year were written by women (Ferreira 1993, 99), while a 1991 publication survey conducted by the Cork-based poetry magazine *The Steeple* further indicated that, excluding Attic Press, women's writing had been taken up by many of the mainstream presses in the Republic: for example, by 1993, 5 percent of Dedalus Press, 16 percent of Gallery Press, 11 percent of Raven Arts Press, and 4.5 percent of Salmon Press books were written by women. In 2003, Dedalus Press estimated that 20 percent of its published poets were women, while the major publishing houses' catalogues indicate that books by women comprise between 14 percent and 20 percent of their total publications. Ann Owens Weekes's *Unveiling Treasures* says, significantly, that since the early 1990s, women and men in the Irish Republic have been publishing at comparable rates (Weekes 1993, 6). And, of course, the continued appearance of Irish women's books in (mainstream) bookshops represents an ongoing and important connection between the production of literature and Irish society, whereby the writing does not exist in isolation from national and international literatures.

Yet this clear connection between improved publishing opportunities and women's writing and publishing has never in itself ensured the quality and consistency of political engagement so evident in contemporary Irish women's writing throughout the period: an engagement that is by no means always in existence in other countries where the women's movement has had an equal if not more profound effect. This remarkable level of politicization in Irish writing can be traced to a number of sources: conservative, repressive, and intransigent ideologies and cultural mythologies in both the Republic and Northern Ireland that were so extreme in their representation and treatment of women they all but invited the radical challenges they have received; the particular histories of the first and second waves of the women's movement in Ireland that facilitated such radicalism; and, finally, the existence in Ireland of a strong tradition of *littérature engagée*; although this tradition has been conventionally associated with Irish men writers, it confirms, when applied to women writers, Carol Coulter's theory that Ireland has long fostered a "subterranean tradition" of women's incursion into public life that is both subversive and radical (1993, 3). In a sense, then, the politics of this body of writing has been revisionist and iconoclastic in intent.

Today, much feminist revisionist work is in the very capable hands of historians, sociologists, and political scientists. But during the early period of women's political activity, it was women's creative practices that provided some of the most important attempts to revise images of women in Ireland, something that reflects the conventional understanding of how different practices and disciplines function, perhaps. Whereas historians, sociologists, and political scientists tend to concentrate on the position of women and men in society, creative production, including writing, is more concerned with images and representations. The effect of these differences, especially evident at an institutional level in the field of women's studies, is that the importance of women's creative practices—as either a mobilizing force or a strategy of resistance—has been seriously neglected or underestimated, more often considered these days as simply a reflection of what is going on in the political arena rather than as a central contributing factor to change.

At the same time, an awareness of the complexities involved in the use of the term *feminism,* to represent the broad philosophical and discursive movement now popularly associated with the women's movement generally, means that a prerequisite of any discussion of women's writing is the need to make explicit certain disjunctions between it—as cultural product—and other aspects of feminism: an acknowledgment that, for instance, not all women writers are feminist, or that not all texts that lend themselves to positive feminist analysis will be written by women. Having acknowledged that *dis*connections exist, however, it is equally important to acknowledge the connections since, in Ireland, so much of this radical women's writing forms an integral part of a discursive, revisionist feminist cultural practice, despite the fact that many of the writers would not comfortably consider their work to be part of any feminist discourse or agenda.

The women's writing under study here was central to the landscape of "popular" fiction of its day. Since the mid-1990s, however, that landscape has changed, along with the kind of fiction that becomes "popular." Poolbeg, for instance, was one of the major publishers of the radical, political fiction produced in Ireland between 1970 and 1995. It is now the major publisher of Irish chick lit, a shift that confirms what we already know: that publishers follow the vagaries of the market rather than committing to any particular politics or genre.

The "passing" of the period and its artifacts provides a pressing reason to examine the changes that led to the creation of the work, as well as the changes that have taken us in a different direction. Since so much is contained within the writing from the early period to neglect it is to lose much of the activism and energy of the period.

As always, however, a significant challenge in any discussion of women's writing from a specific place and time lies in the undefined and often ambivalent relationship between feminist and literary theory, between politics and lived experience. It is evident that not all women writers are necessarily feminist or even politically motivated. Nevertheless, most women writers in print today, old or new, owe something to the women's movement: through re/publishing opportunities created by women's presses, through the challenge to hegemonic literary discourses, through the effect feminism has had on how their work is read, or even through the often unacknowledged space that feminism has created for a broad spectrum of women's voices to be heard. Put simply, it would be difficult to imagine the position of women's writing today without a framework of feminism, whatever internal disputes it may contain. This book takes as a given, then, the fact that the second wave of feminism from the 1970s onward was a politically oriented movement and, thus, any effects that movement may have in the production, writing, reception, or reading of women's writing provide sufficient evidence for a strong connection between feminist politics and women's creativity.

There is perhaps no greater evidence of that connection in Ireland than the justifiable furor that erupted following the publication of the *Field Day Anthology of Irish Writing* in 1991 (ed. Seamus Deane et al.), promoted in America as "a landmark event in twentieth-century literature" and "the most comprehensive exhibition of the wealth and diversity of Irish literature ever published" (Ferreira 1993, 97). Criticism of the three-volume anthology centered not only on its scarcity of women writers and the absence of women from its editorial board, but on its disregard for historical events significant to Irish women generally. The bulk of the criticism came from within Ireland and Europe, spearheaded by prominent Irish feminists— and, importantly, not just writers—and led to the establishment of a women's editorial board of the *Field Day Anthology*, made up of women from both sides of the border, and, eleven years later, to the publication by Cork University Press of two new volumes of the anthology, dedicated to Irish literary women and subtitled *Irish Women's Writing and Traditions* (Bourke et al, 2002).

In one of the first reviews of the new anthology, *Irish Times* literary editor Eileen Battersby criticized the long-awaited project on a number of grounds, not least what she refers to as "the sociological agenda stalking these ambitious, new volumes": "We don't need roll calls or inventories at this stage of our cultural evolution. We want exploration and textual analysis. Sheer force of numbers does not necessarily confer quality" (2002, 10). Later in her review, she writes, "The emphasis and approach in most sections is more sociological than textual or scholarly; as for the conventionally literary, that only arrives halfway through the second volume—and then it is whistle-stop" (10).

The question that is begged here, of course, is why we would still be looking for the "conventionally literary" after all that has gone on since 1970 in terms of the shifts in and challenges to the conventional. In her review, Battersby also criticizes the inclusion of so much journalism in what she clearly feels should have been qualitative literature-based volumes, and she feels that the women's volumes will sit uncomfortably on the shelf with the earlier volumes of the anthology. To some extent, I agree with her, but not for the same reasons. For me, the critical expectations placed on volumes 4 and 5 were simply too great for any project to meet. While the original *Field Day Anthology* exists as a good example of Irish (mostly men's) writing in predominantly historical contexts, volumes 4 and 5 were awaited as something much more: they were going to be, for many, the line in the sand that would divide the history of women's writing on one side from a new beginning on the other, when all that inequality rubbish could be seen to have been dealt with. The fact that no body of work could possibly live up to these expectations seems to have gone unnoticed, and, as a result, in place of any real critical analysis of its achievements (or otherwise), there is an immense sense of disappointment that the "women's anthology" didn't quite live up to the success of the earlier volumes, which were a different literary project altogether. As for any project, there are all kinds of criticisms that could be directed at volumes 4 and 5—the very evident absence of a general editor to oversee the project being just one of them—but to demand that the project be judged by the critical values that had been directly undermined by so much of the writing contained within its covers seems highly questionable to me.

Women's writing has not necessarily been a strictly literary project for a very long time, if, in fact, it ever was. This is not to suggest that standards of literary quality should not or do not any longer apply, but it does point to the fact that the naming of a "women's" anything should introduce alternative modes of analysis, critique, and criticism. Recognizing the multiple purposes of women's writing would involve interdisciplinary approaches that would see women's journalism as an integral component of the *political* aspect of the project. According to Imelda Whelehan, to divide the numerous forms of expression women have used to convey a feminist message is to fragment a body of thought that is entirely symbiotic. She argues, in fact, that the main strength of modern feminist thought is its interdisciplinarity, its resistance to easy categorization. Any attempt to repartition feminist thought into discipline-oriented categories is to perform an act of phallocentric vandalism. Whelehan argues that in order to understand properly the full range of feminist critiques, it is necessary to appreciate that its resistance to categorization is a part of its radicalism (1995, 3). To compare the "women's" volumes of the anthology with the earlier ones, then, is to compare apples and pears.

Equally, the women's writing discussed throughout this book forms an integral component of a multi- and interdisciplinary movement in which such creative practices exist comfortably alongside other forms of writing and feminist practices: Nell McCafferty's journalism, for instance, Pat Murphy's films, Ailbhe Smyth's academic and creative work, Margaret Ward's writing of Irish women's history, and Rita Duffy's paintings. In all cases, at its heart, this body of work has the project of either writing women into Ireland or revising their existing images and places in the traditions.

My rationale, then, for including in my study of Irish feminist women's writing such a broad range of selections is the assertion that there are clear material connections between contemporary women's creative writing as a body of work and the political movement that grew out of the second wave of feminism, which has been so important to the production of that work. For while it is easy to accept that such writing does not always necessarily conform to any strict definition of *feminist*—however or by whomever that might be defined—it is evident that as a body of work it clearly bears the marks of influence of the women's movement. This influence is evident, if not in the forms or themes of the texts themselves, then in their production and reception as related to the positions of women as both writers and readers within societies that have been affected by the contemporary women's movement.

As a result of these relationships between women's writing of the contemporary period and the conditions of its production, I am equally interested in examining a diverse set of contexts that have contributed to the particular shape of Irish feminism as it exists today. This includes popular understandings of Irish (male) history and nationalist mythology, which have played an important part in women's writing in Ireland during the contemporary period. My argument throughout is underpinned by the fact that the ability of creative texts to facilitate or contribute to change is always contingent upon those contexts—social, political, historical, and institutional—that produce them. Women's writing from Ireland, like women's writing from other places, is neither a strictly modern phenomenon nor produced in a vacuum. Rather, it is integrally connected with the many influences that inform it, influences that vary depending on which tradition we are talking about.

The differences in women's cultural production on both sides of the Irish border clearly reflect the development of two distinct political systems. The remnants of Civil War antagonisms, combined with an increasing embourgeoisement of the population and lack of industrialization in the modern Republic all contributed to the marginalization of the Left there, generally. This lack facilitated the development of an oppressive conservative alliance between the Catholic Church and the new Irish state, which is in direct contrast to the development of a sectarian, industrialized working class in the north.

Monica McWilliams, for instance, maintains that the women's movement in Northern Ireland has been most effective in bringing about political change in working-class communities, and in this respect it differs from its more middle-class contemporaries in other places (1991, 91), including the Republic of Ireland. This is also the case in relation to women's creative practices in Northern Ireland, where the production of women's writing, as well as its particular brand of feminism, has been and continues to be most influential at the community level. The retention of an emphasis on class and community activity in women's writing from Northern Ireland is very evident when examined in relation to women's writing from the Republic. In other words, distinctions in the political sphere have played a central role in women's creative practices during the contemporary period.

Chapter 1 of this book concentrates on the Republic of Ireland while chapter 2 examines contemporary women's writing from Northern Ireland. Both show that women's writing of the contemporary period has been almost obsessively concerned with the sociopolitical status of women under hegemonic nationalist regimes in modern Ireland. And while we know that Irish history did not begin with partition, it is the case that the bulk of women's writing in Ireland during the period under study concerns itself, again almost exclusively, with popular understandings of the oppressed position of women in Ireland, which is considered to be brought about entirely by events of the 1920s to 1960s, such as the coalition between the Roman Catholic Church and the nascent Irish nation, the 1937 constitution, and the role of women as family carers.

As a result, the construction of political and cultural myths took place on a number of levels. This myth building not only facilitated the development of an Irish national identity different from that of Britain—as part of the establishment of a postindependence identity in the Irish Republic—but, at the same time, contributed to the development of two separate identities in Northern Ireland. Within the republic and for the nationalist community in Northern Ireland, literature historically played a central role in the construction of nationalist mythology and identity. As a result, there is evidence in the contemporary period of literature equally being put to use by women in a reverse, demythologizing process. No such literary tradition exists in unionist or Protestant mythology, which may well explain why there are so few examples of Protestant or unionist women's writing.

In light of these differences, I will address, particularly in chapter 2, the fact that other genres, especially drama, have played a crucial part in creating a body of work in Northern Ireland that is both wonderfully creative *and* contributory to feminist politics and discourses. In the Republic, women writers of the period have tended to produce novels and short stories in large quantities compared to their writing in other genres. In contrast, Northern Irish women have been less prolific prose fiction writers and have tended to use both poetry and drama as a means of confronting their respective communities.[4] As a result, I will tend to deal in a more emphatic way with the formative influences of women's drama in the north than with drama from the Irish Republic. Again, this is not to assert that one genre is

---

4. I will not be dealing with poetry of the period here since it has been well covered by Patricia Boyle Haberstroh in her *Women Creating Women: Contemporary Irish Women Poets* (New York: Syracuse Univ. Press, 1996).

preferable to another, or that one group of women have been more successful than another, but simply that different material conditions have produced quite different creative practices and products.

Any analysis of contemporary women's writing from Ireland implies
two important things: first, the way in which women and their creative
practices get talked and written about so often belies the existence of important differences between women in Ireland; second, and relatedly, that
Irish women have exploited a framework of feminism to achieve an impressive level of success in interrogating existing notions of themselves, but
have done so relative to the particular contexts in which they write. So
while it may *appear* that women in the Republic of Ireland have achieved
more than women in Northern Ireland, when we examine women and their
cultural practices within the specifics of their production, we can see how
unfair a straightforward comparison is.

Women's writing from Northern Ireland may be compared in several
ways with that from the Irish Republic and elsewhere—in the choice of
realism as a preferred mode, for example, and in the use of a central, female
protagonist who is an integral member of her particular community and
through whom the author chooses to say something about that community.
But women's writing from the two Irelands also exhibits significant differences: the quantity of literary output, for example, as well as differences in
the development of genres between north and south, tells us immediately
that women's writing in the two places has had quite separate production
histories.

In pointing out the differences, I am not attempting to deny that it is
often desirable—for ease of discussion as well as for strategic purposes—
to retain homogeneous categories called "Irish women's writing" or "Irish
feminism." Gayatri Spivak's proposal of a "strategic use of essentialism in
a scrupulously visible political interest" (1987, 205) suggests that even
though we may be generally opposed to notions of essentialism and homogeneity, it is often politically strategic for a group—of women, of Aborig-
ines, of workers—to conceal their diversity and be identified as a cohesive
unit in order to present a political identity and position from which to fight.
But this "strategic essentialism" should not stop us from critical investigations into the ways women's writing or feminism has developed in different

places. And, however much we might want or wish for women in a small country like Ireland to have commonality with each other and with other feminisms, the truth is that life for women, as women and as writers, is very different on each side of the Irish border. Without a close examination of women's work within the specifics of its production, creativity often not only looks impoverished but conservative or, worse, regressive. This is especially the case when women's writing from Northern Ireland is compared with that from the Irish Republic, or when Irish women's writing as a whole is compared with the writings of women from other industrialized countries.

Any examination of the relationship between creative writing and politics involves, by extension, an examination of the ways in which women's writing shares certain features relating to the imaginative or creative re/presentation of women in its various communities. Consideration of the influence of the contemporary women's movement is required in Ireland by a dominant view of history as ostensibly neutral and ungendered, and a heavily gendered body of literature. But they need to be examined also alongside influential theories of revisionism and postcolonialism, which have had a profound effect on critical debate in Ireland. The outcome of the reexamination thus needs to be seen as one example of the many ways in which representations of collective histories, whether of women, nations, or individuals, whether literary or political, are constantly being contested and reproduced.

Clearly, these are vast topics and contexts, and it would be impossible to do justice to them all in one book. But what I will try to do is provide a taste of those crucial determinants that have contributed to contemporary Irish feminism and, in turn, to women's writing of the period. What I will not attempt is an allocation of qualitative critical value to the writing—that is an equally valuable, but quite different project, and one in which much of the writing discussed here would not be included. Some of the writers included here wrote very little and earn their living in ways other than as authors. Others consider themselves to be writers in the broadest and most serious, literary sense, but they all become important in this context because they contributed—in whatever small way—to attempting to alter the representation of women in Ireland during a precious period of literary activity that needs to be recognized and contextualized so as not to be lost to us forever. Rather than in any context of literary achievement, I will discuss the value of this writing as a body of work that is realist, identity-based, and socially engaged and that not only contributed to bringing about changes in Irish society but that clearly represents an example of how certain contexts can create not just a body of writing by women but a feminist oppositional discourse.

As such a discourse, contemporary Irish women's writing from the Irish Republic and from the north shares two particular features. First, to varying degrees, it serves a counterhegemonic function, and, second, it uses certain narrative features associated with feminist writing, such as central female characters, narrative structures, and speaking positions, to retain distinct strategic identities.

This concept of identity has always been central to Irish national politics and writing, of course. But the traditional polarization of Irish politics and historiography into Irish/English, nationalist/unionist, and, more recently, revisionist/postcolonial has meant that women, historically, have not only been forced to choose between such binaries in terms of their personal politics but have been represented as being confined within these political categories. As a result, they have often been trapped by the binaries themselves, or discussed in terms of conforming to one or the other. In contrast, a feminist framework in much contemporary Irish women's fiction has provided an alternative political stance through which issues relating to gender and nationality/ethnicity have been incorporated, permitting the writers to bypass such binaries to some extent.

Equally fundamental to this discussion is the premise that in the two Irelands, dominant ideologies of sovereignty have historically subverted issues of gender and class in favor of what are often outmoded nationalist politics. The effects of this have been varied but consistently detrimental to Irish women. Throughout the analysis that follows, I will be especially interested in the ways in which writing engages with and is affected by such dominant ideologies, and while I acknowledge that creative practices cannot simply be reduced to ideology, I will conclude that, as a cultural practice, the production of literature reflects, reacts to, or interacts with ideology either to affirm or subvert the socially/culturally constructed and, thus, historically changeable categories of "woman," "man," and "literature."

A further part of my interest in this book is the relationship between the evident shift in creative focus and the present condition of political feminism. The health of feminism as a whole relies on the fact that the specific nature of various feminisms—in this case Irish feminisms—be interrogated in an attempt to understand how such local or national movements have intersected with, yet functioned quite separately from, an equally heterogeneous, but immensely influential international movement. According to Irish feminist Anne Speed, for example:

> When we started out in the '70s [in Ireland], we had an expectation that if we in the Irish Women's Liberation Movement took the fundamental issues which women were discussing across the world and applied them in Ireland, then we could move forward in a straight line . . . we have *not* been able to fulfil that aspiration, mainly because of the kind of country we live in. (A. Smyth 1988b, 46)

With the benefit of hindsight, Speed is perhaps preemptive in 1988 in placing so much of the blame on the kind of country Ireland is since we now know that from the mid-1980s, the possibility of moving in a straight line in relation to the dominant Anglo-American women's movement was seriously and legitimately challenged by accusations of exclusivity and elitism from the marginalized voices of those women—black, women of color, working class, lesbian, to name a few—who felt that they were under- or unrepresented in what had become an increasingly homogenized and hegemonic feminist movement. The 1980s generally were not conducive to the possibility of a unified women's movement at either the national or international level, and yet, ironically, this was the most productive period for women's writing. But the shift toward acknowledging "difference" in the international movement, together with the localized split in the Irish women's movement and the apparent impossibility of defining the role of feminism in a nationalist movement within Ireland, complicated what had earlier seemed to be clear-cut objectives.

On the other hand, Speed accurately identifies that it was and is the relationship between contemporary Ireland "and its historical problems
which have carried forward into the present time" (A. Smyth 1988b, 46)
that was in large part responsible for frustrating attempts to fulfil the aspirations of women in Ireland to do what women in, say, England and the
United States were doing at the time. But, like other political movements,
feminism in Ireland has its own distinct history, and apart from a slightly
later start than some other feminist movements, the most obvious difference between it and that in other industrialized countries is that Irish feminism has always been overshadowed by one of the strongest nationalist
movements in modern history.

Specifically in relation to contemporary Irish women's poetry, Patricia
Boyle Haberstroh has shown that if we read between the lines of the debate
concerning what Irish women can and cannot say in their writing, a much
deeper image emerges: "The traditional image of woman in Irish culture lies
at the heart of this problem, and the expressions and ramifications of that
image, so deeply embedded in the Irish psyche, are just beginning to be ex-
plored. If we are to understand the marginalized woman poet, we must first
study the marginalized woman in Ireland" (1996, 13).

Part of the reason for the occlusion of Irish women's achievements, outside the country in particular, is the result of a critical difficulty associated
with the recognition of Ireland as a minority culture, which results from a
number of factors. Geographically, racially, and economically, for instance,
Ireland is perceived to be part of Western Europe and many of its men writers are valued within the canon of English literature, factors that contribute
to Ireland's exclusion from contemporary theoretical debates about marginality and difference. In addition, there is the problem of Ireland's part in
contributing to the population of so many other countries and suffering
(literally) from a romanticized and sentimentalized image that has been difficult to shake. The dominant representation of Ireland and its people, the
centrality of Irish history as well as the enterprise of re/presenting and
re/imagining what it means to be an Irish or Northern Irish "woman" in
order to challenge creatively the presentations and images that have existed for so long, have meant that Irish women's writing has often been
assessed as somewhat retrograde in light of its continued emphasis on

(male-dominated) history and the choice of realism by women writers as a framework in which to discuss that history. This has led to an analysis of the contemporary period of productivity in Irish women's writing as being anomalous or aberrant in some way, rather than as an integral part of an on-going and radical feminist cultural practice. As a result, critical investigations into the diverse ways women's writing and feminism have intersected politically in specific cultural contexts have been neglected.

In expressing their disappointment at the lack of engagement with contemporary women's writing in particular, Batsleer and colleagues point to the failure of critics to extend their critical interest to such writing "so that feminists could really claim contemporary writing as a proper object of study and work, and so that feminist criticism could speak to contemporary readers about contemporary writing as well as about past traditions" (1985, 113; emphasis added). Part of this critical reluctance to investigate the connections between specific examples of contemporary women's fiction and feminist politics is no doubt due to the nature of feminist literary criticism itself, whereby an emphasis on the recovery of lost or marginalized women's texts has been such an important part of its development. This has resulted in limiting the discussion of connections between much of that fiction and a movement that had no apparent historical relevance to its production. However, another reading of this lack of critical interest in contemporary fiction, generally, relates to a recapitulation of a more traditional distinction between the categories of popular and elite culture, evident today in theoretical debates concerning realism and experimentalism in which the latter is privileged.

In their chapter entitled "Remembering: Feminism and the Writing of Women," Batsleer and her colleagues go on to note that "academic literary criticism has a complex relationship with contemporary writing, mediating the formation of literary intellectuals and implicitly informing the practices of publishing and reviewing, while in its own practice ignoring or marginalizing current and recent fiction" (1985, 113). One of the earliest and most influential proponents of such a critical approach was Q. D. (Queenie) Leavis, who thought that art in its popular or mass form was detrimental to the mind and should be clearly distanced from elite art, which existed as an integral component of high culture. In her study of twentieth-century

British literary canons, Karen Lawrence points out that this attempt to separate art and politics was "fuelled by many of the manifestos of modernism, which stress the formal properties of art and discredit the ties between literature and immediate political and social concerns" (1992, 4).

There are, of course, many contemporary critics who argue that the study of popular culture represents one of the most important tools in challenging the whole concept of privileged texts and, thus, undermines the ostensible "naturalness" of literary canons (J. Todd 1988, 94). Nevertheless, many of the features in the dispute between what Rita Felski, in *Beyond Feminist Aesthetics* (1989), calls "instrumental" and "aesthetic" theories of the text are also evident in some contemporary feminist theory debates, whereby many of the differences between, say, French and Anglo-American feminist theories—such as those concerning avant-garde and experimental literature—parallel the earlier debate's differences over realism and modernism.

Feminist literary debates have not been altogether aided either by the incorporation of poststructuralist theories, in which the study of literature is often constructed as an outmoded activity with little relevance to social or political reality. This largely academic shift has its parallel in feminist criticism, whereby poststructuralism is often alleged to have contributed to a decline in those sections of the feminist movement concerned with women's material conditions.

Jo Freeman, for instance, warns that the decline of the women's movement from a political organization to a largely cultural one—reflected, she says, in the growth of women's writing as the most prominent feminist cultural practice—reveals a risk that a focus on the actual conditions of women's material oppression has been replaced by the creative representation of women's deprivation (Freeman 1983, 104). Such a view suggests that the alleged dichotomy of "academic" and "popular" feminism equates, culturally or socially, to a similar dichotomy of "political" and "cultural," implying that the two are (becoming) mutually exclusive.

Part of the necessity for the kind of reexamination undertaken here arises from an acknowledgment that the days have gone of believing that women's writing retained an inferior place in the "malestream" literary world purely as a result of its poor treatment by a predominantly male, conservative, literary critical world. Women's writing still is generally treated poorly by that critical world, of course, but it has other problems to contend with now, not least those that have been brought about by shifts toward notions of post- or third-wave feminisms and the hegemonic influences of Anglo-American and French feminist discourses in controlling contemporary gender theory debates and feminist textual analysis at a local level. Within a specifically Irish context, it is equally curious to witness many of the "popular" women writers from the past thirty years distance themselves from the new popular women's genres such as chick lit because of a neo-elitism that suggests that they wrote serious literature while the latest genres are mere pulp. This attitude points to a perpetuation of the denial that women have almost always operated in the realm of the popular in its many varied definitions.

As mentioned, only rarely has Ireland been recognized as a minority culture, yet, on the other hand, it has suffered from a form of marginalization directly associated with the way women from minority cultures have been contained, not only by mainstream or male critical hegemonies, but by feminist ones as well:

> the source of [my] anger is not in my nationality, but firmly in the apparent non-nationality of certain powerful (it's always relative) others. *SHE/THEY/have nationalities/regionalities/ethnicities*—but *WE do not.* The problem is that whenever the issue is raised—invariably by the ethnicized/ regionalized/nationalized et al.—hegemonic eyes glaze: theories and accounts of other's identities, analyses, experiences are so boring, basic and back in the 1980s—*I can sing this part*—WE don't do (our) identities any more, although of course we fully acknowledge that THEY still need to do theirs, so we've made (a little) space for them to get on with it, over there on the side. (A. Smyth 1997b, 38)

This is a variation of Margaret Ward's 1987 proposition: "What we urgently need to do is to begin to forge an identity as Irishwomen and as feminists living in Ireland, which will not be a pale reflection of the very different problems and concerns of the dominant Anglo-American tradition" (Ward 1987, 60).

For a considerable length of time, the work of Irish feminist critics has been central to critical debates around (Irish) nationalism[5] (Margaret Ward, Maria Luddy, Margaret MacCurtain, Cliona Murphy, Mary Cullen), literature and cultural studies (Clair Wills, Ailbhe Smyth), identity (Mary Cullen, Rosemary Cullen Owens, Diane Urquhart), and religious history (Caitríona Clear, Myrtle Hill, Margaret MacCurtain, Mary O'Dowd), to name just a few. These critics are by no means of one mind on these issues, yet precisely because of the extent of disagreement, the debates generated by their critical and theoretical work have been crucial components of Irish feminism—both culturally and politically—since the late 1980s. Part of my discussion of contemporary theoretical contexts in chapter 3 is an attempt to show how a large part of this important Irish feminist and critical activity has been allowed to slip through the cracks of the major theoretical debates since none of the diverse "Irish" theoretical positions quite fits the "international" positions and, in turn, none of the diverse "international" positions quite fits the "Irish." This is all the more reason, then, why none should be applied unproblematically to Ireland: postcolonial theory too often merges *minority* with *nonwhite* and has failed to develop a critical discourse appropriate for analyzing texts by nonhegemonic (Irish women) writers; postmodernist theories of difference, *écriture feminine*, deconstruction, and psychoanalysis all problematize assumptions of essential identity but may underestimate the politics of material reality and may even deprive (Irish) feminism of its mobilizing force. At the same time, an unproblematic gyno-critical approach to Irish women's writing homogenizes and silences atypical voices, of which there are many.

But chapter 3 is also an attempt to show the difficulty in discussing much contemporary women's writing from Ireland, since it exists not only as a body of feminist oppositional discourse, but as a body of work from a particular place at a particular time, albeit closely connected to the women's movement. The existence of these immensely influential gender and culture theory debates presents us with a dilemma: if we discuss Irish women's writing entirely within the context of contemporary feminism,

---

5. I am using *nationalism* here to denote both nationalism and unionism, which, although different in many ways, display the similar concerns of devotion, loyalty, and struggle in relation to country/nationhood.

then, as a result of its very specific cultural and developmental influences, it will tend to look conservative. Yet if we examine it too closely without a framework of feminism, concentrating solely on the local aspects of its particular identity politics, then it too easily slips by as time-bound, overly particularized, or—worse—parochial. The difficulty, then, is in finding a way to walk the fine line between seeing contemporary women's writing from places like Ireland as part of, and influenced by, a much larger historical movement and, at the same time, allowing the cultural specificity of that writing to emerge. Too often, feminist criticism in Ireland has fallen into the trap of being appropriated by one side or the other, either in contemporary gender theory debates or in terms of the binaries that are such an integral part of Irish and Northern Irish society, rather than undertaking the appropriation of *all* attempts to theorize women and their cultural practices as part of an ongoing feminist strategy.

TWO IRELANDS

1 Undoing That "Other" Conquest

Women's Writing from the Republic of Ireland

PRIOR TO THE MOST RECENT PERIOD of immense social and political change in Ireland, which dates to the 1960s, the marginalized role of women in Irish society is clearly echoed in the world of literary production as it is in the work of writers who grew up in that era, such as Edna O'Brien and Julia O'Faolain. The links between writing and politics are evidenced by the fact that, by the late 1950s and early 1960s, Irish writing was represented by four main streams: the inheritance of the Irish literary revival (led by Yeats), which had invoked the romantic myths of Celtic Ireland in an attempt to establish a cultural identity based on a strong and proud past; the modernist experimentalism of Joyce and Beckett, which abhorred the revival's romantic portrayal of Irish life and the denial of the reality of the Irish identity that, in their view, was fragmented and paralyzed; the realist tradition, which continued to portray the limited and limiting life of the small farmer; and, finally, the Anglo-Irish literary tradition that concentrated on the creation of "Big House" fiction and in which women dominated.

As in postmodernism, the Big House tradition found its most explicit expression through architectural means. But, unlike the nonreferential forms and parody of its modern counterpart, the Big House tradition was firmly rooted in that symbol of power in Ireland, the ancestral home, most often the property of absentee landlords who, by virtue of their class and religious superiority, represented the ruling class in Ireland.

Frank Tuohy notes the tradition's three major characteristics as being the inclusion of a big house of imposing proportions in which the native

Irish are grooms and servants; evidence of an unbridgeable chasm of snobbery, designed to separate the aristocrats from the native Catholic population; and, finally, the representation of deprivation, humorously exposing the boundary between appearance and reality, revealing the contrast between the pretensions of the landowner and the deficiencies of his personal life (Tuohy 1985, 200). In view of this final characteristic, it might be hoped that these often satiric and parodic depictions redeem the works from a position of superiority were it not for the fact that the earlier Big House novelists were themselves Anglo-Irish. In this instance, the term is not limited to its popular literary meaning of having English as a first language but is used in the sociological sense of being of English extraction: usually Protestant, often educated in England and, thus, representative of the ruling class. As a result, much of the early tradition depends on describing, explaining, and, sometimes, defending Irish life from a distanced social position. In general, Maria Edgeworth's *Castle Rackrent* (1800), Somerville and Ross's *The Real Charlotte* (1894) and *The Big House at Inver* (1925) as well as Elizabeth Bowen's *The Last September* (1929) are considered to be early and influential landmarks of the Big House tradition. Conventionally (mis)understood as one of the most conservative strands of Irish fiction, it was this tradition that was, until relatively recently, most closely associated with Irish women writers.

The changes that occurred in Irish society since the 1960s, such as the easing of censorship laws, the shifts away from isolationist policies, an increase in publishing opportunities (including feminist presses), as well as the constitutional separation of church and state,[1] have meant that, unlike their predecessors, contemporary women writers from the Republic of Ireland have been free to challenge traditional orthodoxies—and challenge them they have. But unlike many women writers from revolutionary societies who have used this freedom of expression to endorse an ongoing nationalist struggle (which, for many people in the Republic of Ireland, continues in relation to Northern Ireland) or to endorse an existing national identity, much women's fiction from the Republic of Ireland in the

---

1. Article 44 of the Irish constitution, which granted the Catholic Church a privileged position as "guardian of the faith," was removed in 1972.

contemporary period reveals a rejection and undermining of nationally privileged images, such as the mother figure and women as figures of purity and passivity, as well as challenging the hegemonic role of the Catholic Church in women's lives. Whether through irony, parody, comedy, or tragedy, these literary iconoclasts shatter existing illusions by exposing the absurdity, stupidity, naïveté, and danger associated with such images.

Even allowing for the already acknowledged fact that not all women writers are necessarily feminist or even have feminist sympathies, it is difficult to ignore that of a random 40 contemporary women's novels from the Republic of Ireland written between 1975 and 1995, 34 have central women characters and deal directly with some aspect of women's lives in Ireland, while 82 out of 106 short stories from the same period reveal a similar focus.[2] The production of those novels and stories was first influenced and then facilitated by changes, not only in the society, but, relatedly, in the publishing industry itself.

IRISH FEMINIST PUBLISHING

A full history of feminist publishing in Ireland has yet to be undertaken,[3] and it is certainly worthy of a separate study. However, it is possible to trace the origins of much of the work that appeared from the mid-1970s to five major and interconnected influences: Arlen House, Irish Feminist Information (IFI, from which Attic Press emerged), the Women's Community Press (WCP), the Women's Education Bureau (WEB), and Attic Press, loosely in chronological order, but in many ways integrally connected, not just by many of the same people who moved within and between the organiza-

2. The short stories were from eight collections and two anthologies: Leland Bardwell, *Different Kinds of Love* (1987); Evelyn Conlon, *My Head Is Opening* (1987) and *Taking Scarlet as a Real Colour* (1993); Maura Treacy, "Sixpence in Her Shoe" and Other Stories (1977); Melissa Murray, *Changelings* (1987); Helen Lucy Burke, *A Season for Mothers* (1980); Clare Boylan, *Concerning Virgins* (1989b); Eithne Strong, *Patterns* (1981). The anthologies were "The Wall Reader" and Other Stories (1979) and "A Dream Recurring" and Other Stories and Poems (1981).

3. The most extensive research to date has been done by Alan Hayes, publisher (Arlen House). I have relied on Hayes 1999 in representing the chronology of the five influences here.

tions but by the climate of the times whereby women's publishing became a central component in the politics of the second wave. The overall effect is one of small interconnected events and moments, which, in their entirety, resulted in the majority of recent women's publishing in Ireland.

Arlen House was founded by Catherine Rose in Galway during International Women's Year, 1975, but its early lists were heavily influenced by Louise C. Callaghan and Eavan Boland. Arlen's first publication was Rose's *The Female Experience: The Story of the Womens Movement in Ireland*, but it would be two years before its next effort appeared, journalist Janet Martin's *The Essential Guide for Women in Ireland* (1977). In 1978, the press moved its headquarters to Dublin, changed its name to "Arlen House: The Women's Press," and Janet Martin, Margaret MacCurtain, and Terry Prone joined its ranks. Soon after, the groundbreaking *Women in Irish Society: The Historical Dimension* appeared, edited by MacCurtain and Donncha ó Corráin. Around this time, Arlen undertook a republishing of "lost" women writers, beginning with Kate O'Brien and followed by Norah Hoult, Janet McNeill, and Anne Crone. Arlen also published a series of self-help books beginning in 1979 with Ronit Lentin and Geraldine Niland's *Who's Minding the Children?* and Clara Clark's *Coping Alone* and followed by Máire Mullarney's *Anything School Can Do You Can Do Better* (1983) and Stanislaus Kennedy's *But Where Can I Go? Homeless Women in Dublin* (1983). These books became an important aspect of Arlen's publishing profile, but, importantly, there was not nearly such a clear distinction made between the different genres as we might make today. At this early stage, it was all grist for the mill.

In one of the most important moments of Irish feminist publishing, in 1978, Arlen House and sponsor Maxwell House (the coffee manufacturers) started a literary competition for new women writers, a move that produced three centrally important anthologies: *"The Wall Reader" and Other Stories* (1979), *"A Dream Recurring" and Other Stories and Poems* (1981), and *"The Adultery" and Other Stories and Poems* (1982). These three volumes alone produced a wealth of feminist and women-centered creative work that was in tandem with some of the most important critical work done around the same time: Janet Madden-Simpson's *Woman's Part: An Anthology of Short Fiction by and about Irishwomen, 1890–1960* (1984), and *Irish Women: Image and Achievement*, edited by Eiléan Ni Chuilleanáin (1985) remain benchmarks in women's publishing in

Ireland and, again, opened the way for further research into the representation of Irish women as well as encouraged further creative writing that undertook a re/presentation of the images. Terry Prone's *The Scattering of Mrs Blake and Related Matters* (1985) and Rita Kelly's *"The Whispering Arch" and Other Stories* (1986) represent two of the final publications by Arlen House. After a short-lived reemergence as Rose Publications, Arlen closed in 1987.[4]

Directly resulting from Arlen, however, was the Women's Education Bureau (WEB), founded in 1984. WEB became the national representative body for women writers in Ireland, and its major influence was in organizing writing and publishing workshops. Following Arlen's closure in 1987, the WEB published Mary Cullen's edited volume *Girls Don't Do Honours* (1987), which examined the relationship between women and education in Ireland during the nineteenth and twentieth centuries, and also published Helen Burke's *The People and the Poor Law in Nineteenth-Century Ireland* (1987). The WEB also designed and coordinated courses on "women into writing" for FÁS (the national training authority). Its final publication, in conjunction with Carcanet Press, was Eavan Boland's *Selected Poems* in 1989.

The history of Irish Feminist Information (IFI) is much more closely related to skills training in Irish feminist publishing. Founded in Dublin in 1978 by Róisín Conroy and Mary Doran, the IFI produced a women's calendar, *An End . . . and a Beginning,* and, also in 1979, published the first *Irish Women's Guide Book and Diary,* an annual publication that ultimately ran to eighteen editions between 1979 and 1997 (the subsequent editions were published by Attic). Equally crucial was IFI's training courses for unemployed women, a skills-based course designed to introduce women to the practical aspects of publishing. Funding for the project was obtained from the Industrial Training Authority, AnCo, and from the European Social Fund of the European Economic Community. The first of these courses ran in 1983 under the leadership of Róisín Conroy and Patricia Kelleher, and resulted in three important publications: *Missing Pieces: Women in Irish History* (1983), *Singled Out: Single Mothers in Ireland* (1983), and *If You Can Talk You Can Write* (1983), which represents the first anthology of community writing.

---

4. Alan Hayes relaunched Arlen House in 2000, although the press now has a commitment to publishing a broader range of authors than it did originally.

A second "Women into Community Publishing" course in 1984, coordinated by Róisín Conroy and Mary Paul Keane, produced four more titles between 1984 and 1985. Published in conjunction with Attic Press, which was founded by Conroy and Keane in that same year and which became an imprint of IFI, these titles have come to represent some of the earliest and most important historical and literary work of the period. They are *Did Your Granny Have a Hammer?* (1984), a curriculum guide about the history of the Irish women's suffrage movement compiled by Rosemary Cullen Owens, *Who Owns Ireland, Who Owns You?* (1984), *Rapunzel's Revenge: Fairytales for Feminists* (1985), and *More Missing Pieces* (1985).

As a direct result of the courses run by the IFI, the Women's Community Press (WCP) was established in 1983 after receiving funding from the European Commission's Women's Bureau. Following the printing of a hugely successful series of feminist postcards, the WCP went on to publish Noreen O'Donoghue and Sue Richardson's *Pure Murder: A Book about Drug Use* (1983), the *Irish Feminist Review* (1984), the amazingly successful community writing anthology *Write Up Your Street* (1985), and the controversial *Out for Ourselves: The Lives of Irish Lesbians and Gay Men* (1986), compiled by the Dublin Lesbian and Gay Men's Collective.

Between its founding in 1984 and 1997, when it was acquired by Cork University Press, Attic Press became the major publisher of women's writing of all kinds. Its importance derives from its pioneering role in seeking out and publishing not only women's fiction in an era when serious attention to women's writing as a genre was rare, but Irish women's fiction; it published some of the most important women's writing of the contemporary period, and its influence was great. The void Attic filled was defined in its 1989 catalog: it specialized "in fiction, women's studies, history and practical reference books by, for and about women, with a strong international and Irish profile. Attic has never been afraid of controversy; nor have [they] been reluctant to explore new areas."

From the late 1980s and early 1990s, under the editorship of Mary Paul Keane, Attic began publishing much more fiction: novels and short stories by Irish women like Evelyn Conlon, Mary Rose Callaghan, Leland Bardwell, Éilis Ní Dhuibhne, Ronit Lentin, and Eithne Strong, among others. Much of this fiction compares with that produced by women elsewhere in-

sofar as it can be classified, in either form or theme, by its explicit commitment to feminist politics. The most obvious example in terms of form is
Attic's series of fairy tale anthologies—*Rapunzel's Revenge* (1985), *Ms. Muffet
and Others* (1986), *Mad and Bad Fairies* (1987), *Sweeping Beauties* (1989), *Cinderella on the Ball* (1991), and *Ride on Rapunzel* (1992), all subtitled "Fairytales
for Feminists," and described as "irreverent reinventions of traditional fairytales for feminists of all ages" (cover blurb). Published by Attic in the same
series is Maeve Kelly's *Alice in Thunderland* (1993), also subtitled "A Feminist
Fairytale," which was serialized in some of the anthologies before being
published separately and in entirety in 1993. In their overt feminist stance,
these fairy tales represent a lighthearted look not only at sexual politics but
at a variety of issues such as unionism in Mary Maher's "Hi Ho, It's Off to
Strike We Go!"; environmentalism in "Rapunzel's Revenge" by Anne Claffey and others; class issues in Sue Russell's "Goldilocks Finds a Home"; and
English versions of traditional Irish tales, such as Mary Dorcey's "The Fate
of Aoife and the Children of Aobh."

By the early to mid-1990s, Attic Press catalogs contained more than
one hundred books "by, for and about women," and in 1992, the Arts Council awarded Attic £30,000 to further the publishing of women's writing, the
largest grant given that year to a single publisher (Ferreira 1993, 104).
Apart from its feminist publications, Attic also introduced, under the later
editorship of Ailbhe Smyth, a young adult division called Bright Sparks,
and, in 1994, it launched its general publishing division, Basement Press,
described as "fresh, irreverent, always controversial and entertaining, publishing new and exciting fiction and non-fiction, by both women and men"
(Attic catalog 1994). This description was confirmed by its opening launch
of Des Geraghty's memoir of Dubliners' singer Luke Kelly, as well as
Ireland's first gay list, Queer Views. Between 1989 and 1990, Attic also published ten handbooks for women, including *Emigration Matters for Women* and
Surviving Sexual Abuse.

SURVEY OF WOMEN'S WRITING

Irish women's writing of the contemporary period is by no means confined
to overtly "feminist" literature; as the following sampling will illustrate,

women throughout the decades have written books in a wide variety of genres, both fiction and nonfiction.

Ruth Dudley Edwards, for instance, has been a prolific writer of both nonfiction and fiction. Among her works of fiction are several within the mystery/thriller genre—*Corridors of Death* (1981a), *The Saint Valentine's Day Murders* (1984), *The School of English Murder* (1990), *Clubbed to Death* (1992), *Matricide at St. Martha's* (1995), *Ten Lords A-Leaping* (1996), *Murder in a Cathedral* (1997), *Publish and Be Murdered* (1999), and *The Anglo-Irish Murders* (2001). Similarly, journalist Mary Maher, one of the founders of the Irish women's liberation movement, wrote a murder mystery, *The Devil's Card* (1992), that centers on an Irish-American connection.

Catherine Brophy's tale of one woman's stab at freedom and happiness, *The Liberation of Margaret McCabe* (1985), was followed by a shift in genre with the publication of *Dark Paradise* (1991), which stands as Ireland's first piece of feminist science fiction. Éilís Ní Dhuibhne is a well-respected folklorist and writer in Irish, but she is equally well-known for her novels, short stories, and children's fiction, including *The Uncommon Cormorant* (1990) and *Hugo and the Sunshine Girl* (1991b). Ní Dhuibhne's *The Bray House* (1990), which is set in the twenty-first century, fuses futuristic fiction with recognizable contemporary Irish and British politics.

Irish myth and history are similarly fused in the work of Morgan Llewelyn, who produced five novels between 1984 and 1991, while Patricia Finney's two early novels, *A Shadow of Gulls* (1977) and *The Crow Goddess* (1979), combine Irish and Roman myth. The influence of the Irish language on English is evident in much of Rita Kelly's fiction, poetry, and drama as it is in that of poet, playwright, and short story writer Máire C. Holmes.

As elsewhere, lesbian writing has become a more evident literary category in the canon of contemporary Irish women's writing. Linda Cullen is one of the early writers in this genre whose only novel to date, *The Kiss* (1990), addresses how lesbianism affects the lives of two young successful Dublin women who have shared a close friendship since childhood and suddenly find themselves in love with each other. Cullen and Joni Crone, another writer about lesbian issues, have not published anything for some time.

Mary Dorcey, on the other hand, who has been writing and publishing since the early 1980s, was the only "out" Irish lesbian writer for many years and has produced several books of poetry, short stories, and, most recently, the novel *Biography of Desire* (1997). In more recent years, Dorcey has been joined in the genre by Emma Donoghue, who represents an important voice in Irish literary discourse even though she has lived in Canada for some time. Among other things, Donoghue has written a number of critical volumes, including a history of British lesbianism, *Passions between Women: British Lesbian Culture 1668–1801* (1993b) and *Outlines: We Are Michael Field* (1998b); two novels, *Stir Fry* (1994) and *Hood* (1995); a collection of re-worked fairy tales, *Kissing the Witch* (1997a); and several plays, including *I Know My Own Heart* (1993a) and *Ladies and Gentlemen* (1998a).

In 1988, Joni Crone from the Centre for Performing Arts in Dublin declared that "there is no such organisation as the lesbian feminist movement in Ireland but there is . . . an identifiable political presence within the women's movement and indeed a lesbian feminist sub-culture" (1988, 347). Mary Cummins of the *Irish Times* reported in 1994 that there had been a great deal of activism not just in Dublin but also in Cork, Galway, and other parts of the country and that lesbians had a much higher degree of confidence and involvement in lesbian activism and politics and were coming out in greater numbers than ever: "When [Emma] Donoghue, looking and sounding rather like a competent head girl, turned up on *The Late Late Show* she was an obvious plus for a group who have always been regarded with suspicion. With youth, cleverness, confidence and oozing a 'so what?' nonchalance, I have yet to meet a lesbian who does not speak of her in tones laden with reverence" (Cummins 1994).

Mary Dorcey sees the conjoining of lesbianism and feminism as one of the biggest threats to what she describes as "this virulently misogynistic literary culture" in Ireland (N. Archer 1986, 21). But she also believes, from her own personal experience in winning the Rooney Literature Prize, that literary recognition generally brings its own form of respectability. At the same time, Dorcey sees her work very much as part of a wider feminist program whereby the way lesbians are forced to live in a deeply prejudiced society is simply a reflection of the way women generally are forced to live by a "juggling act." Although juggling is certainly stressful, the survival ability it creates she sees as a great gift and essential for women's lives (22). Thus, the literary success of certain lesbian novels and plays in contemporary Ireland probably represents recognition of literary achievement more than it does an Irish cultural embrace of lesbian writing for its own sake.

In the case of both Dorcey and Donoghue, there is a very clear self-awareness that their work takes place within the contexts of an Irish literary tradition. In Dorcey's *Biography of Desire* (1997), she investigates not only the nature of love and passion between women, but the representation of these things through language and memory. At the center of the novel is a journal that becomes the biography of the title and in which is recorded the intricate details of event and feeling. In this recording in the journal, Dorcey clearly uses literary invention to present the relationship between Katherine Newman and Nina Kavanaugh in a known Irish literary context, which is both familiar and entirely new because of its lesbian content.

The implied audience in a novel like Donoghue's *Hood* (1995) demonstrates one of the most obvious shifts from the earlier tradition of Irish women's writing. Books written in the Big House tradition often assumed a need to explain Ireland to its reading audience, but in Donoghue there is no such attempt: the inclusion of the Irish language as well as certain local personalities, features, and historical events—Nell McCafferty, the "Pill train," and the "Forty foot" swimming hole (Donoghue 1995, 66)—all suggest that Donoghue expects her audience to be at ease with Irish events left unexplained. The echoes of the Big House that do remain in Donoghue's *Hood* are treated ironically: Cara's family home is referred to as the big house (lowercase as opposed to capitals), and we can see how the narrator's place in that house is uncertain. She isn't exactly a servant, yet she keeps the place going almost single-handedly and is actually mistaken for a cleaner by the visiting sister, Kate. Clearly, Mr. Wall, the father of the house, is also meant to represent something from a past age: a man whose sensibilities are not to be offended either by his visiting daughter being found in her dressing gown or by the fact that his other daughter lives in a homosexual relationship under his nose. There is something of the refined Victorian gentleman about Mr. Wall, who never acknowledges anything distasteful. Donoghue's reference to the Big House tradition in *Hood* undermines that tradition throughout by the dysfunctional nature of the family itself, and by the fact that the novel is centrally concerned with a lesbian relationship.

Donoghue also deals ironically with the issue of the Irish language in *Hood*. Mr. Wall insists on calling Kate the Irish Cáit, even though neither he nor his ex-wife is an Irish speaker. Pen (Penelope), the young woman at the center of the novel, is a teacher in a national school and is required to teach her pupils the Irish language. In so much Irish literature, the teaching of Irish is either romanticized as part of a retrieval of a lost past or, alternatively, criticized for its brutal enforcement as part of the nationalist effort. In Donoghue, it becomes something slightly farcical as the children themselves question its usefulness.

There are also the various uses and meanings of "hood" woven into the novel: sometimes indicating a linguistic playfulness (113), but sometimes linked to the references to fairy tales throughout the narrative. The epigraph, for instance, is a lesbian poem about maintaining secrecy, discussed under the guise of "Little Red Riding Hood"; Cara is described as looking like Snow White as a result of the cold (40); there are dreamlike fairy tales concerning a gingerbread house (164) and a cascade of red hair falling from a tower (204); but there is also the image of Pen, herself, as a fairy godmother and nurturer of Cara (185).

This last image of Pen as nurturer echoes that of both Joyce's *Ulysses* and his source, Homer's *Odyssey*, in which both Bloom and Odysseus, or Ulysses, wanders or quests from home leaving his wife, Molly/Penelope, at home to wait. In Donoghue's novel, we can see features of both Homer and Joyce—not least in the narrator's name, Penelope, her abundant size, and the author's construction of her as a sensualist in the style of Molly Bloom. Like Ulysses, Pen's female partner Cara, is said to have been wandering around the Aegean with her friends while Pen waits at home (193–94); always there is Pen as nurturer, as carer.

At its heart, however, *Hood* is a novel about secrecy—the secret of lesbianism, the secret of women's sexuality, secret dreams, role-playing and, of course, secret loss. One of the most interesting aspects of the novel is that, in sharing the sense of grief and loss while at the same time sharing secrets with Pen, we as readers forget completely the sexual orientation of the two characters at the center of the story. *Hood* becomes, like Dorcey's *Biography of Desire*, a story about human love and loss—though in this case, a love and loss that cannot be spoken about publicly. Set in the context of a lesbian relationship, the novel challenges existing assumptions about love and loss: "what would a non-religious lesbian sympathy card be like, I wondered? A postcard with a cartoon on it, no doubt. I tried to come up with a suitable slogan: 'A woman without a body is like a kite without a string' " (194). *Hood* clearly signals Donoghue's awareness, not only of her place as a writer within an Irish tradition, but of literary history and the connections between women.

Two founding members of the Irish women's liberation movement are June Levine and Mary Kenny, although the latter has since repudiated feminism. Levine wrote a history of the movement in Ireland through the medium of an autobiographical novel, *Sisters* (1982), and, together with Lyn Madden, produced a book of nonfiction entitled *Lyn* (1987), based on Madden's twenty-year history as a prostitute. This latter book was published within an impressive fiction list by Attic Press, which was then under the editorship of Mary Paul Keane. Levine's 1992 novel, *A Season of Weddings*, touches on heterosexual and homosexual love as well as cross-cultural issues. Mary Kenny is best known now as a journalist. With the exception of a collection of short stories, *A Mood for Love* (1989), her work has been primarily nonfiction—*Woman X Two: How to Cope with a Double Life* (1978), *Why Christianity Works* (1981) and *Abortion: The Whole Story* (1986). *A Mood for Love* might best be categorized as "internationalist" fiction: that is, fiction written by women in Ireland but with settings and themes that extend into different countries.

In a very different political framework, Ronit Lentin, an academic and writer, has lived, worked, studied, and taught in Ireland since the late 1960s although she was born in Israel. She has written a number of novels, some of which were published in Israel and some in Ireland; an early reference book, *Who's Minding the Children?* (1979), also published in Ireland; a collection of interviews, *Conversations with Palestinian Women* (1982), published in Jerusalem; and other scholarly monographs, including *Gender and Catastrophe* (1997), and *Israel and the Daughters of the Shoah: Reoccupying the Territories of Silence* (2000), and has co-edited others, including *Women and the Politics of Military Confrontation: Palestinian and Israeli Gendered Narratives of Dislocation* (2002). Deirdre Purcell's *A Place of Stones* (1991) and *That Childhood Country* (1992), F. D. Sheridan's collection of short stories, *Captives* (1980), and Dolores

Walshe's plays, poems, and novel, *Where the Trees Weep* (1992), similarly belong in such an "international" category.

Examples of early historical fiction might include Mary Leland's *The Killeen* (1985) located in Cork during the 1930s, Joan O'Neill's *Daisy Chain War* (1990) set during the Second World War, Mary Ryan's *Whispers in the Wind* (1990) in which the Irish War of Independence is central, and Sheila Flitton's *Notions* (1991), which focuses on the 1940s. Alice Taylor's volumes of memoirs/stories of childhood in rural Ireland have proved to be extremely popular both in Ireland and overseas while a similar treatment of Irish rural life can be found in Alannah Hopkins's *A Joke Goes a Long Way in the Country* (1982) and *The Out-Haul* (1985). A much less sentimental vision of contemporary rural Ireland can be found in Maura Treacy's collection of short stories, *Sixpence in Her Shoe* (1977), and her novel, *Scenes from a Country Wedding* (1981), as well as in Maeve Kelly's collection, *A Life of Her Own* (1976).

While there are many individual examples of experimental fiction, it has not been a particularly significant or dominant feature of contemporary Irish women's fiction. Several short story collections, such as K. Arnold Price's *The New Perspective* (1980) and Anne Enright's *The Portable Virgin* (1992), use various experimental styles and narrative techniques. And while a number of writers, such as Evelyn Conlon and Emma Donoghue, have produced individual stories that experiment with narrative style, in general there is no evidence to suggest a widespread interest or movement in experimentalism in Irish women's writing of the contemporary period.

There is evidence, however, of strong links between contemporary Irish women and some notion of "international feminism." Not surprisingly, many Irish women writers of the contemporary period reveal an interest in the relationship between themselves and writers from other countries. Evelyn Conlon, for example, has said that when she started writing there were no Irish literary models and no body of women's literature that related to women like herself, only that of the Big House tradition. Like Mary Dorcey, Conlon's literary identification was with writers from places other than Ireland, such as Toni Cade Bambara and Grace Paley of the United States, primarily because, like her, they did not have "a residual faith in the language and the literature that was already there so, therefore, when they began to write they had the confidence to actually overturn the form and, in a way, the material that I wanted to write about needed that as well because I was fed up with the form of the Irish short story" (Pelan 1995, 111). Conlon also has a particular interest in what she refers to as "the Catholic thing" and the ways in which women from places like Latin America have written about their experiences within Catholicism and the ways they have been able to "burrow their way out from underneath it in a way that Irish men writers from the fifties and onwards didn't or couldn't" (Pelan 1995, 111).

FOUND(ER)ING THE IRISH STATE: NATIONALIST MYTHOLOGY

As might be expected, "the Catholic thing," as well as crucial determinants of national iconography, feature prominently in the work of Conlon and many other contemporary women writers from the republic. These determinants have come to be closely associated with a feminist representation of modern Ireland that, while making for excellent narratives against which to work, do not necessarily represent good history. Nevertheless, within such a reading, the postindependence unification of church and state in the modern Irish Republic of Ireland,[5] which witnessed the construction of a singular, coherent national identity, had serious implications for Irish women in social and political contexts and has remained of central importance to their creative production. The traditional identification of Catholicism as the one remnant of a native Irish tradition unable to be conquered by a colonial regime played a crucial part in the establishment of the Republic of Ireland as an independent nation. In its rejection of British (Protestant) imperialism, postindependence Ireland wholeheartedly embraced the Catholic Church as its leader and savior to the extent that the laws of the newly created Irish Free State adopted Catholicism and its moral values as a vehicle for nationalist goals.

The struggle between the two major political parties (led by William Cosgrave and Éamon de Valéra) between 1922 and 1932 included an at-

---

5. I am using the term *republic* for convenience. However, from partition in 1922 until 1949, what is now known as the Republic of Ireland was known as the Free State.

tempt by each to gain the support of the powerful Catholic hierarchy. The bids for endorsement resulted in a series of restrictive laws, many of which directly affected women. The Juries Act of 1927, for example, excluded women from jury service, and the Censorship of Publications Act of 1929 empowered a five-"man" board not only to censor any publication it considered obscene but to prohibit any literature that advocated contraception of any kind.

In an impressive study of the role of the Catholic Church in Ireland, J. H. Whyte explains that in the years following the Civil War, although a deep pessimism existed among the Irish clergy regarding intemperance, gambling, and violent crime, the most prominent area of concern was a decline in sexual morality, encouraged by an influx of magazines and films from abroad and manifested in the increased number of dance halls in rural areas. A joint pastoral of 1927 entitled "The Evils of Modern Dancing" reflects the concern of the Irish bishops at the time:

> These latter days have witnessed, among many other unpleasant sights, a loosening of the bonds of parental authority, a disregard for the discipline of the home, and a general impatience under restraint that drives youth to neglect the sacred claims of authority and follow its own capricious ways. . . . The evil one is ever setting his snares for unwary feet. At the moment, his traps for the innocent are chiefly the dance hall, the bad book, the indecent paper, the motion picture, *the immodest fashion in female dress*—all of which tend to destroy the virtues characteristic of our race. (cited in Whyte 1980, 27; emphasis added)

Whyte makes it clear, however, that while it is difficult to find comparative material from other countries, there is evidence that the Irish obsession with declining moral standards was part of an international anxiety that emerged following the 1914–18 war. Distrust of the dance-hall craze, for instance, was reported from countries as diverse as Italy, Turkey, Hungary, Cuba, and the German state of Thuringia (33).

In 1932, de Valéra's Fianna Fail party won control from Fine Gael and remained in power until 1948, during which time further significant legislative changes were made that were to have a direct effect on the lives of Irish women for some time to come. In 1935, for example, the prohibition of the sale, advertising, or importation of contraceptives was incorporated into the Criminal Law Act. Most of the repressive laws passed at this time relating to employment remained in force until the 1970s, as did the constitutional link between church and state.[6] According to Seamus Deane, "this desperate search for purity, for the political thing-in-itself, was focused by the Treaty (1921) and by the earlier Government of Ireland Act (1920). De Valera was its metaphysician-in-chief" (Deane et al. 1991, 3: 683).

Possibly of more importance to women was the creation of a new constitution in 1937 that, for the first time, not only explicitly acknowledged the role of the Catholic Church in the new nation but that of women and the institution of the family also. The much cited article 41 of this constitu-

---

6. Initially, as elsewhere, changes for women in Ireland were slow to be introduced, but things did change throughout the 1970s and 1980s. For example, in 1973, the Civil Services (Employment of Married Women) Act removed the ban on employing married women; the 1974 Anti-Discrimination (Pay) Act established the right to equal pay for equal work; the Juries Act of 1975 extended jury service to all Irish citizens; the 1977 Employment Equality Act was intended to ensure that a person's sex or marital status would not be a determining factor with regard to vocational training, recruitment, or work experience. Throughout the same period, reforms were slower, more limited, or totally nonexistent in the area of personal liberty. Family planning centers were initially established in central cities, but they could only promote "natural" family planning. Limited reforms were introduced in 1981 relating to rape by other than husbands. Divorce is now possible, although abortion remains a contentious issue in Irish society. More recently, while progress remains slow, fragmented, and inadequate, as elsewhere, there have been many material changes that have had a significant impact on women's lives in Ireland. For instance, there has been an improvement in women's pay rates since the early 1990s. Contraception has been fully legal in the republic since 1992, which means that family planning centers (and other health clinics) are legally entitled to prescribe the contraceptive pill and other contraceptive devices. Changes in family law have also been significant, whereby domestic violence, rape, and child sexual abuse have been major issues on the policy and legislative agenda for the last decade. Considerable legal reform has occurred as a consequence of feminist lobbying. Marital rape has been a crime since 1990. (See *Irish Feminist Review '84* 1984; Ailbhe Smyth 1983; M. Daly 1989).

tion clearly reveals the influence of the Catholic Church in its attitude to the family unit:

> 41.1.1. The State recognises the Family as the natural primary and fundamental unit group of Society, and as a moral institution possessing inalienable and imprescriptible rights, antecedent and superior to all positive law.
> 41.1.2. The State, therefore, guarantees to protect the Family in its constitution and authority, as the necessary basis of social order and as indispensable to the welfare of the Nation and the State.

Of more significance, however, is article 41.2, which states that, "by her life within the home, woman gives the State a support without which the common good cannot be achieved." Measures to assist the achievement of the "common good" fortuitously also solved the problem of women's growing demands for equality by placing them firmly back in the domestic realm, a status achieved by idealizing the role of wife and mother within the family unit. As a legislative safeguard, the constitution also included provision for the protection of that unit:

> 41.3.1. The State pledges itself to guard with special care the institution of Marriage, on which the Family is founded, and to protect it against attack.
> 41.3.2. No law shall be enacted providing for the grant of a dissolution of marriage.

In theory, article 41 could be interpreted as an acknowledgment of the contribution made by those women who dedicated their lives to the family unit by free choice. But what of women who didn't choose marriage and motherhood? No allowance was made for them in the constitution, yet, as a result of economic factors from the 1930s until the 1960s, a high proportion of Irish women remained unmarried. For example, the first government payment for care of senior citizens was introduced in 1968. Eligible people over seventy years old could pay for care from a female relative living with them. Married women were excluded from being paid carers on the assumption that they did not work and were, therefore, already in the home and available to care for the elderly parents or parents-in-law. Only in 1971 did male relatives become eligible as carers (Comhairle). Article 41 became a legislative fortress impermeable to the realities of modern family and economic life. Eiléan ní Chuilleanáin elucidates:

> The Irish state's laws and social provisions up to 1970 remained repressive of liberty in the two areas of sex and work. The outlawing of contraception, the fact that women at work accepted lower wages and, if married, were taxed at a higher rate than men, had the result that in both areas women paid a higher price for less. A choice was offered by the state to women in its employment between work and marriage. It was a false choice, dividing economic autonomy from sexuality and commitment in personal life. (1985, 6)

More recently, Molly Mullin has stated that the language of the constitution provides one of the best illustrations of why struggles over definitions are important since "not only does the Constitution assume the right to define 'Family,' but it also assumes that 'woman' can be used interchangeably with 'mother,' and that both are automatically associated with domesticity" (1991, 42).

The legislative changes in the Irish Republic were echoed in cultural myths of moral and religious purity, which, in turn, contributed to the overall construction of a nationalist mythology that encapsulated a number of other features of the new republic, including political insularity or isolationism, belief in an idyllic Celtic past or Golden Age, and a vision of communal as opposed to societal organization, the latter standing for modernity with all its evils. In the midst of such nationalist mythology is a very clear use of a literary contribution to the political project. In his Wolfe Tone lecture, given in New York in 1904, W. B. Yeats stated his vision of an ideal Ireland as a place where:

> If there are few rich, there shall be nobody very poor . . . a place where men plough and sow and reap, not a place where there are great wheels turning and great chimneys vomiting smoke. Ireland will always be a country where men plough and sow and reap . . . We wish to preserve an

ancient kind of life. Wherever its customs prevail, there you will find the folk song, the folk tale, the proverb and the charming manners that come from an ancient culture. (cited in Richard Ellmann 1988, 116–17)

In his now famous St. Patrick's Day radio broadcast of 1943, Éamon de Valéra echoed Yeats's imaginative vision by stating that his desired Ireland would be "a land whose countryside would be bright with cosy homesteads, whose fields and valleys would be joyous with the sounds of industry, with the romping of sturdy children, the contests of athletic youth, the laughter of happy maidens, whose firesides would be the forums for the wisdom of serene old age" (Valéra 1943).

This image of the stoic Irish peasant is pervasive in Irish literature and film of the early twentieth century. The fact that it offered a positive image of an existing, negative stereotype is only one reason for its immense and continued success. In a society with at least two distinct ethnic groups whose differences were most often based on class division, as well as the increasing growth of a Catholic middle class, the concept of a respectable and proud peasantry forming the bulk of the population perfectly fitted the emerging political vision of Ireland as an insular, rural, and, thus, pure society existing amidst the corruption and modernity of western Europe—but particularly England.

Difficulties for women in postindependence Ireland were by no means confined to legislative changes, however. As part of the same process of decolonization and construction of foundation myths, the attempt by Irish nationalists—many of whom were writers—to redress existing, negative images of colonial Ireland served to further marginalize women in their own society. According to Clair Wills, the feminization of Ireland and the Irish in colonial discourse shaped postcolonial attempts to redefine Irish identity, and, as a result, the traditionally nationalist postcolonial "renaming" of Ireland served only to reconfirm the mythology of woman (1993, 52). This "mythology of woman" is very evident in plays of the revival period. In the work of Synge and O'Casey, in particular, there is a constant denial of "real" women through the portrayal of a feminized/idealized Ireland sacrificed in exchange for freedom. David Cairns and Shaun Richards have pointed out that the trope of the "Poor Old Woman" and the practice of using "woman" as a symbol of sovereignty, although widely understood, were often subject to deconstruction, however (1991, 132).

Despite the literary glorification of women found in much modern Irish men's writing, the reality for many Irish women, and particularly those from working-class and rural backgrounds, was their removal and exclusion from every aspect of public life. They were trapped in a domestic sphere in which they could rarely own property due to the patrilineal structure, and were permitted no access to contraception, abortion, or divorce, yet held responsible for the moral well-being and upbringing of their children. As Jenny Beale notes:

> A woman who married in the countryside lived out a closely defined role. Often in an arranged marriage, she was supposed to be subservient to her husband. Economically, and often emotionally, this subservience was real, though it was offset to some extent by the strength women developed through their responsibility for the children and the domestic economy. (1986, 29)

So the response to one colonial regime produced another form of cultural imperialism in which women paid a high price. The literary reflection of political goals responded to imperialist stereotyping by implicitly reinforcing women's dependence as a response, confirming Rona Fields's assertion that:

> The subordination of women is exacerbated within groups that are oppressed groups in the context of the larger society. In such groups the male is forced into a subordinate, subservient role to his masculine counterparts in the majority group. Since power and masculinity are generally equated, his only recourse for expressing his "masculine potency" is through sexual domination of the women in his group. (1976, 115)

This reads as a more sophisticated version of James Connolly's "slave of slave": "the worker is the slave of capitalist society, the female worker is the slave of that slave. In Ireland that female worker has hitherto exhibited, in her martyrdom, an almost damnable patience" (cited in Innes 1993, 61). On this level alone, the effect of this codification of second-class status was disastrous for Irish women who, denied access to political and literary power, were further subjugated by a literary stereotype that belied the reality of their lives. Most writers of this early period—at least those accepted by the establishment—conformed to nationalist goals in their writing, adding weight to the illusion that, in Ireland, the dominant ideologies have no "underlying dominant ethnicity, that theirs is a 'universal' culture, [which] is a carefully crafted and maintained illusion of great use politically and culturally" (Tovey 1989, 17). But even the most superficial investigation into concepts of nationalism, imperialism, or myth makes clear that they are all-encompassing terms that allow for little discussion of other issues. An emphasis on nationalism or imperialism, for example, implies that issues such as class and gender exist in an undifferentiated relationship to the larger ones of race or ethnicity. But while such myths, and the notion of nationalism itself, remain ostensibly ungendered, they have been, on both political and ideological levels, almost exclusively masculine.

AN "ALTERNATIVE REVIVAL"

Since the mid-1980s, influential literary and cultural critics like Declan Kiberd and Seamus Deane have been usefully interrogating these fixed notions of identity as they had existed and been understood in Ireland for a long time. Kiberd points out that at the time of the Irish literary revival led by Yeats, there was an alternative revival led by James Connolly and James Joyce—"men who began with the courageous admission that there is no such thing as an Irish identity, ready-made and fixed, to be carried as a passport into eternity." The writers of this "alternative revival" had no ready-made insignia of Ireland, says Kiberd, but only a desire to create the objective conditions within which the "pursuit of freedom might begin. They hated the past with its dreary toll of defeats and the inevitable sentimentalization of failure" (1984, 13–14).

Kiberd goes on to say that, in contrast to Connolly and Joyce, Yeats, "having dazzled himself with [an] Ireland of stolen children and fairy forts, of serene towers and violent highways, of big houses and cosy cottages," went on to employ his immense rhetorical powers to enrapture everybody else and thus contributed substantially to the modern notion of what it meant to be Irish (1984, 14). Though this is probably an opportunistic interpretation of Yeats and his project, there is little doubt about the ways in which the poet's images became exploited for purposes of nationalistic mythmaking.

In slightly different terms, Seamus Deane also suggests that the repercussions of the Yeatsian myth have survived long after the conditions that helped to produce it have vanished, a result of the Irish mythmakers' attempts to "historicize in order to politicize, and Ireland, in consequence, begins to cease to be an actuality and begins increasingly to become a metaphor of the self. It's a strange and vicious circle" (1985, 321).

The "actuality" that Deane refers to is the heart of what contemporary writer Mary Dorcey, specifically in relation to lesbian writing in Ireland, has called the "second Ireland": an Ireland that the outside world rarely sees (or wants to see), but that is central to any alternative tradition of contemporary Irish writing and identity generally, and to contemporary Irish *women's* writing and identity specifically:

> Public attitudes and laws and institutions in Ireland very much reflect the older generation, people born before the fifties. The reality of life for the younger group—whether it is the drug culture, permissive sexuality, the breakdown of the nuclear family—none of these find expression at the institutional level and are just beginning to find expression in the artistic world. So there is a thirst for an expressive theatre, cinema, music and literature which acknowledges and comes out of this *second* Ireland, this concealed Ireland, this Ireland which up to now has *been silenced* by emigration. (N. Archer 1990, 22)

THE FATE OF IRISH SUFFRAGE

In the face of Yeats's literary and de Valéra's political visions, Connolly's and Joyce's alternative traditions have gone virtually unnoticed as a result of their appropriation into nationalist mythology. Similarly, more than thirty years of Irish feminist research and scholarship into the role and contribution of women to the achievement of Irish independence has certainly challenged, but hardly altered, the dominant perception that women such as Constance Markievicz, Maud Gonne MacBride, and Hanna Sheehy Skeffington threw their weight behind the nationalist cause wholly and exclusively *as* nationalists, rather than as women who had nationalist aspirations and sympathies as well as hopes of freedom for all Irish women and men following independence: once again, an appropriation into a nationalist mythology, and part of what Sheila Ryan Johansson has called the "collective amnesia" of male historians (Ward 1991, 7). As Mary Cullen has explained, "a woman like Markievicz may be seen as part of Irish history when she is participating in nationalist or labour political or military activity. She and other women are *not* seen as part of Irish history when they campaign in support of women's claims for civil and political rights" (1985, 6).

There is no evidence that the women of this earlier period saw their role as an either/or choice between nationalist and feminist movements. Constance Markievicz, for example, is most often used as representative of the earlier period as one who was prepared to put her nationalism before her feminism. She was a commandant in Connolly's Citizen Army and a leader of the *Cumann na mBan* or Women's Auxiliary Army of the Irish Volunteers. But she also addressed nationalists in 1909, saying, "Fix your minds on the ideal of Ireland free, with her women enjoying the full rights of citizenship in their own nation" (Beale 1986, 5). As a further example of her view of the relationship between nationalism and feminism, she published an article in *Bean na h-Eireann* entitled "Free Women in a Free Nation," in which she argued that "no one should place sex before nationality or nationality before sex" (Innes 1993, 138). Rowbotham declares that there were clear strategic conflicts between Sinn Féin women and the suffrage movement:

> For nationalists the Irish suffrage movement was merely another branch of the British movement. On the other hand, for some feminists the self-reliance fostered by Sinn Féin was wrongly posited on assumptions of women's domestic sphere. Hanna Sheehy Skeffington . . . criticized the Sinn Féin approach because it did not free women as individual citizens, recognizing them in their role only as mothers and housewives. (Rowbotham 1992, 78)

Liam O'Dowd provides one possible reason why such a strong Irish women's movement was subsumed following independence and partition. By examining the dissipation of the earlier women's movement in contexts of nationalist political ideology and religion, as well as international conservative retrenchment and economic protectionism, O'Dowd reveals how factors within and without Ireland contributed to the contraction of women's public and political role between the treaty and the outbreak of World War II (1987, 4). His conclusion is that women's roles in politics were denigrated in the 1920s, unlike those of men, and as a result, women "had precious few ideological resources or opportunities to extend their political influence, even in areas which might be regarded as 'women's issues' " (11). After 1921, those women who had once been prominent in the major political movements became supporters of minority causes that touched only tangentially on the overriding political concerns of the new state. Margaret Ward explains this retreat to lost causes as resting on two factors, namely "the inherent anti-feminism of Catholic nationalism and its leaders, and the failure of politically active women to develop an autonomous and relevant programme for the extension of women's rights" (1987, 9–10). Frances Gardiner confirms the apparent ease with which feminism was subsumed into nationalism by pointing out that five of the six women in the lower house in 1922 were related to men executed in 1916 (19). Feminist historian Margaret MacCurtain's germinal essay on the historical image of women in Irish history continues the story:

> The participation of women in the national struggle was a short-lived phenomenon. Overtaken by the forces of counter-revolution (again, a familiar pattern in Third World revolutionary uprisings in the twentieth century) Irish women retreated into a secondary role with the setting up of the northern State in 1920 and the Free State in the south in 1922. (Ní Chuilleanáin 1985, 49)

Yet while it has been so often acknowledged that Ireland's continued struggle to gain independence from Britain was achieved at an enormous cost, both to human life and economic resources, it is rarely acknowledged, certainly outside feminist analyses, that one of the highest prices paid for

Irish independence was paid by its women. That such a significant number of women took part in its achievement held the promise of liberation to women in postrevolutionary Ireland. Instead, the reverse is true since, despite their contribution, and despite the fact that Irish women were in the vanguard of the suffrage movement, their legal and institutional position in postindependence Ireland became one of continued inferiority and subservience, allegedly for the good of the state. There were exceptions, as always, such as James Connolly's daughters who became senators in the newly formed nation, but such women were rare enough to suggest that they were both token and symbol.

Such strictures within modern Irish society, enforced for purposes of political expediency, led to the construction of cultural and literary images that have functioned as one of the most insidious yet effective methods of serving dominant interests, and that fundamentally led, in independent Ireland, to the disintegration of what had been one of the strongest and most militant women's movements of the twentieth century. Quite distinct in genesis and function from similar movements in, say, England, America, Canada, Australia, or New Zealand, Irish feminism has never been in a position to concentrate solely on "women's" issues or to disassociate itself from Irish nationalist politics.

According to David Lloyd, what was at stake in the recurring images of Irish identity and nationality in the earlier part of the twentieth century was "the gradual transformation of a counter-hegemonic concept within an oppositional nationalism into a hegemonic concept within a new nation state, a transformation which is . . . written already into the precepts of bourgeois nationalism" (1993, 3). Declan Kiberd concludes that the rights of the individual, which had been the informing principle of the whole cultural revival, were now subordinated to the so-called interests of society, especially in matters of sexual behavior and private morality (1995b, 22).

Despite their enormous contribution to the attainment of independence, and despite the fact that they were enfranchised earlier than their English counterparts, then, the early Irish feminists were in a significantly less powerful position, politically, in 1952 than they had been thirty years earlier (O'Dowd 1987, 3). While a number of studies have asserted that on both a collective and individual level, these women were consistently confronted with the choice of supporting either the nationalist or the women's movement, others have concluded that such a dilemma, if it existed, was not necessarily a major contributing factor to the fact that following independence, Irish women were in a weaker political position.

C. L. Innes has pointed out that the women of this earlier period, such as Anna Parnell and Augusta Gregory, were more concerned with liberation of the groups (woman and nation) than they were with individual liberation (Innes 1993, 44–45). Therefore Augusta Gregory could approve of Yeats, as spokesman for the literary revival (as political movement), being named as sole author of plays that she, in fact, wrote or co-wrote. This was an admirable thing to do, but then Yeats appropriated the work and, in turn, became appropriated by the literary establishment, thus totally obscuring Gregory's original aim and replacing it, for many years, with a false picture of her as a less creative being who deferred to a great master.

The early aims of suffragists like Hanna Sheehy Skeffington who, along with James Connolly, believed that the liberation of Ireland as a nation went hand in hand with the liberation of women as part of that nation, became representative of a socialist/feminist idealism that could not be attained in the new republic in the face of ever-strengthening capitalist/ patriarchal/religious bonds. With each successive stage in Ireland's political development, the position of women in the south continued to regress, to a point that made resuscitating the women's movement of the earlier period ever more difficult. Two major political events had especially serious consequences for the achievement or maintenance of a representative women's movement. First was the partitioning of Ireland in 1922 into the Free State (republic) in the south and a British province in the north; this provoked the development of fierce nationalism and sectarianism on both sides. Second was the passage of the 1937 constitution, which enshrined a woman's/ mother's place in the home over workplace rights. Each had a direct and profound effect on women's lives.

The ways in which a certain kind of nationalist mythology entered the cultural iconography of the Republic of Ireland have been well documented. Sexuality, however, as represented by powerful female figures, was simply written out of an Irish history that had no place for active heroines— whether mythological ones like Queen Maeve or real ones like Constance

Markievicz, who was granted a reprieve from execution despite her part in the 1916 rebellion. Not surprisingly, one of the most powerful and prevailing female images associated with the mainstream nationalist sacrificial myth has been that of the mother figure whose role is that of a breeder of sons for sacrifice in the name of their country. Alternatively, women can exist as supporters and nurturers of men who are fighting for Irish freedom. Both images have come under fire by a significant number of contemporary women writers. From the early-twentieth-century nationalist phase until the late 1950s, in fact, when nationalist history was challenged by early revisionists, Irish "nation" and Irish "woman" were conflated into the largely literary figures of Kathleen ni Houlihan, the Dark Rosaleen, and Mother Ireland, among other symbolic representations.

Brian John believes that the awful character of Irish heroism, which Yeats turned to advantage, is its fatality, whereby the hero gains his spiritual triumph in physical defeat (1979, 182). However, this is a spiritual/physical experience from which women are excluded—or, at the very least, in which they play only a maternal role. Luke Gibbons, in his study of landscape, narrative, and memory in Irish film, maintains that in the artistic reconstruction of Irish history undertaken by the leaders of the literary revival, the past was transformed into a stirring narrative of heroes and battles, of "gods and fighting men" inspired by the warrior virtues of chivalry, purity, and violence: "The mere presence of a woman posed a threat to this ascetic, male universe, so when in the most famous of all the historical sagas, the *Tain Bo Cuailgne*, Ulster is invaded by Maeve, the warrier Queen of Connacht, we find O'Grady's narrative powers stretched to their very limits." Gibbons quotes Philip Marcus's description of O'Grady's predicament as attributable to his need to make Maeve more feminine and, thus, "to endow her with some of the personality traits traditionally associated with the weaker sex . . . at times, the proud amazon of the sources seems more like the delicate fainting heroines of the nineteenth-century novel" (1983, 150).

Not surprisingly, during such a fiercely nationalistic phase, a rejection of these images by nationalist women would have represented a rejection of the Irish nation itself, a problematic choice when the nation's existence was so tenuous. But rejecting the Irish nation and its mythology has not been a problematic issue for women of the more recent period.

Conventionally presented as a long-suffering sacrificial victim mod-
eled on the Virgin Mary, the literary adaptation of the Irish mother is at
once venerated and despised, existing only to breed sons who will fight for
Irish freedom and daughters in whom she can instill purity and obedience.
Domestically powerful but socially powerless, the image of the traditional
Irish mother conforms to the literary image of Ireland itself as woman: natural, passive, and possessed. It is toward such images that contemporary
Irish women writers have directed much of their attention in an effort to
undermine and reject the model as having any value.

The rejection of role models is by no means entirely new to Irish
women's writing, of course. Writers who were active in the 1940s, 1950s,
and 1960s, such as Julia O'Faolain, Edna O'Brien, Mary Lavin, and Kate
O'Brien have, throughout their literary careers, focused attention on the
plight of women within restrictive Irish sociopolitical structures. This
makes them remarkable women writers in a way that many of the later examples are not, since these earlier writers "took on" the political and literary
establishment without the benefit of any political movement or framework.
They focused a good deal of attention on the "mapping" of the circumstances that led to the position of women in Irish society and, as a consequence, implied an inevitability of direction or fatalism for their women
protagonists. This often attracted criticism from early feminist critics who
alleged a lack of agency or analysis being included in the writing of that era.

CHALLENGING THE ENTRENCHED:
WOMEN'S WRITING FROM THE REPUBLIC

By contrast, women writers from the 1970s on, perhaps building on
the groundwork laid by the earlier ones, reveal much less interest in why
things are as they are than on the strategies developed for coping with and,
hopefully, changing them. It is surely no coincidence that in stories such
as Clare Boylan's "Housekeeper's Cut" (Casey and Casey 1990), Maura
Treacy's "Made in Heaven" (Desalvo, D'Arcy, and Hogan 1989), and Kate
Cruise O'Brien's "Losing" (Casey and Casey 1990), the narrators' rejection
of the maternal role model goes hand in hand with the rejection of, or by, a
male partner whose expectations of the women's behavior implies a view of

women as domestic, subservient, and dependent; none of which applies to these protagonists. In these stories, as in much of the fiction under discussion, in fact, tradition and conservatism are embodied predominantly in either the mother figure or the male partner while the female protagonists, almost without exception, look to a very different set of values.

In contrast to the noble, devoted, and hardworking mother evident in much twentieth-century Irish writing and exemplified by Sean O'Casey's Juno (O'Casey 1963), the fictional mothers of contemporary Irish women's fiction are often absurd, pathetic, childlike characters who, far from achieving a goal of programming their daughters into a narrow-minded world of subjugation and imprisonment, cause them to seek escapes of one form or another. The mother presented by Helen Lucy Burke, for example, in "A Season for Mothers," reveals not only the narrator's spatial distance from Ireland through her life in Italy, but a psychological distance from the mother (known throughout the story only as Mrs. McMahon) who comes to visit her. Dressed in all the "black glory" (Burke 1980, 5) of her recent widowhood, wearing a sort of raven's wing attachment on her hat and carrying her rosary beads over her wrist, Mrs. McMahon's first flight and first visit to Italy is presented as a temporary and trying interlude that is barely tolerated by her daughter, Martha, the narrator of the tale, in the name of duty and little else.

Burke takes the image of the Irish mother beyond stereotype into the realm of caricature. Mrs. McMahon is a pathetically comic representation of the generic Catholic mother; one of a type rather than an individual entity as reflected in the title and in the opening lines of the story:

> Spring brought to Rome the first of the wild asparagus and the baby new potatoes from the South of Italy. It also brought the first and heaviest crop of mothers. Considerable bargaining about them went on between the girls. "I'll drive yours to Castel Gandolfo if you have mine twice to dinner," and "I'm giving a party for mine, and you can bring yours if you introduce mine to the Cardinal." (5)

At work in an Irish diplomatic department, the daughters compare notes on the foibles and trials of visiting mothers: one sits all day in the entrance lobby of the apartment building knitting a brown garment that is thought to be a Franciscan shroud; one has struck an Italian with a bottle during an argument over a cat; and one has to have gruel in bed every night, a demand that sees her daughter, Catherine Kelly, forced to buy oats from a racetrack stable and grind them in her coffee mill. Like Martha, all their usual routines are placed in a temporary state of paralysis during the visits. Martha's relationship with her lover, Giorgio, a married man, is put on hold for an indefinite period since, although she desperately wants to know, she is unable to ask when her mother's air ticket expires.

Obsequious, devout, xenophobic, and parochial, Mrs. McMahon sees only what she wants to see. Burke portrays her as frequently childlike, complete with tantrums. The beauty of Rome is lost on this woman who came only to pray all day, every day, in the pope's own church, which, ultimately, is an enormous disappointment to her. Prostrating herself in reverential awe at the entrance on her first visit, she is roughly hauled up by an official telling her to clear the way for the queue forming behind her. Further disappointment ensues with the discovery of holy statues, which Mrs. McMahon considers "no fit sight for modest eyes" (10). She finally settles for one with wings, a halo, and a dress that, although close fitting enough to show two large nipples, at least covers it from throat to ankle: "Kneeling, she wondered if it could be the Angel Gabriel, for she had always thought of Gabriel as a male angel; and besides (if he wasn't) he would surely have had the decency to wear a brassiere when making the Annunciation" (11). Mrs. McMahon's view of the natives as "horrible staring oily people" and "pagans in palaces" leads her into the clutches of a young, alcoholic Irish priest, "a Maher from Tipperary" (14), a good family in Mrs. McMahon's view since "his mother was a Nugent from Ballinasloe" (15). Despite Martha's protests that there is no such thing as a poor priest, her mother continues to supply the young man with Martha's brandy, cigarettes, and money.

The mother's disappointment is further revealed in her news to Martha that Maura Cregg, a girl who was one year ahead of Martha at school, has nine children with a tenth on the way: "She [Martha] knew that what appeared to be a question was really a statement: that she was being condemned for living an empty frivolous life in a foreign capital, instead of the penitential meritorious life of an Irish wife and mother" (22). A pleasant Sunday lunch attended by Martha, Mrs. McMahon, Father Maher, Olive Whiteside (a colleague of Martha's), and Olive's English mother turns into a battle between the mothers when Mrs. Whiteside has the audacity to suggest that Father Maher is not only a drunk but a lecherous parasite who preys on lone women. Furthermore she hints that there are unanswered questions concerning Martha's promotion, big car, and easy lifestyle, to which Mrs. McMahon retorts:

> "And if a poor priest drinks too much occasionally, isn't it a disease? Who and what drives him to it?"
>
> "Oliver Cromwell, I suppose. All you Irish are the same, anyway."
> (30–31)

Close to blows, the two "aged gladiators" (33) are led away by the daughters, Mrs. McMahon being calmed by the promise of lunch with Martha and Father Maher at Castel Gandolfo, the palace of the pope where, Mrs. McMahon hopes, she might meet up with a cardinal or even His Holiness himself. Totally placated by Martha's apparent shared outrage at Mrs. Whiteside's suggestions, Mrs. McMahon settles comfortably in the back seat of Martha's car and addresses Father Maher: "You must be tired . . . that little tiny airless room of yours you told me about—sure you could never get a decent night's sleep" (34). Instantly, Martha realizes what her mother is planning, and she also knows that in such matters her mother always wins. Mrs. McMahon confesses that she has been dreading the journey home on the plane, and expressing her view that she is sure that Martha, too, has not been looking forward to being left on her own, Mrs. McMahon adds in a cosy tone: "Sure it just goes to show you, that the Irish never appreciate each other until we encounter the foreigners, the Italians and the English" (35).

Ultimately, then, Burke exposes Mrs. McMahon as a complex figure: conniving, manipulative, and interfering, immensely powerful and dangerous yet remarkably pathetic. The childlike self-centeredness remains, whereby it is incomprehensible that Martha could possibly want a life other than that which the mother herself would choose, but the comic aspects vanish in the tradition of the best use of satire with the realization that beneath the surface lies a great seriousness and sadness.

An interesting aspect of Burke's work is that she is not primarily acknowledged as a writer in Ireland but as a well-respected restaurant critic, among other things. This is no way takes away from the quality of stories such as "A Season for Mothers" but points to the fact that much of the early writing from this contemporary period was not exclusively the property of "writers," or the literary establishment, but was, instead, an instrument of change that permitted Irish women to express themselves in relation to various aspects of their society.

Burke is only one of a number of Irish women writers to have re/vis(ion)ed the image of the Irish mother into comical, pathetic, or terrifyingly powerful figures. Different altogether are Clare Boylan's stories such as "The Picture House," "L'Amour," "Concerning Virgins," "A Model Daughter," and "A Little Girl, Never Out Before" (Boylan 1989b), all of which investigate various forms of exploitation of motherless children at the hands of both women and men.

Escape from or rejection of mothers appears often and in many different forms in contemporary Irish women's fiction. Catherine Brophy's *The Liberation of Margaret McCabe* (1985) and Ita Daly's *A Singular Attraction* (1987) are just two examples of different forms of escape, which both lead to the realization that there is basically no such thing as freedom. But, at the same time, both novels confront the idea of a fresh start, or cutting off from the past—a past that is often represented by the mother figure.

Brophy's protagonist, Margaret McCabe, is a teacher at a Catholic school for children from deprived backgrounds. She leaves her parents' middle-class Dublin home at the age of thirty-four to move in with her first lover, Oliver, after her parents find out she has spent the night with him. Arriving home after the discovery, Margaret finds her mother in the kitchen doing the ironing and quietly weeping: " 'Oh, where did I go *wrong?*' she cried. 'I thought I did everything I could. I tried to bring you all up as good Catholics. I thought I was doing everything for the best. I knew not going to mass would lead to something like this' " (1985, 151). For a week, communication is reduced to "sad reproaches and long sighs" (151). Margaret's mother tells her that it will kill her father while her father assures her that it will be the death of her mother, although "both seemed in excellent health" (152). When the realization dawns on Margaret that she is as oppressed by Oliver as she ever was by her mother, she leaves him, moves back into her parents' home temporarily, and, finally, ends up living alone in a flat. In response to her tyrannical boss, the Reverend Mother, she acknowledges that "being your own woman isn't only about dealing with men, there are lots of oppressive women too," (164). Although Margaret has dealt with Oliver, the novel ends inconclusively, with Margaret in a state of resigned confusion over the uncertainty of her work situation and the possibility of ever being free: " 'Of course you're the liberated type,' an assistant said to me in a shop the other day. It made me think. Am I? I don't know. A lot of the time it doesn't feel like that. I suppose I'm less tied up in knots than I used to be, but then is anybody ever fully liberated? I don't know" (165).

Pauline, the protagonist of Ita Daly's *A Singular Attraction* is also a teacher and in her late thirties, but her release comes only when her mother dies: "And in one hour's time Pauline will close the door on these newly painted walls. With one suitcase containing all the worldly goods she cares to take with her, she will walk down the front path and never come back" (1987, 10). Pauline, who for more than ten years had left her house every Sunday morning "when Mammy was alive" (73) ostensibly to attend mass, is intensely aware of her own narrowness and insularity represented more than anything else by the "burden" of her unwanted virginity—something represented for so long in Irish society as a valuable dowry to be taken, intact, into marriage. Totally unfamiliar with how one actually gets rid of this burden, Pauline considers the idea of a male prostitute but is uncertain whether there are any about "for heterosexuals like herself. . . . At least she assumed she was heterosexual, but could you be sure without having had a nibble? That's why supermarkets put on wine-and-cheese-tastings. Pauline was a great fan of these—sometimes, on a lucky week-end, she'd had a three course snack-with-wine in a supermarket. But to the matter in hand" (25).

Daly critiques many aspects of Catholic Ireland through the narrative, sometimes quite comically:

you know as well as I do that up to a few years ago girls who got into trouble would be read off that altar and their parents told to show them the door, ordered by the priests of the parish to do so. . . . And as for homosexuality, my poor mother went to her grave believing it to be an invention of the English gutter press . . . (76)

Sometimes the critique is tragic, for instance, when one of Pauline's favorite students tries to self-abort and is found "bleeding in a field with a knitting-needle sticking out of her" (113).

Friendship, followed by a fumbling, disastrous sexual encounter with a Danish neighbour, Jens, appears to provide a means of Pauline's "escape from the miasma" (91) that is Catholic Ireland. But her attempt to rid herself of her "burden" by sleeping with Jens without telling him that she is a virgin leaves her initially mortified and even more aware of the pointlessness of her life; ultimately, though, Pauline is remarkably at peace with herself and the world: "She savours the last of her tea with pleasure and then beckons the waitress. . . . Then she stands up and walks towards the door, a handsome woman of thirty-nine—one who walks with some measure of serenity and assurance into the autumn sunshine" (143). The experience also acts as a catalyst for her newfound contentment, which lays her mother's ghost to rest once and for all: "May she rest in peace. There is no percentage in resentment against the dead, it doesn't pay off. . . . Since that night, Pauline had stopped blaming Mammy, and now the cry 'it's all your fault' is as much a thing of the past as a pair of perpetually grazed knees" (142).

While mothers are central to the fiction, fathers or father figures are also dealt with occasionally and in much the same way. Helen Lucy Burke's "All Fall Down" tells a touching story of a father who is an "oddity" in the village because he doesn't beat either his wife or his daughter when drunk but, unfortunately, falls down in the same spot outside his daughter's school window every afternoon after having been chased out of the pub, thus causing her immense embarrassment: "Quite simply, I hated him. At night, lying with the blankets drawn over my head and tucked in the far side of the pillow, I used to scheme how I would kill him before I was eighteen. A push down the stairs from the top landing—now that would be a fine thing!" (Burke 1980, 84). In the event, the narrator is saved the trouble. When she is sent to a convent school after her father is knocked into a ditch by a straying cow, the narrator tells everyone that he is dead. Enjoying her new life among the nuns and fellow students, she is horrified when she receives word that her mother and father will be attending her confirmation. She writes back telling her father her true feelings about him and, in return, receives a note explaining that the mother and her "uncle" will be coming instead: the fact that she has no uncle and her parents, in order to see her confirmed, are prepared to go along with the charade, is of no immediate concern to her at all.

As is usual with Burke's stories, there is a twist in the tale. Upon his arrival at the convent, it becomes clear that the narrator's best friend and heroine, Frances Boylan, along with another friend, Una Sheedy, are infatuated with her "uncle," who is clearly totally sober: " 'He's lovely looking,' said Frances. Flabbergasted, I realised that she meant it; and that she was comparing his emaciated elegance with her stout common father. And I realised that she too was ashamed of her father. Did all children hate their parents, I wondered?" (89).

Having won the girls' renewed respect by introducing them to her "uncle" who charms them into awe by his politeness, however, the narrator's newfound prestige is short lived when, at the top of the marble staircase, the father turns to wave to her friends and falls down the stairs. The narrator's response is to run to the bottom of the stairs, pick up her father's walking stick, and beat him with it: "It took the combined strength of my mother and two nuns to get me away from him. As I struck, his eyes looked up at me for each blow and winced away as the stick fell. He said nothing, although his mouth writhed. He did not cry out" (90). A short time later, the narrator learns of her father's death by alcohol poisoning. Burke uses equally incisive prose to address issues of Irish (male) politics in "Battles Long Ago" and "Sensible Middle-Aged Men."

Clair O'Connor's "Hyacinths" captures the sadness and desperation of a woman who is trapped in caring for her aged, alcoholic father. Like Burke, O'Connor allows the reader to identify entirely with the protagonist, Kate, in her desperate situation. But the desperation is mixed with a good dose of pathos for the old man who, for four years, has been Kate's unwitting captor:

> "Answer me," Kate's voice was loud and angry.
>
> Frank moved his gaze from *The Irish Times* to Kate. He stared blankly for a second. "Scrambled or boiled?" she repeated. . . . "Dermot is coming today Dad," Kate said as she put the scrambled eggs in front of him. No reaction. She was used to being ignored by him. She was looking forward to her brother Dermot's visit. At least it would give her the chance to share her worries about Frank.
>
> Surely Dermot would agree to pay for him to dry out. She looked at her father. He was attempting and failing to fork some scrambled egg to his mouth. His hand shook and the egg fell onto his plate. She heard herself say, "Daddy." She hadn't called him Daddy since schooldays. He looked at her, then at his plate and left the table, stiffly formal. In his room, he climbed into the bed fully dressed, the hood of the bedclothes obliterating the daylight. He sobbed his shame into his fists, his teeth grazing his knuckles. (Walsh 1993, 94–95)

Ita Daly's "A Family Picnic" portrays the parents of the young protagonist/narrator as remarkably childlike and ineffectual. The protagonist, on the other hand, does "brain work," knows her way around Dublin, drives a car, has been to Spain, and, during a summer outing, plays the role of parent to her mother and father: "She liked this dream mother who seemed so much younger than herself in many ways. Her mother would always have that vulnerable air about her, she realised, looking back at her sitting there, playing with a blade of grass" (Desalvo, D'Arcy, and Hogan 1989, 129).

One of the interesting aspects of this story is its third-person narrative style, which is very simplistic, in keeping with the story itself. In many ways, it is even reminiscent of the "Dick, Jane, and Spot" stories often used in primary schools, stories reeking of innocence and purity. In Daly's story, however, this idyllic narrative is periodically disrupted by a sense of unease, as when we are told that two of the family's children (both sons) have been the antithesis of Mary's "goodness." The mother, dreaming of where they might be or what they might be doing, checks herself: "But she mustn't think of them today. They were all going on a picnic and the sun was shining. And if she didn't hurry they'd be late" (124). Equally disturbing is that we readers get only glimpses of Mary herself through a narrative that is subtly ironic: "Mary handed her father a plate which she had just rinsed. How he had enjoyed himself today. He reminded her of when she was young, and he would take her to Mass on Sunday, holding her hand tightly, and telling her stories of his own childhood. Her parents. She felt close to them again; today they were a family" (129).

As already mentioned, the vast majority of stories and novels written by contemporary Irish women have female central narrators or protagonists. When these writers do feature men as central protagonists, most do so strategically; in Mary Walker's ironically titled "Cherubim," for example, the male narrator allows the author to investigate an aspect of Irish society normally closed to women.

Having recognized his old pal, Lorcan Burke, "all biz and importance at the Pope's elbow every turn he made on his visit to Ireland," (Walker 1981, 20) the male narrator, Lavelle, goes on to relate his and Burke's humorous, though somewhat unrighteous, involvement in the competitive business of being altar boys in Duneen during the 1950s. He uses the memory as a means of explaining why it is no surprise that Burke is at the pope's elbow, implying a less-than-flattering image of the connection between religious life then and now.

In a Ginger-Meggsish-type tale, Walker reveals the absurdity and financially rewarding all-male world of religious ritual and elitism: "Tomorrow morning, July, the third, 1955, a contest will be held to see who gets off the altar fastest, Father Gonzaga served by Kevin McEllin, or Canon Fennessy served by Lorcan Burke. The server of the slower celebrant then agrees to retire from altar service" (28). Needless to say, Burke wins, hence the adult narrator's lack of surprise when he turns up as aide to the pope looking every bit as smug as he did the day he won the contest with "a saintly expression on his face [and] his years of experience about his head like a halo" (29).

Leland Bardwell, one of the most prolific of the contemporary writers, uses a central male narrator in a different way again, however. Bardwell was forty-two years old when her first book of poetry, *The Mad Cyclist*, was pub-

lished in 1970. Since then she has produced many novels as well as a number of short story and poetry collections, several plays, and an unpublished
musical, *No Regrets,* based on the life of Edith Piaf, performed on both Irish
and English radio.

Bardwell's fiction is most often discussed in terms of being concerned
either with the life of Irish men and women who return to "home" and see it
as observant outsiders, or with Protestant (and thus minority) middle-class
life in the Republic of Ireland. In this latter case, a central male character is
most often associated with an inability to alter what is portrayed as an entrenched, yet stagnant class system. Mothers and/or fathers are frequently
not present in Bardwell's fiction, and her stories often focus on the effects of
favoritism within families. It seems likely that Bardwell uses a male narrator
in this latter kind of fiction in order to distance it from that of the Big House
tradition.

Her novel *The House* (1984) and a short story entitled "Cedric Dear"
(Bardwell 1987) appear to use the same, or similar central character called
Cedric who returns to his Protestant, middle-class family near Dublin. In
both novel and story, Cedric's narratives investigate the family's confused
national identity, what he calls the "Protestant spoil-sport ethic" (1987,
107), emotional barrenness and restraint, as well as aspects of familial loyalty and love. In both the story and the novel, the reader is encouraged to
sympathize with Cedric as someone who is a product of, but who has rejected much of, his own background.

Class barriers and madness form the basis of another of Bardwell's stories, "Night Rider" (Bardwell 1987) which focuses on a "half-wit," Patrick
Gallagher, who has spent much of his life living in a box and who is rescued
by the local nuns for whom he does menial tasks. Patrick is compelled by a
brief glimpse of sanity and, thus, potential escape, after watching Cathcart's
daughter, Deborah, out riding, and he steals into the stud farm of the
wealthy Cathcart family for six successive nights and rides one of their
horses. On the seventh night, he is discovered, shot at by Deborah, and
then turned over to the police, who charge him with trespassing. Although
the charges are ultimately dismissed, the reader's sympathy lies with Patrick
who glimpses one more possible means of escape after the trial when he attempts to flee from the accompanying nun and drown himself. Failing in his

attempt, "Patrick was, as before, an extinct creature caught in a lock of time" (1987, 58).

Bardwell, however, is too often thought of and described as a writer who deals only with sympathetic characters (male and female) who exist as outsiders looking in at situations that were once familiar. A number of her best stories, in fact, deal with very controversial material (certainly in Ireland) specifically related to women, such as incest in "The Dove of Peace" (1987), domestic violence in "Outpatients" (1987), and women's madness in *There We Have Been* (1989a), but, unlike the previously mentioned male narratives, such material is always dealt with through central women characters or narrators.

In contrast to the family themes discussed above, domestic violence and the entrapment constituted by conventional marriage in Catholic Ireland appear as central concerns in much of the fiction of contemporary writers. In Catherine Slattery's "Moving," for example, the narrator, following years of violence, is finally beaten by a legal system in which her rights always seem to be just a few steps behind those of her estranged husband. Having returned to Ireland with her children, who, unlike her, settle in quickly and comfortably, the narrator realizes that "after the initial sobbing, week by week she would watch relations give her children tenpences and gasp and nod and tuttut until she believed she would burst. She began to understand that the huge anchor of their various sympathies would eventually weigh her down, and she knew that she couldn't come back. Things had changed. She just couldn't" (*Departures 5* 1993, 51).

She discovers through her brother-in-law that her husband has also returned to Ireland and is in rehab to sober up. When he gets out, he will want to move into the house in which she is living because it is, after all, his property. The narrator takes her children to school one morning and leaves them there. She promises them that they can come and visit her at Christmas time and go swimming, the implication being that she is going somewhere hot, and as far away from Ireland as possible.

The reaction of women to violent situations is dealt with in many other examples. Mary Ellen Fean's "Spring Cleaning," for instance, tells of one woman's new start in life, represented by her beginning spring cleaning not because it is spring but after her husband has died of a heart attack in the middle of one of his violent attacks on her. Having decided not to advise anyone of his death, she cleans all the other rooms, but leaves his body in the kitchen where it fell: "She became accustomed to the motionless figure in the armchair by the stove, the house was as silent as it had always been. . . . No one seemed to notice the strange smell that pervaded the house that summer" (18).

This kind of retreat into madness as a means of escape is sensitively dealt with in much of the fiction. Clare Boylan's "Technical Difficulties and the Plague" (Boylan 1989b), Melissa Murray's "Space Invaders" (Murray 1987), and Evelyn Conlon's "My Head Is Opening" and "In Reply to Florence" (Conlon 1987) are just a few examples, which vary greatly in terms of style and technique. A further retreat, to suicide (a major sin in Catholic teaching), is the subject of Conlon's "The Letter" (Conlon 1987) and Murray's "Flights of Angels" (Murray 1987).

Infanticide is the focus of Éilís Ní Dhuibhne's "Midwife to the Fairies" (Desalvo, D'Arcy, and Hogan 1989) and Clare Boylan's "The Little Madonna" (Boylan 1989b), while abortion, the "fallen woman," and unwanted pregnancies/babies are central to Maeve Binchy's "Shepherd's Bush" (Desalvo, D'Arcy, and Hogan 1989) and "The Custardy Case" (Walsh 1993), Liz McManus's "Midland Jihad" (Walsh 1993), Leland Bardwell's "The Quest" (Bardwell 1987), and Harriett O'Carroll's "The Day of the Christening" (Desalvo, D'Arcy, and Hogan 1989). A mental breakdown caused by the death of a child is the subject of "The Garden of Eden" by Éilís Ní Dhuibhne (Walsh 1993).

While in most cases the themes of contemporary Irish women's fiction are extremely serious, one of the most enjoyable aspects of the writing is the way these themes are dealt with. Rita Kelly's "En Famille," for example, is a story of contemporary family life viewed through the eyes of a close observer. Via a mixture of sardonic wit and irony, Kelly reveals just how mundane and absurd traditional family life and values can be. Visiting her sister Barbara, brother-in-law James (a teacher), and niece Niamh, Catherine senses that the whole show is hanging together by a thread:

> But, [she] felt, as with the pretty curtains and labelled jars, a certain playing at *Hausfrau*, grown-up babyhouse, which a normal sane remark might

shatter. Like weighing out clay and pretending it was sugar, or mixing mud in a paint-tin and pretending it was sweetcake. If someone, tired of the game or finding themselves outside the circle of make-believe, remarked on the mud, everything would stop suddenly, then pouting, tears, and a smashing of jam-jars on stone. (Kelly 1981, 99)

Barbara holds up the strain and "choking archetype" of her pregnancy as a piece of good luck, given that she and James barely sleep together. Barbara is dissatisfied with the couple's sex life, to the point to resorting to aphrodisiacs: "The lot, from wheatgerm to shock tactics. Then it finally dawned on me. That school, all those girls, even the nuns, it does something to them, I mean it's bound to, siphons off the sexual energy, then he comes home absolutely spent" (102). Hardly a traditional or orthodox view of the role of nuns in Irish education, but it is only one of a number of stories that takes a very unorthodox view of sisters religious generally.

Even less conventional is Maura Richards's second novel, *Interlude* (1982), which is also an early example of women's erotic/lesbian fiction. Richards challenges several social mores in the novel, beginning with the opening scene of passionate sex between two women who have never met before, which takes place in the dressing room of one of Dublin's more respectable and fashionable Grafton Street stores. Something of a "bodice ripper," the novel's main focus is on the steamy sexual encounters between the two women and, less centrally, on the conflict experienced by the one married woman in deciding whether she loves her husband more or less than her new lover. It closes, in a fittingly melodramatic way, with the revelation that one of the women is a nun and has decided to return to the convent:

> Going back to what? You, a raving lesbian, going back to a convent full of women like you, is that it? What do you do? Come out every now and again and prey on some helpless woman like me, destroy her life and then return to the safety of your stronghold? I should squeeze the hypocritical sneering sanctimony out of your face . . . I was so easily taken in! I was happy, so happy with Richard, never knowing that I was a latent lesbian, now what is there for me? Oh, Sheila, how can you leave me, you said you loved me, how can you leave me? (124)

But the role of nuns and convents, too, is broached in a way that would almost certainly displease traditionalists: "I know you find all this hard to rec-
oncile with my lesbian feminism," says the 'nun' in *Interlude*, "but there is no
real conflict. . . . No, the modern communes which I know are thriving
groups of strong-minded independent women, who basically have a greater
loyalty to Mary than anything the Patriarchy wants to foist on us" (128).

In quite a different way, Mary Rose Callaghan's "Rita" (also published as
"Underwear") is a funny, moving story of an aging, sensitive lay nun who
shoplifts fancy underwear from a Dublin chain store and who, when confronted by the Mother Superior, confesses that she was thinking of a boy
she once knew:

> "Ah, yes, Mother . . ." The old eyes hazed over. "We'd go up the fields to-
> gether, and lie in the long grass and the cows would come and gape at our
> nakedness. Sometimes . . ."
>
> "Stop it! Do you hear me? Stop it . . . You'll never go out alone
> again! . . . What was his name?" she asked when they joined the snake of
> traffic sliding homewards through the dark. (Callaghan 1990a, 16–17)

Rita Kelly's "Trousseau" (1986) is also concerned with nuns and underwear. This story considers the painfully embarrassed and "inadequately
proportioned" Sister Frances's day of shopping with Mother Margaret and
Sister Oliver during which they are confronted by a young man who thinks
Frances's brassiere size is a joke and from whom she flees.

Eithne Strong's "The Bride of Christ" centers on the loneliness and sadness of a woman for whom the church represents an asylum or sanctuary,
while Clare Boylan's "A Particular Calling" uses religious imagery to de-
scribe the lonely life of Patricia Higgins, a "travelling electrolysis lady" who
removes hair from "lips and loins and throats and ears" and who applies herself "with deft detachment to the parts most usually associated with love,
tenderly removing hormonal surfeit while the women faintly groaned and
murmured on about the pains of life" (1989c, 163). Largely removed from
the "pains of life," dealing only with the world of women and their "hormonal surfeit," Patricia Higgins's life, in many ways, is like that of a nun.
Upon arriving in a town, she pins up her card: "Miss Patricia Higgins is in

Sinnott's Hotel from Tuesday 14th to Friday 17th for the usual services" (155). The notice, ironically, leads to her being mistaken for a prostitute and almost raped after a group of drunken men see her go upstairs with a man whose company she welcomes as a break to her loneliness.

While she is often surprised by the amount of body hair on other women, Patricia herself hardly has any on a body that is described in iconic religious terms:

> Under her clothes her skin was smooth and cool as marble, as pale as a grey pearl. Her breasts were parchment pale and rather flat but wide in circumference, like saucers of cream. It was not a beautiful body, but it was flawless. In bed she liked to think of those cool unblemished curves beneath her nightie as a temple for the Holy Ghost. (158)

These stories, which reveal the vulnerable, lonely, and joyless side to the lives of single, devoted Irish women—whether nuns or nun-like—are very different from traditional portrayals of religious women in Irish society. Most often associated with either angelic devotion to God and the good of society or with images of cruelty and deprivation, even stories from the "transition" period of Irish women's writing, such as those by Edna O'Brien, include images of religious women and often incorporate the mother figure, most often as idealized heroines for the female protagonist or as despised figures whose main aim in life is to reproduce themselves through their daughters or students. Once again, then, in the more recent fiction there is an attempt to engage with "tradition" by juxtaposing modern images of religious life—good and bad.

Interestingly, priests do not appear to any great extent in the fiction other than as shadowy, authoritarian figures who are alluded to rather than examined in any depth. Like male narrators, in fact, they most often serve a strategic function in the fiction, such as their role in Evelyn Conlon's "The Last Confession" (1993), which, perhaps more than any other example, encapsulates the way Irish women writers have mediated both their gender and their nationality through their fiction.

Significantly, Conlon's story is also narrated by a male, the brother of the story's subject. According to the local bishop, she has deliberately set out to sleep with a number of priests and then take photographs of them as a revenge against their hypocrisy and judgmental attitude toward others. Disbelief on the brother's part that his sister is capable of blackmail soon turns to shock when his sister contacts him and tells him the truth: "She said she was doing it to blow apart the *total* hypocrisy—I mean TOTAL—and I got impatient thinking, yes, yes, yes, but you can't do that. I then said, but didn't it bother you, sleeping with priests? yuk; she said that it wasn't only men who could enjoy revenge" (Conlon 1993, 144).

The following Saturday's newspaper contains an unsigned statement from his sister saying that the photographs do exist and that she has no objection to priests having sex as long as they did not pretend that they were not and as long as they admitted it openly and changed the laws accordingly. The paper also carries a statement to the effect that a blackmail note from "some nutcase"—whom they didn't know—has been received saying that a number of "constructed" photographs, allegedly of priests, were in the blackmailer's possession:

> Didn't know who she was, hah! Well, how come next morning there were police cars everywhere around our street? They stayed there for a month, so soon the neighbours had the whole story. . . . so we sold our house and moved out here to the wilderness. The neighbours don't see the police cars, there are no neighbours. My wife doesn't talk about my sister. Neither do I, but oh, I do love to think about her often, sometimes, like now. (145)

There is an underlying tension in the story, evidenced in these last lines, between the brother's need to conform and a grudging admiration for what his sister has done. Aware that his humiliation at the hands of the priesthood could never be as great as his sister's—because he and the priests are men—and, initially, at least, prepared to defend his sister against the power of the bishop, the brother is ultimately revealed to be as powerless against the Catholic hierarchy as his sister is. However, she has taken an active part in breaking the rules that attempt to keep her in her place.

In a story like this, Conlon manages to traverse the fine line between sexuality and nationality to show that the two are interconnected. It is conceivable, for example, that some feminist critics would find the story unacceptable on the basis that no self-respecting woman would desecrate her body just to prove a point about priests' hypocrisy. The point is, of course, that it is only within a country with strong Catholic links that such a story has any relevance at all: the connections between the protagonist's gender and nationality are so close, they cannot be separated.

Conlon, like most of the other contemporary fiction writers from the Irish Republic, generally portrays quite "normal" women: in other words, not women who can be read as atypical members of their society, thus disallowing readings of the texts as examples of "one off" or aberrant characters. Such a portrayal also forces the question of how many of those existing alongside the protagonist have also internalized their gender/class/national oppression. In doing so, the writers politicize their characters by allowing them to be commentators on their communities from within the community: the "enemy" is no longer an abstraction, "out there," but is identified in real terms as an integral part of the community itself.

This can be seen quite clearly in many of Conlon's early stories. "The Park" (1993), for example, focuses on a few friends the night before the pope's visit to Dublin while they paint anti-pope slogans on prominent walls around the city. In relation to the story and the activity itself, Conlon has said:

> I think it's taken the country the best part of a decade to get over the psychic damage that was done over the whole nonsense of his [the pope's] coming. There were people who went out and painted anti-Pope slogans the night before he came and I felt that that was as valid a thing to write about as any other aspect of his visit. . . . A lot of the psychic oppression suffered by Irish women comes from being reared strictly in the religions that they come from. (Pelan 1995, 113)

In another of her stories, "Park Going Days" (Conlon 1987), set in a working-class suburb of Dublin, Conlon focuses on a group of women preparing to take their children to the park, who choose to wait until one of them has cooked dinner for her husband—the only man in the community to have a job. But it is clear that this is done less in deference to the husband than to the wife as a member of the "park-going" community.

In "On the Inside of Cars" (Conlon 1993), Conlon addresses what happens to women when they find themselves with time on their hands. In this story, the estranged husband takes the children out for the weekend and what we, as readers, share with the narrator is a sense of her abandonment to thoughts of pleasure and leisure that never actually come to fruition because of an unfamiliar paralysis brought about by having time to spare.

Conlon's work also reveals her awareness of the connections between writing, literary history, and women's lives, something that is evident in much of the writing from the Irish Republic, more than in writing from Northern Ireland. But even in this context, an awareness of literary connections is quite distinct from earlier periods, a difference that almost certainly arises from the fact that Irish women writers traditionally emerged from the ranks of the Ascendancy (ruling Protestant middle classes) and, consequently, were much less concerned with notions of national identity than with cultural ones. As a result, much of the tradition of these earlier Irish women's writing depends on describing, explaining, and, sometimes, defending Irish life from a somewhat distanced social position. While this writing was usually carried out with great skill and sensitivity, it largely concerns itself with maintaining the status quo of "conservative . . . middle-class morality" (Madden-Simpson 1984, 7).

In Conlon's "My Head Is Opening" (1987), a story about a woman's coming to terms with herself after withdrawing from the antidepressants that have kept her functional for so long, Conlon uses the woman's reading habits as a gauge of the various stages in her life:

> There was the very bus stop where she [Louise] had sworn that nothing was going to change, when she was eight months with her first. And Timothy had promised. At that time she still read. But more babies came and her husband started talking to the shadow beside her. She read less. Books dissatisfied her and left her yearning. There were no books for this side of things. Another baby. (Conlon 1987, 17)

As a child, Louise had written an essay, "When I Grow Up," in which she had said "I'm not sure what I will do but I do know that I won't do certain things, like getting married and/or having children" (18).

> Louise grew in fits and starts, reading books to suit her moods—romantic, sharp, doomed, hopeful. Books where people chose, prison books, busy books, quiet books. Stories where no one chose, where everything happened in deluges from the sky and everyone was forced to go on, regardless . . . she read the books where no one chooses and felt so bad she went to romances. (19)

Ultimately, it is books and the imaginative escape they offer her that allow Louise to repair herself:

> Louise, meet Louise. She heard voices from lost women relatives and from books where people choose. . . . when she shopped in the supermarket she didn't see the crowds of children, didn't hear the voice of too many people—no, she moved in the pleasant parts of imagination as she put her ailed body and mind back on the earth of the thinking living. (20)

All her husband, Timothy, knows is that she is not taking tablets any more and seems to be all right at the moment, but "She did talk a lot about books, but books were books after all. She also talked about herself much more than before, but Timothy Sorohan, as he was now, was not one for either of these topics" (20).

The title story to Conlon's anthology, *Taking Scarlet as a Real Colour*, perhaps more than any other encapsulates her views on the role of literature in the life of "ordinary" women: "A person is only ordinary when they're slipping out of the womb and haven't been told anything yet. What did this man think an ordinary woman is? a woman who had read only a few books? a woman who has a few books but has never read any of them? a woman who has read the books that give her only the right words?" (1993, 171). The entire story, written in a monologue addressing "Susan," discusses what has and has not been said about women in books, the ways they have been mis- and underrepresented:

How could anyone be an ordinary woman; our mothers . . . were sent out
of rooms when a baby boy's nappy was being changed, Mother of Divine
Jesus, it's no wonder some of us pick at penises as if they were going to
bite us. Ordinary? Ordinary? . . . I'm going to order champagne for us and
tell you what I think we are that was never said in the books I read. (171)

There are many other examples of explicit engagement with traditional
and modern views of literature, such as Helen Lucy Burke's "The Last Infirmity" (Burke 1980) and, perhaps the most experimental of all in this area,
Ita Daly's *Dangerous Fictions* (1989), whose title alone implies the powerful
potential and danger inherent in women imaginatively playing around with
tradition. In this novel, a different kind of family is central—one where the
mother has deliberately distanced herself from the child:

She [the child] would demand her place in the sun; Martina [the mother]
had seen to that. It had not been easy, they had both suffered pain . . . as
she turned her back on the piteous little face, walked away from the cries
of "Mummy, don't leave me." . . . It is good for her, it will make her independent. She may suffer a little now but she will grow up needing no one.
Her back will be straight and her heart will be light and she won't even
know how to cringe. (Ita Daly 1989b, 20)

The whole notion of the traditional family is rejected by the main protagonist, Martina, in what appears to be a coldhearted and calculating way. A
crucial part of the rejection is established early in the novel and centers
on the domineering figure of Charlotte, Martina's mother-in-law who feels
that Martina is an inadequate wife and mother. In turn, Martina believes
that Robert, her husband, is like most men in his unnatural and unhealthy
love of his mother. Following Charlotte's death, Robert is disturbed to receive word from the caretaker of the cemetery that someone has been defe-
cating on his mother's grave. The "someone," of course, is Martina:

He had to get a divorce—too late to worry now about what came out.
One could be got quickly, he believed, in Honolulu or the Cayman
Islands or some such place. He would stand up in front of the black judge
and say, "Your Honour, I wish to have my marriage dissolved because

my wife desecrated my mother's grave. My wife shat on my mother's grave." (82)

Daly directly addresses the way women and men can become differently fossilized by the institutions of marriage and family. Robert, the husband/father, is associated throughout with a search for heat as a source of comfort. He lives in the basement of their Georgian terrace house and uses a variety of heating methods to keep warm. The character of Robert is weighed down and immobilized by a search for warmth and comfort, often located in whiskey, as a means of representing his inertia:

On occasion he had walked in the garden of the square or sat there on a bench on sunny mornings. There was seldom anyone else around and, as he sat or walked, he was made aware of the unbearable weight of the city crowing down. He listened to the screaming of car engines, the hysterical tap-tapping of high-heeled shoes, and it seemed to him at such moments that the city was occupied by frantic people and that there was no choice between that state and his own lethargic dullness. (49)

By contrast, Martina lives mostly in the upstairs part of the house where it is cold, drafty, and unwelcoming. Everything associated with her character is symbolized by coldness, of temperature and aloofness of nature. By the end of the novel, however, Martina has abandoned the family, Ireland, and all signs of coolness and aloofness for a life in temperate Spain as a live-in English teacher to a wealthy family. The distancing of herself from all that she has known acts as a cathartic release for her, emotionally and physically. Having written to her husband and daughter for the first time in an effort to offer some kind of explanation for having walked out on them, Martina confronts the depth of her now released feelings:

I know that this is no sort of explanation, but it is the best I can do, for the moment . . . I've only given you a Poste Restante address, just in case you are tempted to come looking for me. You mustn't try to find me or worry about me. My new life is busy and satisfactory and I do have hopes for the future but it will be a slow process. In an emotional sense you two are my life and always will be. (149)

Clearly, the fiction discussed so far is not meant to be a definitive or exhaustive catalog of contemporary women's literary work from the Republic of Ireland—an impossible task given the sheer volume of work produced since the 1970s. Hopefully, however, it is evident from this selection of representative examples of contemporary fiction that women writers from the Republic of Ireland engaged with traditional views of various aspects of women's lives in modern Ireland in an effort to redress perceived imbalances. It would be quite possible to continue cataloguing the vast majority of such fiction in this way: within themes of the family, domestic violence, the church and state, sisters religious, literary history, and so forth. It would be a difficult task, in fact, to find any substantial amount of women's writing from the republic between, say, 1970 and 1995, that was not involved in imaginatively challenging the entrenched images of women in Irish society through a variety of means.

In *Imagined Communities,* Benedict Anderson offers a further valuable perspective on writing in his analysis of the historical development of print languages through a combination of capitalism and print technology; these provided sociopolitical contexts that created the potential for a new form of imagined community that, in turn, encouraged the development of a sense of national identity (1991, 46). In a similar way, Irish women's writing from the contemporary period can be seen to use different, though equally significant sociopolitical contexts, founded on a framework of international feminism and national women's presses, to develop a sense of identity again—one that makes room for both a gender and a nationality as opposed to just the latter. But while women are generally central to such writing, there is little evidence that men are the main enemy. Rather, it is political and ideological structures that are under attack: religion, the family (most often through images of mothers and fathers), patriarchy, and the cultural/national myths that, in themselves, became institutionalized tools of female oppression. It is possible to argue that the Republic of Ireland's decolonization resulted in a cultural imperialism within which Irish women became as oppressed in relation to Irish men as Irish men and the nation had once been in relation to Britain. When the position of women in the modern Republic of Ireland is viewed as a microcosm of the larger, historical imperial/colonial relationship between England and Ireland, then it is possible to see that Irish women adopted in turn as subversive and counter-hegemonic a tradition in their fiction as once existed in that produced by Irish (colonized) men in response to similar conditions.

In general, much of the writing from the contemporary period represents a fictional world that neither ignores nor necessarily denigrates men, but decenters them and the power bases they have held for so long. The major achievement of contemporary Irish women's writing from the Republic of Ireland lies in the debunking of what were essentially national myths, specifically as they related to women. In some cases, this process takes on complex forms, both in terms of literary devices and narratives. But often it is undertaken in amazingly simple ways. For example, the number of novels and stories written by contemporary Irish women that have central characters named Mary or Martha indicates both a religious—or, more often, antireligious—*and* postcolonial significance: first, in undermining of the Mary/Martha dichotomy (Mary as Holy Virgin/figure of purity, Martha as pagan figure of duty and obedience), and, second, in allocating such names to indicate generic colonized and Catholic figures.

2 The Unfinished Revolution
Women's Writing from Northern Ireland

IN HER INTRODUCTION to *The Female Line* (1985), which was the first substantial published collection of writing by Northern Irish women, editor and poet Ruth Hooley (now Ruth Carr) celebrated the arrival of the 1980s as a decade in which the setting up and expansion of women-only publishing houses throughout the world heralded the arrival of a "whole new commercial apparatus" that allowed women's voices to be heard as never before. But her enthusiasm was somewhat tempered:

> Here in Northern Ireland there is little evidence of any such revolution . . . few female authors find their way onto reading lists for higher and further education courses. Few female authors stare out from the covers of locally published fiction and poetry. (For instance, The Blackstaff Press's ratio of single-author poetry books is in the region of two female to fifteen male poets.) (Hooley 1985, 1)

Sadly, little has changed, although in 2004 the ratio in Blackstaff's list was five female to eighteen male poets.

Interestingly, evidence of feminism in other areas appeared quite early in Northern Ireland. For example, women's studies programs were established at the University of Ulster in the late 1980s and were extended by the early 1990s (though they no longer exist), while women's studies programs at Queen's University began around 1991. WEA (women's adult education) programs in the north received substantial support and finance throughout the 1980s. Meadbh Publishing, an independent and relatively short-lived venture of the late 1980s, did have considerable impact, and the important and ongoing *Women's News* was for a long time the only feminist magazine in Ireland. Despite such a strong start, however, women's studies and feminist publishing did not thrive in Northern Ireland the way they did in the Irish Republic throughout the 1980s and 1990s. Again, this should not be taken to imply that there are no problems left for women's studies, feminism, or women's publishing in the Irish Republic—far from it—but, rather, that the hard work to get women and their cultural practices on political and social agendas in the republic is a reflection of the use women there have been able to make of existing traditions of activism and education. But it also points to the fact that it has always been much more difficult in Northern Ireland than in the Irish Republic to discuss women's lives, their politics, or their cultural practices as distinct from the broader politics of Northern Ireland.

WOMEN'S PUBLISHING IN NORTHERN IRELAND

Blackstaff Press remains the major publisher of women's writing in Northern Ireland and has always claimed a particular interest in local women's work. Its (recently retired) editor, Ann Tannehill, has stated that the press's inability to focus exclusively on women's writing or even to develop a specific feminist program has much more to do with what is submitted for consideration than with any bias from within the press itself. According to Tannehill, they simply do not receive a sufficient number of manuscripts from northern women writers to be able to concentrate on women's writing, yet they receive a great many submissions (often of poor quality) from northern men. Tannehill blames the paucity of northern women's writing at least partially on a lack of confidence (personal communication with author).

Ruth Carr believes that most women writers in Northern Ireland in the contemporary period write poetry that is published in magazines because there is nowhere else to send it. But these magazines tend to be U.K. based, rather than Irish or Northern Irish, which means that Northern Irish women tend to get lumped in with British women writers and are often pressured to write about the same kinds of issues, rather than those that relate specifically to life in Northern Ireland. Carr also believes, however, that there is a north/south divide that particularly excludes Northern Irish women writers from inclusion in the southern literary scene, on the one hand. But on the other hand, there is a regular critique from critics and others that Northern Irish women do not include "the Troubles" in their poetry, despite the fact that they very often write "troubled" poetry (personal communication with author).[1]

The most immediate and obvious difference between women's writing from the republic and from Northern Ireland during the contemporary period is its reduced volume, even allowing for the difference in population size in the two places. Here, too, though, it is important to take into account conditions that go beyond demographic statistics, such as the fact that the Republic of Ireland offers substantial tax benefits to creative artists. This policy has had a very positive effect, keeping many writers in Ireland. Also, many Northern Irish women writers are included in publishing figures for Britain or the United Kingdom, rather than Ireland or Northern Ireland. In addition, most of the women's writing from the 1970s and 1980s is now out of print, and this has particular implications for feminist literary history. *The Female Line*, for instance, has been out of print for many years, and with it goes a crucially important creative recording, not only of the ways in which women in Northern Ireland initially experienced the Troubles, but also, and more importantly, a record of the nature of their early collective action as feminists. Since the fragmentation of the women's movement in North-

---

1. Since the mid-1960s, Northern Ireland has experienced what is euphemistically called "the Troubles"—a period of often severe civil unrest marked by conflict between nationalists/republicans (Catholic) and unionists/loyalists (Protestant). The British government sought to contain the unrest by sending a strong contingent of the British Army there, which remained on active duty from August 1969 until the very recent peace agreements were implemented. Its presence, far from calming matters, acted as a strong irritant. In light of the Troubles, everything about Northern Ireland is contentious and based on a binary of Protestant/Catholic. The religious divisions equate into political and paramilitary/activist terms, which tend to represent the spectrum of binaries through which the two communities understand and talk about each other: Protestant/unionist/loyalist versus Catholic/nationalist/republican.

ern Ireland, publications such as *The Female Line*—which incorporates writing from both the Catholic and Protestant communities dealing with a wide variety of topics across a number of genres—have been rare.

SURVEY OF WOMEN'S WRITING

The Female Line included, in whole or part, work by some forty-five writers. Of these, approximately twenty-five had not been published extensively and nine had never been published before, and while some of the writers included—such as Mary Beckett, Jennifer Johnston, and Frances Molloy—are still readily available in print, others are not. Even a brief sample of this writing demonstrates that it is a sad loss. Standing somewhere between community and mainstream publishing, *The Female Line* as well as other, similar, publications, such as the Northern Ireland Arts Council–assisted *Passages* series, represented a crucial publishing avenue for northern women throughout the early period.

As with the Irish Republic, one of the most significant features of contemporary writing by Northern Irish women is the number of writers who first appear in print relatively late in life. Frances McEnaney, for example, was born in 1916, yet had her first story, "The Cage," published in *The Female Line*. McEnaney's story tells of the initial fear of marital entrapment experienced by a middle-aged farmer following the death of his sister when he realizes he cannot care for himself. His ultimate insensitivity toward his new wife, who has basically been sold through economic bargaining from one life of servitude to another, is made more poignant through the distancing and decentering of the woman throughout the narrative, making it clear to the reader who the "caged" one of the title actually is.

Although she had some stories first published in the 1950s in *The Bell*, *New Irish Writing*, and *Threshold*, Mary Beckett, born in 1926, did not have her first collection of stories, *A Belfast Woman*, published until 1980. Her first novel, *Give Them Stones*, was published in 1987. Beckett's work focuses on women whose lives are in turmoil as a result of their class, politics, and gender. *A Belfast Woman* and *Give Them Stones*, in particular, deal with the lives of nationalist women and their families in working-class Belfast during the two troubled periods of the 1930s and the 1970s. However, Beckett also deals with themes such as mother-daughter relationships, primarily their difficulties.

Her story "Under Control," for instance, takes the form of a long letter from Kathleen in Ireland to her sister Peggy in England, in which Kathleen pours out the pain she is feeling after her daughter, Stella, has told her that she hates her for ruining her life. The hatred manifests itself in cruel, callous comments designed to destroy the joy that Kathleen is feeling in raising Stella's illegitimate and unwanted daughter as her own: "She [Susan] is the loveliest, happiest child, Peggy, mischievous and energetic. Stella says I make a fool of myself running after her, that I am too old and too stout and that if I'm going to bend over on the footpath to lift up a struggling child I should wear tights and not stockings. Oh she can mortify me with her tongue" (Hooley 1985, 99). Kathleen's outpouring is concluded with a return to controlled politeness: "I will never refer again to her outburst of this morning. That's why I'm getting it off my chest to you. I don't expect you to make any answer to all of this. Don't worry. Everything is again under control" (101). This sense of life being held barely "under control" is a prominent feature of much of the women's writing from Northern Ireland, wherein there is a sense of impending eruption kept in check by the frailest of social mores.

The late Frances Molloy is an example of a northern writer who makes good use of satire as a means of exposing the way women in Ireland are subjected to the whims of politics, religion, and insecure men. Her novel *No Mate for the Magpie* (1985b) tells, in Northern Irish dialect, the story of Ann Elizabeth McGlone, whose tale of growing up in Northern Ireland reveals the stupidity and senselessness of the *us* and *them* mentality, especially for working-class Catholics and Protestants. In her short piece, "An Irish Fairy Tale," Molloy uses the same satirical method to reveal Saint Kevin of Glendalough as "the patron saint of woman beaters" (Molloy 1985a, 148).

Jennifer Johnston, one of Ireland's best-known writers, addresses the mythology associated with Northern Ireland in her fiction. Between 1972 and 1979 she produced five novels—*The Captains and the Kings* (1972), *The Gates* (1973), *How Many Miles to Babylon?* (1974), *Shadows on Our Skin* (1977), and *The Old Jest* (1979)—all of which center on Ireland's troubled politics and culture from either an historical or contemporary perspective.

Born in 1930 to a literary father and theatrical mother, Johnston was forty-two years old before she published her first novel. This fact and her earlier concentration on what Shari Benstock refers to as "tales of the lonely individual storyteller" focused on "the furthest reaches of artistic alienation" (Benstock 1982, 216) are reflected in Johnston's own description of her early confusion as a writer:

> Almost from the moment I started thinking, I really would have preferred to have been a man. I wouldn't want to be a man now, but it seemed to me as a child that it was a man's world. The world was for men and I couldn't work out where I fitted into it. I certainly didn't see myself taking up the women's role and in all my dreams and imaginings I was always a boy. It took me quite a long time to work out the fact that you had to take what you were and attack the world from that standpoint . . . I hated being seventeen. I found the world a very daunting, at times terrifying place. In fact, I didn't much like being anything until I was thirty. (Quinn 1987, 57, 59)

Yet, as early as 1977 in her fourth novel, *Shadows on Our Skin*, Johnston reveals a concern with issues that were to become central to critical discussions of Northern Ireland's future direction. Setting the view of Joe, a young native of Derry, against that of a southern woman visitor, Johnston addresses the already-evident political divide between north and south:

> "You're not from Derry, are you?"
>
> "I've only been here a couple of years. My parents would turn in their narrow graves if they knew where I was."
>
> "Why?"
>
> "That was a silly thing to say. I don't think they'd really mind. Worry. They'd worry. They were never too keen on the North. Like a lot of people down there. They looked on the border as a sort of necessary protection. Keeping out some awful plague." She sighed. "They were simple people. Nice. Very nice when you look back on them." (Johnston 1977, 88)

Later in the novel, the shooting of two British soldiers in a Derry street leads to this exchange:

> The old man began to sing again. "A nation once again . . ." An ancient, destroyed voice.
>
> She dragged her eyes away from her hands and looked at him. "It's old buggers like you should be shot, with your talk and your singing of glory and heroes."
>
> "Freedom . . ."
>
> "What's freedom?"
>
> "Don't be a fool, woman. You know well what freedom is. Didn't I fight for freedom? Didn't I give my health? What did Pearse, God rest him, say about freedom?"
>
> "Well, you don't remember, that's for sure. Have they any more freedom down there than we have up here?"
>
> "You misunderstand . . ."
>
> "Is there a job for every man? And a home for everyone? Have all the children got shoes on their feet? Are there women down there scrubbing floors to keep the home together because stupid, useless old men are sitting round gassing about freedom? Singing their songs about heroes?" (154)

Joan Lingard, born in 1932, published six novels for adults, the first in 1963, before turning to children's fiction. Given her religious background as a Christian Scientist raised in a "Protestant stronghold with just a few Catholics around" (Quinn 1987, 95), Lingard's early novels, not surprisingly, focus on the divides of Northern Ireland, primarily during the years of World War II. This idea of a divided community is a focus of a great deal of the writing from Northern Ireland. Marjory Alyn's *The Sound of Anthems* (1984), Julie Mitchell's *Sunday Afternoons* (1988), and Kitty Manning's *The Between People* (1990) are just a few of the better-known examples.

Shirley Bork's first published story, "The Palm House," which appeared in *The Female Line*, centers on the confusion, sadness, and identity crisis experienced by the middle-aged narrator as she sits waiting for her lover to meet her to discuss his proposal for a ménage á trois. All around her are the signs of a disturbed and divided society. The woman's reflections and meditations take place in the Palm House, an extended part of the Botanic Gardens that are next to Queen's University in Belfast, two sites which symbolically represent conservatism in the form of tradition (the gardens) and radicalism (the university). The narrator undergoes a crisis in which she is physically and metaphorically situated between the two: "a rather pathetic, middle-aged woman. Someone I don't recognise" (Hooley 1985, 110), who wishes it were summer and the park full of "teenage lovers and dogs and babies in prams" as she sits crying "for all the people in the park" (110) as well as for herself.

Virtually everything in Bork's story relates to age as a way of symbolizing the dichotomy of old and new, which is representative of Belfast itself: the two soldiers who guard the gates to the park are "scarcely more than boys" and are confronted by an old lady who solemnly presents them with an ice lolly before scuttling on about her business (107); the youthful students juxtaposed with the "tweed-suited, silk-scarved ladies heading for the Extra-Mural Department" of Queen's (106); the man with his "brain-damaged" son who sparks memories of her own, similarly damaged child (108). It is not insignificant that the narrator, a woman trapped between the old and the new, past and present, can see and understand both sides.

But while the theme is a common one, the divisions are, of course, portrayed in the contemporary writing in many different ways: sometimes from a fixed perspective within one or other of the communities; sometimes through the eyes of a child who doesn't yet understand the divisions or the significance of her or his unformed, though inevitably predestined, political affiliations and cultural identity. This sense of inevitability or predestination is the most evident way in which the entrapment or siege associated with Northern Irish politics appears in women's writing. However, while there are many different portrayals of the divisions, there are very few examples in which a partisan view is expressed. The writers seem to be much less concerned with who is at fault than they are with representing the effects of the political conditions on women's lives.

Another late starter, Caroline Blackwood (1931), did not have her first novel, *For All That I Found There*, published until 1974, when she was forty-three. Like Jennifer Johnston, Blackwood is most often associated with a modified continuation of the Anglo-Irish Big House tradition in which the

decline of the ascendancy in Ireland is witnessed through the disintegration of its most evident architectural symbol. Like Johnston's, however,
Blackwood's fiction is much more complex and interesting than this critical description suggests. More accurate, perhaps, is Ann Owens Weekes's
assertion that Blackwood focuses on "decay: of ideals, marriages and Big
Houses, ultimately seeing deterioration as the human situation, much en-
livened by eccentric or mysterious characters" (Weekes 1993, 38).

There are some interesting thematic points of contact between
women's fiction from Northern Ireland and that from the Irish Republic
during the contemporary period also. Jan Kennedy's first story, "June 23rd,"
for instance, has as its protagonist Martha, who has been forced to give up
her job and flat in Coleraine after her mother's accident and father's stroke
and now cares single-handedly for her aging parents. Once a year Martha's
sister Edwina arrives from England to allow Martha to visit the seaside at
Greystones for two weeks. The story focuses on the day of Edwina's arrival,
June 23, with Martha attending to lists, notes, and orders so that everything
will be in place for her sister to step in and care for the parents without too
much disruption to all of their lives. The extent to which Martha is forced
to ensure that, even in her absence, her parents' needs are attended to is
only answered by resentment shown by her mother and father toward her
for "deserting" them every year (Hooley 1985, 180).

Similar to stories from the republic such as Catherine Brophy's *The Liberation of Margaret McCabe*, Ita Daly's *A Singular Attraction*, and Clairr O'Connor's
"Hyacinths," everything in Kennedy's story points to repression from parental control, seething resentment and bitterness on the part of Martha who,
at thirty, is destined to spend her life being a "good daughter" (Hooley 1985,
179), nursing her parents while her sister's life continues without interrup-
tion: the entire story reflects a variation of the sacrificial myth represented
here by the dutiful daughter. The end of the story, then, both surprises and
shocks the reader, although not without providing a certain sense of satis-
faction. An unexpected note arrives within a few hours of Edwina's expected
arrival and states:

> I know I should have let you know earlier, should at least have phoned to
> say I wasn't coming. Cowardly of me perhaps, but *I know you will understand.*

I just cannot go on with this charade of the dutiful daughter. I can't go on pretending to enjoy my stay at home. I come back here to Michael, at the end of the fortnight, exhausted. He feels the strain is too much for me and I really cannot be expected to go on doing it. *I know you'll understand,* Martha, and think of some excuse for me.

Your loving sister,

Edwina. (181; emphasis added)

Martha understands everything clearer than ever before. She tells her mother and father that Edwina has telephoned to say she has a puncture and will be a little later than usual, and then "The dishes washed, best summer coat over her arm, Martha closed the door behind her, checked it was secure, and walked briskly up the hill" (182). Like Clairr O'Connor's "Hyacinth," the narrator is "let down" by a sibling who fails to turn up and take her or his fair share of parental caring, thus causing a radical change in the behavior of the carer herself.

Maggie Sands's first published story, "The Calling of the Green," takes the theme of revenge against parental control even further, although the sacrificial culprit in this instance is a man named Michael Feeny. The story opens with Feeny, who has spent seven years in America, fondly contemplating his return to Ireland for his brother's wedding. The jungle green airport sign saying "Welcome to Northern Ireland" and the protagonist's delight in seeing Seamus, his brother (both of which appear on the first page), are the only positive events in the story. The mood is broken when, within minutes of arriving, Michael asks about their mother:

"Is Mammy not with you?"

"No, she's all worn out with the excitement of seeing you again. She missed you a lot even though she had myself to look after her. She has been praying night and day to Our Lady this seven years for you to come back and stay in Ireland. It'll do her a power of good to have both sons around her again. What with Daddy dying and yourself leaving, sure her aul heart's nearly broke." (*Passages* 44)

But any discomfort Michael feels at the implication that he is somehow responsible for his mother's unhappiness pales into insignificance when he sees her and realizes that, having gotten away once, he will never be able to leave Ireland again:

> She was trying to paralyse him with that look. Michael winced. In the brevity of the moment, he saw her as he had seen her then—a broken and hoggish old woman who took her religious beliefs to the point of insanity. A pair of artless wooden Rosary beads lay in her lap, twisted between the spindly fingers of her fleshless left hand, and beyond her the face of the Sacred Heart burned against the whitewashed walls. Michael could see that self-same crippling look coming from the eyes in the print. He was literally rooted to the spot. (45)

Later, lying beneath "the figure of the crucified Christ," (45) Michael realizes that he will never see America again because "she would not let him leave. She wanted her son" (46). Michael sees only one escape: "They intercepted Michael at the airport next morning, his bag still unpacked and the pair of wooden Rosary beads with which he had strangled his Mother clutched tightly in the whitened knuckles of his left hand. As they led him away he was heard to say, 'Ireland never lets go of her sons, does she?' " (46).

Polly Devlin, born in 1944, has focused much of her fiction on the crisis of identity experienced by Catholic children growing up in Northern Ireland. In her memoir, *All of Us There* (1983), she captures what she sees as the sense of struggle and fatalism associated with Northern Ireland's Catholic population:

> All children born in segregated places are born with a dark caul, a web of ambiguities around them, from which it is difficult to struggle free. But the Roman Catholic children of the province of Northern Ireland have a darker, stronger birth-membrane imprisoning them against which they have to struggle, since the loyalties and love we feel towards our putative nation and powerful religion are subversive. Loyalty towards the idea of Ireland and love for Mother Church are inextricably entangled, yet neither feeling can be open, proud or free, since neither religion nor country has status, official sanction or respect. (47)

Devlin is one of those writers whose work crosses a number of genres: in addition to the memoir, she has produced, among other things, a history of photography, a collection of children's stories entitled *The Far Side of the Lough* (1983), and a novel called *Dora, or the Shifts of the Heart* (1990) in which she investigates aspects of cultural and sexual identity through the central figure of a woman writer.

THE NORTHERN CONTEXT

While this use of the woman writer as central figure is fairly common in stories and novels by writers from the republic, it is quite rare in works from Northern Ireland. There is, in fact, very little explicit investigation of the relationship between women and creativity in the fiction produced by women in the north. Rather, central female protagonists in northern women's fiction are more likely to be either directly involved with sectarian politics or determined to avoid politics of any kind.

This focus on the political rather than overtly creative can be explained at least partially by the fact that the women's movement became visible in Northern Ireland at roughly the same time as the Civil Rights movement (and, by extension, the Troubles), which has meant that the politics of feminism, class, nationalism, ethnicity, and sectarianism have developed as ostensibly different features of one source problem of inequality. The reality, of course, is that while not unrelated, such politics are fed by quite separate—and often antagonistic—inequalities and by the binaries that inevitably dominate divided societies and imply, oversimplistically, that people belong to one polarized grouping or another: Irish/British, Catholic/ Protestant, nationalist/unionist, republican/loyalist. At the same time, the blurring of the lines between nationalist, ethnic, and gender politics in Northern Ireland created a modern, northern version of the nationalist/ feminist binary *within* the Irish women's movement, something that caused untold damage to the development of feminism in Northern Ireland.

At first glance, it would seem that the high-profile political involvement would foster feminism. Between 1976 and 1983, for instance, women prisoners in Armagh jail were involved in a no-work protest designed to gain political, as opposed to criminal, status. Between November 1972 and the end of 1973, about 650 republicans in all were interned, and approximately 60 of them were women. However, between 1973 and 1975, the women prisoners had almost full control of Armagh jail.

Between February 1980 and March 1981, the women of Armagh joined the "dirty protest" undertaken by the men of Long Kesh[2] prison, which included a no-wash protest and the smearing of excrement and, in the women's case, menstrual blood, on their cell walls. The debate as to whether this action was a feminist or a nationalist issue became the most divisive in the history of Irish feminism:

> Many feminists were emotionally torn between their desire to support the sufferings endured by the women, and their concern lest this feminist solidarity be translated into unconditional support for the Provisionals . . . women within Sinn Féin who are fighting for greater equality for women, isolated as they so obviously are, felt betrayed at the lack of public support by the feminist movement. (Ward 1983, 3)

Irish playwright and activist Margaretta D'Arcy was one of eleven women arrested as part of a protest by Women Against Imperialism. She spent three months in Armagh in 1980 during the period of the "dirty protest," and she was requested by the women of Armagh to "tell . . . everything" once she was released. Her book, *Tell Them Everything: A Sojourn in the Prison of Her Majesty Queen Elizabeth II at Ard Macha (Armagh)* was published in 1981. D'Arcy's account of life in Armagh reveals an acute awareness of her own double vision: "I was not only an observer, I was also a participant and I had to retain my own individuality as a civilian. Mairead's [Farrell's[3]] task was infinitely more intricate—to ride the everchanging currents and winds

2. Her Majesty's Prison Maze (known locally as the Maze) was on the site of a former Royal Air Force station at Long Kesh, on the outskirts of Belfast. The prison became known to Irish republicans as Long Kesh or H Block (the area where political prisoners were detained), and was so called because of the shape of the prison "cages" or buildings when seen from the air.

3. Mairead Farrell was arrested and sentenced to fifteen years in prison in April 1976 for allegedly planting bombs as part of an IRA campaign to protest against the withdrawal of

affecting life in jail from society outside" (D'Arcy 1981, 68). Such nonfiction exists as a very different kind of political discourse from the creative writing produced by contemporary Northern Irish women, which is much more politically ambivalent.

The tightrope between nationalist goals and rights for women continued to be a difficult one on which to balance. By the late 1980s, the split between the Northern Ireland Women's Rights Movement and the Socialist Women's Group over strategies of anti-imperialism, followed by a further split between the Northern Ireland Women's Rights Movement and the Down Town Women's Centre, again over political differences, exposed the complexities involved in forming a women's collective in Northern Ireland. In turn, these events have had an effect on the development of institutionalized feminism in the north and on women's writing and publishing. These divisions represent a fairly straightforward reflection of the broader political sphere.

NATIONALIST MYTHOLOGY IN NORTHERN IRELAND

Seamus Deane has said, "The principle of continuity which [Yeats] established in literature, stretching from Swift to the Revival, and that which Pearse established in politics, stretching from Wolfe Tone to the men of 1916, are both exemplary instances of the manner in which tradition becomes an instrument for the present" (Deane 1985, 158). The result has been that the cultural machinery associated with the republic's earlier battle for independence, evident in the politics of Ireland during the late nineteenth and early twentieth centuries, has been transferred to Northern Ireland during the contemporary period, so that features of cultural nationalism that have faded in importance in the Irish Republic remain central to the struggle in the north—and not exclusively for the nationalist community; as Deane puts it, "the figure of Cú Chulainn is now very small in the Irish Republic, but

---

special status for political prisoners. She became the OC (officer in command) of A Wing, Armagh, during the hunger strike and "dirty protest" periods. She was shot dead along with two comrades, Dan McCann and Sean Savage, in Gibraltar in March 1988 by British soldiers from the Special Air Service (SAS).

in east Belfast he looms larger" (1991, 1: xxiii). Cairns and Richards see this as regressive since "identity formed in a narrative of the past, informed by tropes whose vital moment is over, is incomplete" (1991, 137).

Generally speaking, the dominant features of this "instrument" are centered on the recycling of three concepts that were central to the earlier republican politics and mythology: that of a coherent national identity that is essentially "green," indigenous, Catholic, and republican; the appropriation of the blood sacrifice myth most often associated with Pearse and the Easter 1916 rebellion; and a belief that the Troubles in Northern Ireland are a straightforward continuation of Ireland's earlier struggle for independence from British imperialism.

The first of these concepts has manifested itself most often in the nationalist population of Northern Ireland being portrayed, and often portraying themselves, as a body of disenfranchized native Irish who always have had and always will have a closer relationship with their indigenous comrades in the republic, based on a shared nationality, than they could ever have with the alien "British" unionists with whom they share a culture. Yet as Liam O'Dowd, among others, has pointed out:

> In the South the state has definitively replaced the Catholic Church as the framework of intellectual activity. The Anglo-Irish Agreement, the EC and growth of a more specialised intelligentsia have reduced intellectual interest in the "national question." This has meant a distancing of the "Northern conflict" and a re-working of a national identity more congruent with the twenty-six-county state. This has isolated the republican movement in the North. (O'Dowd 1991, 170)

The second recycled concept, the blood sacrifice, is especially evident in the mid- to late 1980s. Cairns and Richards have pointed out that to read Bobby Sands's poetry, prose, and polemics, for example, is to realize that he recycles Pearse's images of suffering and sacrifice, translating them to the situation of the H Block and the dirty protest.[4] He links the republican

4. Bobby Sands was a sentenced "special category" prisoner in Long Kesh. In 1980, the British government refused to grant five demands to political prisoners, which resulted in

Volunteer to the suffering Christ in, for example, "The Torture Mill-H Block":

> Blessed is the man who stands
> Before his God in pain,
> And on his back a cross of woe
> His wounds a gaping shame,
> For this man is a son of God
> And hallowed be his name.
> (Cairns and Richards 1991, 132)

One of the most dominant of these images emerged as the result of a distinct shift in the cultural myths of Ireland between the nineteenth and twentieth centuries. In nineteenth-century Irish nationalism, the two most important myths were a belief in an ancient unified Gaelic nation and in the struggle of the Gaels from the twelfth century onward against an alien English occupation (J. R. Archer 1986, 24). Following the 1916 rebellion and the execution of its leaders, however, there developed a new foundation myth in which "the blood sacrifice awoke the Irish nation from her slumbers to begin the struggle for independence in earnest" (J. R. Archer 1986, 33). Cairns and Richards have pointed out that, with regard to the pre-Rising revival tropes, "in terms of impact there can be no doubt that the trope of Ireland, and those who fought for Ireland, as Christ Crucified/Christ Risen was far more significant—culturally and politically. Pearse's

---

what became known as the H Block/Armagh hunger strikes. On 27 October 1980, seven H Block prisoners began a hunger strike, which lasted until 18 December (fifty-three days) when a thirty-four-page document, agreeing in principle to the five demands, was presented to them. The British Parliament led by Humphrey Atkins later reneged on the agreement. Bobby Sands was one of the prisoners who went on hunger strike on 1 March 1981 in response to the collapse of the agreement; he was elected as a member of Parliament for the nationalist electorate of Fermanagh/South Tyrone while on strike and died on 5 May 1981 after sixty-six days on hunger strike. Sands's death was followed by nine others: Francis Hughes, Raymond McCreesh, Patsy O'Hara, Martin Hurson, Thomas McElwee, Mickey Devine, Joe McDonnell, Kieran Doherty, and Kevin Lynch. Sands's poems and short stories were published under the pen name of "Marcella" in the late 1970s and early 1980s.

plays, stories and poems are redolent with these images" (Cairns and Richards 1991, 132).

Similarly, D. E. S. Maxwell quotes Eamonn McCann that "one learned, quite literally at one's mother's knee, that Christ died for the human race and Patrick Pearse for the Irish section of it" (Maxwell 1982, 157). Richard Kearney considers that it is precisely the ability to solicit sympathy through the fictional construction of such figures of suffering (as in hunger strikes, for instance) that has, historically, been one of Irish republicanism's strongest weapons (1980, 21). Certainly, Sands's and the other hunger strikers' political martyrdom in Northern Ireland is easily equated to that of Pearse and the leaders of the Easter 1916 rebellion.

But the recycling of such images is evident in much nonfiction too. In *An Interlude with Seagulls: Memories of a Long Kesh Internee*, for instance, Bobby Devlin recalls how the production of harps, Celtic crosses, music boxes, and spinning wheels formed an important part of the handicraft activities in the prison: "These items were much sought after, especially with the name of Long Kesh written on them, as this name is now symbolic to the republican struggle. Long Kesh harps and crosses take pride of place in many households in many countries of the world" (Bobby Devlin 1985, 13). Devlin also recalls taking Irish lessons during his time in Long Kesh (something that became known locally as "jailtecht"), and relates how he and other prisoners looked forward to the Easter messages that appeared in the *Irish News*: "To my son Liam, Cage 3, Long Kesh Concentration Camp. The season's greetings to a true felon of our land. I who gave birth to Cuchulainn the Brave. From your mother" (48). Such reenactments of political martyrdom are also evident in publications like *The Captive Voice/An Glór Gafa*, which publishes writings by both male and female Irish republican prisoners.

The third concept, that all Ireland is not yet independent, is perhaps the most straightforward and politically strategic in that it is the one that is renewed consistently by those involved in the republican movement as a means of invoking an historically based justification for political action. In this, the Troubles exist as part of the "unfinished revolution" between Ireland and England, and the context in which they are discussed is clearly within the discourse of imperialism, as seen in these two passages written by members of the nationalist Northern Ireland Civil Rights Association:

Whatever else it's about [the struggle in Northern Ireland], it is certainly
not about religion, certainly not about theology, certainly not about religious intolerance. People are at last beginning to realize that the issues
in the north of Ireland are historic issues, based on the problem of imperialism. They have to be resolved by correcting the historic wrongs. (Bernadette Devlin McAliskey 1994, 36)

The sectarian divide in the North is of very long standing. It's rooted
very deeply in the history of Ireland—it goes back 400 years. The politics
of Northern Ireland, the dominant political structures of Northern Ireland, have always been based upon the sectarian divide. So we mustn't
underestimate the depth of the division in Northern Ireland. (Eamonn
McCann 1994, 17)

Both Bernadette Devlin McAliskey and Eamonn McCann were part of
the original Northern Ireland Civil Rights Association (NICRA), and have
been deeply committed to and involved in northern (nationalist) politics
since the 1960s. However, despite the fact that Devlin McAliskey has consistently called for a rethinking of women's role in Irish politics to take account of the interrelated categories of gender, race, and class, she is still
most often associated with a kind of ungendered republican activism. This
construction of political women such as Devlin McAliskey is one feature of
a traditional association of sectarian politics with religion, which is integral
to Northern Ireland's political history and identity and which, in turn, is
most often seen to be a continuation of the (privileged?) political history
and identity of the Irish Republic.

In contrast to so much of the nationalist mythology kept alive in
Northern Ireland, however, the concept of nationalism in the Republic of
Ireland has shifted ground several times and today often represents little
more than an important feature of Irish history or, alternatively, something
that is still important, albeit distantly, to an ongoing struggle in the north.
Either way, it is inaccurate, if not nonsensical, to speak of a single cross-
border nationalist community or ideology.

According to Felix ó Murchadha, for example, nationalism in the republic is seen in terms of tradition, culture, and history "with the appendix
of vague irredentist aspirations to the North," while in Northern Ireland,

particularly in the working-class areas of Derry and Belfast, nationalism is an ideology of revolt, "the galvanising force of historical and contemporary justification for a struggle against oppression" (1993, 1–2). Ó Murchadha goes on to maintain that in concepts such as tradition, culture, religion, language, and identity:

> words such as "Catholic," "Nationalist" and "Irish" have different connotations, different emotional associations, North and South. Until nationalists in the Republic realise this, until they see that nationalism in the Republic is part of the establishment ideology and in the North, for the most part, an ideology of rebellion, they will never come to grips with the Northern situation. (2)

For most people in the Republic of Ireland, however, coming to grips with "the Northern situation" has not been a crucial aspect of life for a long time. Other issues have taken precedence, not least a confrontation with shifts in self-identification from a romantically isolated, rural, and agricultural nation—such an important part of a nascent national independence—to an ostensibly economically prosperous European one.[5]

More often than not, Northern Ireland represents to many of the republic's institutions, including the Catholic Church, little more than an example of what not to do. In 1994, for example, the *Irish Times* quoted Bishop Cahal Daly, on behalf of the bishops to the New Ireland Forum, saying that Northern Ireland's threefold increase in marital breakdown was an example of what happened when divorce laws were liberalized (*Irish Times* 8 February 1994, 12). Many people in the Republic of Ireland view Northern Ireland as a negative place, beyond comprehension and therefore best left to its own devices. Margaret Ward indicates that this attitude toward Northern Ireland extends to all facets of intellectual as well as popular debate and has created long-term problems as a result:

5. I say "ostensibly" because there remains much discussion in the Republic of Ireland concerning its place in Europe, as well as ongoing debates concerning identity, made all the more complex these days by an influx of refugees, asylum seekers, and returning immigrants.

The academic community in Ireland failed in its task of engaging with
the issue [of partition], so discussion seldom moved on to more fruitful
levels . . . the difficulties involved in understanding the complexities of
the North of Ireland were solved by the simple device of erecting an intellectual border, shutting off the troublesome six counties from the rest
of Ireland. (1995a, 128)

Ward goes on to infer that this quarantine has had a particularly negative
influence on Irish feminist history, since, in failing to come to terms with
events in the north, feminists missed the opportunity, first, to understand
why British suffragists chose to establish a presence in Ireland during the
earlier part of this century and, second, to raise political questions regarding the ways in which feminism can overcome differences when the "protagonists are locked into a colonial relationship" (1995a, 129). Regardless
of what could or should have happened, the reality of the situation is that,
since its birth in 1922, Northern Ireland has always contained two distinct
communities that developed within distinct cultural and political systems,
and this has been important in the development of equally distinct feminist
politics, north and south.

The decade 1974–84 was Northern Ireland's most turbulent in terms of
sectarian violence. In their study of northern women's experiences of the
time, Fairweather and colleagues found that one in ten adult men from the
nationalist community were imprisoned during that decade. But they also
point out that when the status of male prisoners was changed from "political" to "criminal," it was women who organized the demonstrations through
the Relatives Action Committee, a political campaign that was "unique in
nationalist history in that it was the only mass organization started and led
almost exclusively by women" (Fairweather, McDonough, and McFadyean
1984, 50).

Brenda Murphy perhaps best exemplifies how women writers from
Northern Ireland at the height of the Troubles negotiated the line between
art and politics, nationalism and gender, or, in Murphy's case, the way
writers/activists creatively shape political material. A writer from the age of
seventeen, Murphy spent six years in Armagh prison for republican activi-

ties and is often associated with community writing. Apart from *The Female Line,* her work was published in Desalvo, D'Arcy, and Hogan's *Territories of the Voice* (1989). Murphy has also been involved with Dubbeljoint Productions, a theater company formed in 1991 in West Belfast. She was coauthor of *Binlids* in 1997 with Danny Morrison, Jake MacSiacais, and Christine Poland, and sole author of *Forced upon Us* in 1999; both are unpublished.

Murphy is known for short, razor-sharp prose pieces that confront various aspects of women's lives. Her most widely published piece is "A Curse," which relates one woman's discomfort and humiliation at the hands of the prison system when she is being detained for questioning and her period arrives—known as "the curse" colloquially. Apart from an intense sense of confinement and powerlessness, Murphy's story addresses two problematic aspects of gender politics in Northern Ireland: what women are permitted to speak about, and the failed notion of female solidarity. When confronted by a policeman after banging on the cell door, the protagonist asks for a policewoman, but the request is refused by the impatient, puritanical man:

> "I've taken my period," she said simply. "I need some sanitary towels and a wash. I've not been allowed to wash since I was arrested, days ago." He looked at her with disgust. "Have you no shame? I've been married twenty years and my wife wouldn't mention things like that." . . . "Look, mister, I asked for a policewoman. I'm filthy, I'm bleeding, I need a wash and a change of clothes. Ask them to ring my mother. She'll bring them down for me. I don't think even your wife would stand here and bleed in silence."
>
> "Don't you foul-mouth my wife, you wee hussy!" His face contorted with rage as he slammed the cell door. (Desalvo, D'Arcy, and Hogan 1989, 236–37)

Even more unsettling is the arrival, hours later, of a policewoman with a sanitary towel who tells the protagonist to "follow me and hurry up about it. You have to go to the interview room again" (237). Taken to a room containing a (blocked) toilet, a washbasin (minus hot water, soap, or towel), and a urinal, the woman cleans herself up and, hopeful of some semblance of solidarity or, at least, humanitarianism, attempts to appeal to the policewoman's womanhood: " 'Look, could you see if I can have a change of clothes and a proper wash? You know what it's like when you have your period?' The woman officer appeared not to hear, looking away as she repeated, 'Hurry up. You're wanted for interview' " (237). Murphy is only one of many overtly "political" women from Northern Ireland to negotiate aspects of life from a distinctly female perspective.

HOUSING AS A CENTRAL THEME

Given that housing was a central issue of the contemporary period in Northern Ireland—the catalyst for the Troubles was a housing dispute—it is not surprising that many contemporary northern women have creatively dealt with the politics of that particular issue. From 1945 until 1968, in the largely Catholic town of Dungannon, County Tyrone, almost three-quarters of the public housing was allocated to Protestants. The eviction of Mary Teresa Goodfellow and her three children from a council house in Caledon, County Tyrone, in June 1968 finally exposed one aspect of government corruption in Northern Ireland: Catholics could not vote unless they had a house, but the allocation of housing was in the hands of the local unionist-controlled council. Goodfellow's involvement in the organized squat was the result of negotiations between the republican clubs that existed at that time and the newly formed civil rights movement and was the first direct political action taken by that group in Northern Ireland. Significantly, it was women who brought it about.

Jill McKenna's first published story, "The Reprisal," is just one example of short fiction that deals with local government corruption and the deterioration of the old political order in Northern Ireland. The story exposes some of the complexities of life in the north when unionist farmer Joe Best and his son Tom discover two boys planting what looks like a bomb in their barn. One of the boys escapes; the other, taken into the parlor at the front of the house—as far away as possible from the barn—is presented with an almost stereotypical example of Ulster Presbyterian domesticity:

> They took the boy through the narrow hallway into the front room— gloomy and austere, with a leather horsehair sofa, two straight-backed chairs and a heavy Victorian table with a vase of dried flowers placed

mathematically in the centre. The fireplace was concealed by a glass-covered screen, with "Simply to thy Cross I cling" embroidered painstakingly on it by some long-dead hand. Yellowing photographs of stony-faced couples stood stiffly on the upright piano; and a framed copy of the Ulster Covenant took pride of place above the mantlepiece. (Hooley 1985, 140)

Joe recognizes the boy as the son of a former girlfriend, Catholic Kathleen Donnolly, whom he was forbidden to marry. Instead, he married Margaret, "a nice enough woman, but his father's choice, not his" (144). Joe's genuine puzzlement as to why his barn has become a target reflects a blindness common to those for whom ideology has become hegemonic: since Joe is not a member of the UDR (Ulster Defence Regiment) or any political or paramilitary organization, he cannot understand the boy's explanation of the attack as a reprisal for the fact that his father was not hired as a veterinarian's assistant with the local council:

> "Sure you'd have voted against me da anyway, even if you'd have known. The D.U.P. [Democratic Unionist Party] says jump and you jump. That's what me da says anyway."
> Joe was silent. The boy pressed on. "You want to see the place we're living in. You wouldn't put a dog in it. It's got black stuff growin' up the walls and no bathroom or anythin'. Your animals are better housed than us."
> "That's not our fault. That's the Housin' Executive."
> "Aye, but you and your mates voted against the housin' estate they were goin' to build at Kilbeg."
> "That's because we reckoned it was a waste of public money."
> "Oh aye. A waste of money—to rehouse the likes of us?" (143)

Confronted with the individual (and emotionally evocative) face of deprivation for which he is at least partly, albeit unwittingly, responsible, Joe has nothing to say in his own defense and decides to let the boy go:

> The boy's face lit up and he jumped to his feet. "My da was right, Mister Best," he said. "You're not too bad—for a Unionist." At the door he paused, and a smile flickered across his face. "Sorry about your barn."

He was gone. Joe heard the front door closing softly at the same moment as a car door slammed in the [back] yard.

Seconds later, the peaceful calm of the summer afternoon was shattered by a loud explosion. (145)

In McKenna's story, the past, the present, and the future are represented entirely by either impotent or vicious men; women play no part at all except as absent or silent figures. This absence reflects the fact that women have played only a marginal role in unionism. But by their continued silence, the women are also represented as being implicated in maintaining the status quo of dominant patriarchal (in this case, unionist) ideologies.

McKenna's story encapsulates a number of different issues beyond that of housing, not least the futility of attempting to interpret the situation in Northern Ireland in terms of straightforward binaries of good and bad; Joe is a good man, and so is Francie McBride. Yet all of the men in the story are either products (Joe and Tom) or victims (the boy and Francie) of elitist ideologies that dictate fixed places in society. To a large extent, the generation of Joe and Francie is blind to those ideologies and live peacefully, if unequally, by accepting their roles, while the next generation (the boy and Tom) is destined to live in conflict if the inequities of the society are to be exposed and redressed. In this way the story resembles, among others, Deirdre Madden's *Hidden Symptoms*, in which the violence of Northern Ireland represents a necessary airing of previously hidden and invisible, though insidiously dangerous, cancers that had eaten away at the fabric of society.

This generational difference in the need for confrontation is evident, too, in Anne-Marie Reilly's "Leaving," another first-published story in *The Female Line* by a writer who had completed no serious writing before joining a writing group (Reilly, 1985). Reilly, however, is less ambivalent than McKenna in her portrayal of the ways in which housing and women's lives in the north are intermingled with issues of class and politics. The first-person narrative of "Leaving" begins: "Ever since I can remember my mother wanted to move house. 'Up the road' was what she called it. I wasn't sure where 'up the road' was, but even then I knew it would be somewhere wonderful" (Reilly 1985, 55). The narrator's aunt lives "up the road," in the longed-for paradise, which exists anywhere past the Falls Park: "She [the Aunt] had 'married well.' Her husband drove a car. My father disliked them intensely. They had achieved material success, my father never would. I loved going there, so did my mother. They had a garden and a bathroom and a proper sitting-room with a piano in it" (55). By contrast, the narrator and her family live in a small rented house in a street off the Falls Road. In this "parochial and very clannish" street, "everyone gossiped and borrowed and visited" (55)—everyone except the narrator's mother, who stays apart from all the activities of the street because "she wouldn't be there for long, she hoped" (55) although at the time of the narrator's birth she had already been there for fifteen years.

Sadly, another fifteen years would pass before the narrator's mother is finally able to move to exactly where, thirty years before, she wanted to go, but the circumstances of the move are not what she expected: "Our street was one of the first to be burned and my parents had to run from the house they had lived in for thirty-two years, clutching a very few personal belongings" (56). Re-housed in a top-floor maisonette, the mother realizes that what she'd hoped to escape has simply come with her, as "up the road" becomes the new Catholic ghetto following the gutting of many streets in the Lower Falls Road neighborhood. The story poignantly deals with the ways in which working-class women and men are alienated from their own class by myths of "bettering" themselves through identification instead with middle-class or aspirant Protestant values and materialism.

In many ways, the mother of this story is like Joe of the previous one: both are members of a "lost," defeated generation that has internalized hegemonic notions of "bettering" oneself. In Joe's case, however, he is a privileged member of the dominant society while the mother in "Leaving" is someone who has internalized aspects of her own oppression: "They have never settled in their new home. They won't buy a fitted carpet 'in case they move,' or new furniture 'in case they move.' Yet I know my mother has long since given up hope of that much-wanted house. Strangely, it's for my father's sake that she keeps up the pretence" (Hooley 1985, 56). In contrast, the narrator is a member of a new generation that has a different approach: "The consequence of my mother's life is now surfacing in mine, I won't waste time longing for something better, I'll go out and fight for it and that is bringing its own heartache" (56–57). Again, Reilly creates a sense in which the time has arrived to expose or release what has been held under the surface for so long, no matter how painful or difficult this may prove to be.

Housing is also the central topic in Ellen Pollock's "Scene Around Six," one of the winners of the inaugural Women's Press/Maxwell House short story competition in 1978. Pollock's story skillfully and humorously focuses on serious class issues relating specifically to Northern Ireland. The story opens with what seems to be a sense of random selection:

> Belfast. Royal Avenue. Five p.m. Rush hour.
> Quickly, pick a person, any person . . . That one!
> Henry John Shiels, about fifty, ex-machine tool operator.
> Quickly, quickly, pick another, any other . . . There! That woman.
> Rose McCusker, early forties, mother of five. Good. (*Passages* 83)

The story then alternates between narratives dealing with Henry John, a working-class Protestant, former B-Special policeman who lives on the Shankill Road, and Rose, a working-class Catholic woman. We first meet Henry John sycophantically buying pints of Guinness for a British Army captain. Almost immediately, Henry John is established as another example of blind loyalty to a political system that he is attached to through alliance rather than allegiance. He sees nothing peculiar in buying drinks (specifically pints of Guinness) for an English army captain who dreams of a pint of Ruddles (an English beer) while, at the same time, proudly relating the nature of his own exploitation and dismissal at the hands of a capitalist economy that he is prepared to defend. Rose, too, is introduced as a slightly comic figure in a waiting room, reading a women's magazine: " 'Listen to this,' said Rosie. 'Warm the brandy, set it alight and pour it over the pigeons!' She looked up from the magazine and turned to her neighbour in the waiting room. 'Do you ever feel that you don't exist?' " (*Passages* 85).

Pollock makes particularly good use of Belfast dialect to capture working-class accents and patterns of speech, and, like Reilly's "Leaving," she portrays the mother as family arbitrator and ultimate defender of masculine values. Just as the mother in Reilly's story keeps up appearances for the sake of the father, so Rose defends her husband's beliefs against the onslaught of a younger generation for whom those values are outmoded and futile. As members of an oppressed group within the larger society, the women always feel an underlying solidarity with their men:

> "I regret the fact, for example, that my husband lived and *died* and never had a decent house to live in. And this here is the irony of it," said Rosie, turning to the other woman. "Do you know what his trade was?"
> "What was that?"
> "He was a bricklayer! Aye." Rosie laughed quietly. "Been out of work for ten years." She picked up the magazine again. "That's what I regret." (87)

We meet Rose again during an interview with the Housing Department—an event that clearly takes place on a regular basis:

> "Evening Brian," she beamed, closing the door behind her and going over to the counter. "Is this the housing department?" She hesitated before taking her seat.
> ". . . Yes, Mrs McCusker, this is the housing department."
> "Great. Any sign of a house?" She sat down, arranging all round her.
> "Name?"
> "Mrs Rose McCusker," she said, very matter-of-fact. (89)

Having confirmed for Brian the same details she confirms every week—such as the fact that she is Rose McCuskey of 23 Talbot Street, Falls Road, widowed with five children, one of whom is in jail for burying guns in a back garden they don't have—Rose is informed that there is still no house for her: "What about the proposed 4,000 houses out at Poleglass there? Come on, Brian, put us down for one of them. That there would be dead handy for me, just up the road like that, tucked in between my sister-in-law in Andersonstown and the brother out at Twinbrook. Eh?" (91).

Rose tells the reader as well as the housing official that she is one of 600,000 people living in substandard housing in Northern Ireland and one of 300,000 people living in a house unfit for human habitation. Brian regurgitates the official, bureaucratic decision that it is unlikely the 4,000 houses promised will be built at Poleglass:

> It has simply been brought to the attention of the planning department by certain people at present holding office on the council in question, Mrs McCusker, that the linking of Andersonstown and Twinbrooke estates by another estate housing the overflow from West Belfast would only, and I quote: "serve to create a solid working-class Roman Catholic ghetto the whole way out to Twinbrooke, a hot-bed of republican discontent and a threat to security and law and order." Now, Mrs McCusker, would you or would you not say there is some sense in refusing to create the very breeding grounds for violence and discontent? (92)

The final section of the narrative is reserved for Henry John's disappointment following a visit to the captain to complain that local Catholics are restoring some of the bricked-up houses on their side of no-man's-land, a "southerly encroachment" (92) that worries him and his Protestant neighbors because of the possibility of marauding Catholic bands attacking their defenseless women and children. The captain reminds Henry John that the houses were bricked up in the first place because the Catholic population had to flee from marauding Protestant bands. Henry John later relates the outcome of events to Sammie, the local bartender:

> "Do you know how much money is spent on defence every year, Sammie?"
>
> "I don't indeed," said Sammie.
>
> "£2,000 million is spent on defence every year. Do you know what we got?"
>
> "What?"
>
> "Four large concrete flower pots full of daffodils." Henry John nodded sadly over his Guinness. "Oh, I went back. I went back and I says could they not send us round a few radar controlled ground-to-air geraniums, for the daffodils wasn't even keeping out the dirty flies from their stinking Fenian kitchens! A bunch of daffodils between life and death! And we're talking hereabout the best bloody army in the world!" (93)

Passages such as this comically (and tragically) emphasize the ideological blindness of men like Henry John to the fact that, as a working-class member of Belfast society, he has more in common with Rose and her community than he ever could with the captain or his England. Yet even when confronted by the fact that the captain has done the wrong thing by the Protestant community's standards—in pointing out historical facts and failing to take seriously their fears of being massacred—Henry John sees no distinction between the needs and values of Protestant Belfast and those of England.

Pollock and others capture much of the political complexity of Northern Ireland by showing how capitalist and imperialist ideologies have functioned to obscure issues such as class and ethnicity. This story, again like many others, demonstrates reluctance on the part of contemporary Northern women writers to endorse any sense of "good" and "bad" or "us" and "them." Much of the fiction produced by northern women in the contemporary period depicts an understanding of the complexity between entrapment and freedom, heroes and villains, individual and society, safety and danger.

Fiona Barr's award-winning and often-anthologized story, "Wall Reader," for instance, engages complexly with these issues. Forced to flee Belfast after the woman of the story forms an innocent relationship with a British soldier in a park, the couple central to this story head for Dublin, although they originally see London and Dublin as equally safe places. The story shares with many others a central female protagonist, a challenge to any simple dichotomous understanding of Northern Irish society, and a minimal identification of the "enemy." The soldier with whom the woman shares nothing more than conversations about children and families, hopes and ambitions, is humanized yet depersonalized to the extent that he remains an anonymous voice and barely distinguished face peeping out from a gun turret during her afternoon walks in the park with her baby. The woman's boredom, suffocation, and her need to escape is enforced throughout the story in her reading of walls and, ultimately, in her association with the anonymous soldier, activities that link her to a world beyond the claustrophobic Belfast: "It was a meeting of minds, as she explained later to her husband, a new opinion, a common bond, an opening of vistas" (Hooley

1985, 85). The woman seems to read Belfast's walls as a form of political activity from which she can remain objective, but the power of sectarian politics proves to be larger than any individual desire for liberty.

An interesting aspect of Barr's story is the intertextual allusions to a
number of Robert Frost's poems. American Frost was passionately pro-
nuclear-disarmament, antiwar, and left wing by American standards of his
time, and was the guest speaker at John F. Kennedy's inauguration. Apart
from the very strong thematic links between Frost's poem "Birches" and
Barr's story, there is a direct reference to the poem when the protagonist of
the story thinks that "one could do worse than be a reader of walls" (*The
Wall Reader* 47), echoing the poem's final line: "One could do worse than be
a swinger of birches" (Graves 1963, 79).

"The park is ugly, stark and hostile" (Hooley 1985, 84), of Barr's story,
echoes Frost's "The Woods are lovely, dark and deep" in Frost's poem "Stopping by Woods" (Graves 1963, 140), and reflects not only Barr's protagonist's ties to domestic and other responsibilities but also her reflections on
existence and death. "Stopping by Woods" explores the finality of suicide as
an escape from routine family commitments and responsibilities. Suicide/
death is tempting, but it is ultimately rejected by the poem's persona because of "promises to keep" to others. This, again, is linked to the responsibilities of the woman in Barr's story to her child, husband, and community,
the latter now labeling her a "TOUT" and from whom she must escape for
her own and her family's safety.

Similarly, Frost's poem "Mending Wall" is dense with references to the
human territorial demarcations that fly in the face of nature. Barriers, walls,
and so forth represent exercises in futility: primitive, selfish, counterproduc-
tive behavior—"just another kind of outdoor game / One on a side" (Graves
1963, 23). The poem's focus on the generational transmission of the act of
building walls and the reiteration of past follies strongly tie to Barr's story
and her protagonist's desire to get away so that her child does not have the
same legacy of generationally transmitted bitterness that is Northern Ireland today. It is, ironically, April when the crisis in Barr's story occurs—the
"spring mending-time" of Frost's poem—suggesting that Barr used the allusions to contrast regenerative forces with those of thoughtless destruction,
further exposing the futility of the political situation in Northern Ireland.

Barr captures the lack of choice and sense of fear and entrapment that has been such an integral part of life for many people in Northern Ireland. This is evident in much of the fiction of the period. However, it is important not to confuse this fear with a sensationalizing of the Troubles. The fact that contemporary fiction by northern women has had to compete with the most popular form of writing to come out of the north—namely, the largely male-produced thriller in which women are either nonexistent or conform to well-recognized stereotypes—has meant that much contemporary women's fiction has been inappropriately analyzed as part of that genre.

WOMEN'S WRITING AND THE THRILLER

Eamonn Hughes argues that the thriller has been the major response to Northern Ireland on the part of its novelists (1991, 6). But perhaps he should have specified male novelists; for while the genre has done well out of Northern Ireland, it is almost exclusively one produced by men: Gerald Seymour's *Harry's Game* (1980), Benedict Kiely's *Proxopera* (1979), Bernard MacLaverty's *Cal* (1983), Tom Clancy's *Patriot Games* (1987) and Brian Moore's *Lies of Silence* (1990) are the examples most often used in discussions of the genre in a Northern Irish context.

Bill Rolston argues that, in popular novels such as the thriller, women are generally confined within a limited set of stereotypical roles in a plot that surrounds an individual (masculine) republican "villain" whose impetus for action arises not out of an organized collective politics but out of "personal need or psychological inadequacy" (1991, 42). Within such narratives, women's roles are restricted to those of the mother who fears for her children (44), the seducer/lurer of men (47), or a central female political villain whose "curse is that, having abandoned their natural vocation of motherhood . . . can never be 'real' terrorists like men" (51). Sarah Edge takes this point even further:

> Women's involvement and interest in national identity struggles . . .
> causes a problem because it disrupts traditional and dominant ideologies
> surrounding femininity on a number of levels. Women who are involved

in violence disrupt dominant ideologies of the feminine as passive and peace-loving. Similarly, women's involvement in the public world of politics disrupts ideologies surrounding women's space in the private world of home and family. (1995, 176)

Certainly, it could be argued that (women's) novels such as Una Woods's *The Dark Hole Days* (1984), Linda Anderson's *To Stay Alive* (1984), Deirdre Madden's *Hidden Symptoms* (1986), Niki Hill's *Death Grows on You* (1992), or stories such as Fionna Barr's "The Wall Reader" and Anne Devlin's "Naming the Names" (1986) are thrillers insofar as the Troubles are central to the narrative: Devlin's female "villain" in "Naming the Names," in particular, could be interpreted as not only an active female republican but a lurer of men to their deaths (a representation that also appears in Neil Jordan's film *The Crying Game* [Edge 1995]). But, like Hill's *Death Grows on You*, Devlin is ambiguous as to whether the protagonist lures her English lover into the hands of the IRA and death because that had been her "political" aim all along, or because she, as a woman, has been rejected by him. Similarly, Barr's scenario in "The Wall Reader" contains at least some of the features associated with the thriller genre as a category in which:

> what is needed is no more than an adventure playground in which "heroes" can confront "villains." At its most mechanical the thriller moves to a closure which projects its locale as a closed but always unresolved system: the Cold War can never end, the forces of corruption can never be defeated, and the problems of Northern Ireland will inevitably endure. (Hughes 1991, 6)

But in Barr's story, there are no "heroes" or "villains" to confront each other. Instead, both women and men (symbolically, in the story, an English man and Irish woman) are identified as powerless members of societies that remove individual choice: once again, a complex depiction of the debilitating effect dominant ideologies have on the individual.

Woods, Madden, Hill, Devlin, and Barr, among other women from Northern Ireland, also frequently problematize the whole notion of "heroes" and "villains" as well as "right" and "wrong" by showing individual (almost exclusively women) protagonists who, by one means or another, confront the reality of life in Northern Ireland as one symptom of a long, serious, largely static, yet by no means incurable illness. Joe and Colette of Una Woods's *The Dark Hole Days* cope with unemployment, tragedy, and a descent into private madness by physically retreating from the public madness that surrounds them and that seems only tangentially connected to the politics of the north. Deirdre Madden's *Hidden Symptoms* focuses on the problems of Theresa Cassidy, a Queen's University student who is at odds both with her Catholicism and her home of Belfast following the murder of her twin brother, Francis. However, Theresa's acknowledgment of the ugliness of Northern Irish society is never portrayed as acceptance or defeatism. Rather, the Troubles represent an exposure of an insidiously poisonous society hidden behind a facade of civilized behavior, a society barely under control:

> Ulster before 1969 had been sick but with hidden symptoms . . . Belfast was now like a madman who tears his flesh, puts straws in his hair and screams gibberish. Before it had resembled the infinitely more sinister figure of the articulate man in a dark, neat suit whose conversation charms and entertains; and whose insanity is apparent only when he says calmly, incidentally, that he will club his children to death and eat their entrails with a golden fork because God has told him to do so; and then offers you more tea. (Madden 1986, 26)

Linda Anderson's *To Stay Alive* (1984), published in the United States as *We Can't All Be Heroes, You Know,* is an equally disturbing story of Dan and Rosaleen's ultimately unsuccessful attempts to avoid the violence and sectarianism of everyday Belfast. Sadly, the novel was well received as another example of the thriller subgenre. While such analyses of Anderson's work see her as contributing to this category as an existing and very popular tradition of northern writing, they also perpetuate the notion of Northern Ireland as a closed, static, and fatalistic society, a depiction that does not fit comfortably with a feminist reading of Anderson's work. Rather than reading the impossibility of avoiding the divisions in northern society as negative and inevitable, and thereby continuing the "game" of sectarian blindness, Anderson—in common with much of the fiction discussed—can be read as encouraging engagement, sometimes quite confrontationally, with those same divisions, particularly as they are experienced by one (representative) woman.

Clearly, some outstanding writers have emerged from Northern Ireland in the contemporary period: Jennifer Johnston, Frances Molloy, Mary Beckett, Linda Anderson, Christina Reid, Marie Jones, Anne Devlin, to name a few. Given that issues of nationalism, ethnicity, and class—as well as gender—have traditionally formed a pressing part of emergent, contemporary identity politics for nationalist women, it comes as no surprise that the vast majority of contemporary women's fiction from Northern Ireland has emerged from within that community. Yet writing by women from Northern Irish nationalist communities shows very little evidence of an allocation of political responsibility on individuals of the "other" community, especially not on unionist women. Rather, responsibility for deprivation is placed firmly on the systems of oppression that keep both communities in subservience. Interestingly, it has been in the field of drama, rather than fiction, from Northern Ireland where the most extensive engagement has appeared with the sectarianism of both communities.

DRAMA AND NORTHERN WOMEN'S WRITING

Changes in the feminist political landscape throughout the 1980s were paralleled by a similar divergence in the impact of both fiction and drama on both sides of the border so that there are substantial differences between the Republic of Ireland and Northern Ireland in the production of drama. During the 1980s in the republic, a significant number of women became involved at an administrative level both in the major theater companies and in the setting up of new groups, and, since that time, the production of feminist drama there has generally lagged behind that of women's fiction and poetry. Interestingly, this administrative path evident in the republic is one more often associated with geographic areas less troubled by questions of identity and regionalism, such as the south of England. In Northern Ireland, however, women's drama followed the path of both regional and indigenous theater by producing women's drama that interrogates identity politics through the local and contingent, something Elaine Aston refers to as an "identity politics of regionalism" (1995, 76) or, more generally, drama that reflects economically or otherwise divided societies.

Northern women's drama throughout the 1980s and most of the 1990s was greatly influenced by the work of Marie Jones (chief scriptwriter for Charabanc Theatre)[6] and by Christina Reid and Anne Devlin, and much of this drama was community based. Drama for women writers in the north came to represent a genre that allowed a head-on confrontation with Northern Irish politics at the community level. Anne Devlin's *A Woman Calling, Ourselves Alone,* and *The Long March,* published as a trilogy in 1986; and Christina Reid's *The Last of a Dyin' Race* (1986), *Tea in a China Cup* (1987), *Joyriders* (1972), *The Belle of the Belfast City* (1989a), and *Did You Hear the One About the Irishman* (1989b) were all well received in Northern Ireland and beyond. These playwrights set many of their plays within the confines of strictly sectarian settings in order to examine the position and representation of women within those communities. But with the demise of Charabanc in 1995 and the shift in interest of writers like Jones, Devlin, and Reid, northern women's drama is no longer particularly in evidence and is certainly no longer visibly connected to anything resembling a feminist cultural practice—possibly, again, precisely as a direct result of its extraordinarily localized nature.

The drama of Anne Devlin, Christina Reid, and the Charabanc Theatre Company nevertheless represents the most successful attempts to challenge both the nationalist and unionist communities of Northern Ireland with various representations of sectarian life, particularly as it has affected women. *Ourselves Alone* (in A. Devlin 1986b), Devlin's first staged play, remains her most overtly political one. It centers on two sisters, Frieda and Josie, and Donna, the de facto wife of their brother Liam; the women are

6. Sadly, Charabanc folded in August 1995, but its members have continued to be involved in other, diverse community theater projects in Northern Ireland and beyond. Marie Jones has achieved great success with her Dubblejoint production of *Women on the Verge of HRT,* initially produced as part of the West Belfast Festival in 1995; with *A Night in November* (2000a); and, most recently, with *Stones in His Pockets* (2000b), which has been critically acclaimed in Ireland, Britain, and the United States.

together in only two scenes, yet there is no mistaking the dramatic juxta-position of their varied and fractured voices and experiences, both personal and political, and the much more singular, ideologically bound and driven voices and experiences of the men in the play, all of whom are involved in the republican movement.

Heterogeneity in the play is represented differently, then, for men and for women. Devlin draws even the more complex male characters as complex only in relation to sectarian politics; they are never personalized in the way the women are but are portrayed instead as representatives of shifts and factions along party-political lines:

> FRIEDA: My brother's changed his political line three times at least since 'sixty-nine. He joined the Officials when they split with the Provos, then the INLA when they split from the Officials; the last time he was out on parole he was impersonating votes for the Sinn Féin election. And I hear lately while he's in the Kesh he's joined the Provos! Now what does that tell us—apart from the fact that he's a relentless political opportunist? (Anne Devlin 1986a, 243)

But the men are all represented ultimately as traitors—differing in kind rather than degree. Practically no distinction is made, for instance, between Joe as a political traitor to the IRA and Liam and John as personal traitors to Donna and Frieda.

While the men of Devlin's play are simplistically, even stereotypically, drawn, her women reveal a range of complexities based on personal, political, social, cultural, and, of course, gender differences, not only between the women and men but between the women themselves: Frieda has no interest in politics and longs to be in an environment where she can sing what she likes rather than feeling forced into singing republican songs for a republican audience; Josie is an active, high-ranking member of the IRA; Donna is very much a domestic figure. In common with a number of writers discussed, Devlin draws the women as being different not only in their overt responses to republican politics but in their definitions of "good" and "bad," "danger" and "safety," and, even, "Irishness." At the play's conclusion, for instance, Frieda decides to leave after being ostracized by the community; she is asked by Donna "why not go South" and she answers "I'm not that kind of Irish" (307).

In terms of "danger" and "safety," Devlin makes it clear that the women are in as much danger from the men of their own community as they are from anyone else. Violence against women is an integral, disturbing part of *Ourselves Alone*. The discussion about Bobby Sands during a scene of impending violence between father and daughter articulates a view of Sands that runs counter to dominant republican ideology:

> MALACHY: You'll not make little of me. Siding with the people who condemned Bobby Sands.
> FRIEDA: (*Backing away towards the door*) They didn't condemn him. They said he beat his wife! Hard to believe, isn't it? . . . They say when he was dying she was so afraid of him she wouldn't go up to the prison to see him. In fact she wouldn't go near him until she was sure he was definitely dead. (260)

Like Patrick Pearse before him, the strength of Sands's position as political martyr makes voicing such opinions a sacrilege. But in the absence of their articulation in any other arena, the appearance of such views in the creative arts suggests that writers like Devlin are refusing to participate in the perpetuation of nationalist mythmaking. More importantly, by using domestic violence as a context in which to discuss him, Devlin goes beyond existing polarized representations of Sands as either a political martyr or a political enemy. The emphasis is altogether removed from Sands as either of these things and is transferred instead to his wife and the issue of domestic violence itself, which, along with various other so-called nonpolitical forms of violence, has gone relatively unchecked in Northern Ireland over the period of the Troubles.

In contrast to Devlin, Christina Reid more often uses the domestic world of Belfast's working-class (usually Protestant) women to challenge binaries of personal, political, and communal identity. Like Devlin, Reid uses the women not to present a united front of domestic solidarity but to show the differences between the women at the domestic, political, and generational levels. In *Tea in a China Cup* (1987), for instance, mother Sarah and daughter Beth differ greatly in their political beliefs. For Beth, the meanings of cultural/political events such as the July marches are antithetical to those of her mother. Beth, like many of the young protagonists of the fiction, is part of a generation that is no longer willing to turn a blind eye to the inequities of Northern Irish society, regardless of how difficult it might be to confront them.

Reid uses Beth's relationship with her Catholic best friend to draw further contour lines between rather than through women. Acting as the central narrator, Beth also participates in the action of a play that consistently provides a feminized view of life. Sarah (the mother), is a product of the aspirant society at the heart of Protestant Belfast; she values above all her best china tea set. Reid also sharply contrasts heroic male war stories with women's perception of war as an experience of abandonment, loneliness, and isolation. Such a feminized view reveals extraordinary differences between women of different generations, something that Reid is generally interested in and most often works into her plays through the relationship between mothers and daughters.

Reid creates a world of women, principally through Beth's narrative flashbacks, which link her and her mother to her grandmother and her great-aunt Maisie, who are involved in communal activities like laying out the dead. Whereas in Devlin's play the women are rarely seen together and the drama revolves around their often antagonistic and rebellious relationships with men and their politics, Reid uses her world of women to show how dramatic conflict with the past is experienced primarily through flashback. This is a world where women and men rarely confront each other overtly. Instead, the women's voices (comprising the main narrative) criticize the men from within their world of domestic ritual, such as when Maisie tells Grandfather Jamison that he was a "vindictive oul bastard" (Reid 1997, 9) but only after he is dead.

The most prolific example of Northern Ireland's women's drama from this period is, of course, the work of Charabanc Theatre Company, which achieved great success in challenging both nationalist and unionist communities of Northern Ireland with various stage representations of sectarian life, particularly as experienced by women. Between its formation in 1983 and 1993, the company performed fifteen plays, four of which had all-

female casts. It also included collective productions, such as its first play
(unpublished), *Lay Up Your Ends,* by Martin Lynch and Marie Jones, which
focuses on everyday conditions of Belfast life. Though by no means exclusively a women's theater company, Charabanc described itself as a "touring
theatre company, which devises and promotes plays with strong female
roles" (Charabanc brochure 1992).

But Charabanc also performed work not created by the company, but
which it felt had "something to say to the Northern Ireland community"
(Charabanc brochure 1992), including *The Stick Wife* by Darrah Cloud,
which is set in a suburban backyard in Birmingham, Alabama, in 1963; *Cauterised* by Neill Speers, about two women who work in a hardware shop in a
rural Northern Irish town in 1959; *Me and My Friend* by Gillian Plowman,
which focuses on four people coping with mental illness; and *Bondagers*
(1995) by Sue Glover, set on the vast farms of the Scottish borders. (None
of these plays have been published.) Charabanc performed throughout
Ireland, as well as visiting London and Glasgow, and conducted five tours
of America. In 1984 the company visited Moscow, Leningrad, and Vilnius
and was a guest of the World Stage Festival in Toronto and the International Theater Festival in Munich. Despite this level of international success, however, the central focus of Charabanc's philosophy has been its
own communities and, most often, on issues of gender and class in those
communities.

The plays deal with a variety of themes, including the intersection of
sectarian politics and domestic violence. Company members were not
averse to rewriting play endings during performance runs to ensure that audiences couldn't easily categorize or appropriate the company's work as belonging to one side or the other:

> In our third play [*Now You're Talkin'*] we couldn't find an ending . . . We
> were frightened of leaving it at a moment where people could say, "Ah,
> that's what Charabanc thinks, that's a statement." We invited people we
> trusted to come and see it and asked them what they thought of the end-
> ing. People made different suggestions and we tried them. (Carol Martin
> 1989, 92)

Charabanc also performed several plays by Marie Jones, a founding member and main scriptwriter of the company: *Oul Delf and False Teeth, Now You're Talkin', Gold in the Streets,* and *Girls in the Big Picture* (all unpublished), *Somewhere Over the Balcony* (M. Jones 2001), *The Hamster Wheel* (M. Jones 1990) and two unpublished one-act plays, *The Blind Fiddler of Glenadauch* and *Weddins, Weeins, and Wakes.* In February 1995, Charabanc performed *A Wife, a Dog, and a Maple Tree,*[7] which deals with the issue of domestic violence. The play was written by Carole Moore, one of the company's artistic directors, and Sue Ashby, a founding member of the Manchester Women's Theatre Group, and was performed at the Playhouse, Derry. Charabanc's other artistic director, Eleanor Methven, believes that the choice of subject matter is a brave one for a theater company in Northern Ireland:

> It would make life a lot easier if we always produced plays which are not so demanding, but I think we're well enough known now that people know that they will be entertained regardless of the theme[,] the added bonus is that they'll also be presented with some dilemmas, something to think about for the first time or, to think about in a new light. We all need our prejudices challenged every now and again. (*Women's News* Feb./Mar. 1995, 20)

All of Charabanc's work reflects Marie Jones's extraordinary ability to confront a northern audience with humorous and poignant (though nonsentimental) images of itself by drawing on the most traditional and communal features of life within both the Protestant and Catholic communities. That these are also the most political and sectarian features becomes of secondary importance as a result of her knowledge of and very evident fondness for working-class people from both communities in Northern Ireland, as well as her concentration on everyday life rather than on "important" events.

7. To date, most of Charabanc's work remains unpublished, but copies of scripts are held in the Dublin Writers Centre and the Linenhall Library, Belfast. *Somewhere Over the Balcony* was anthologized in Gilbert 2001.

Somewhere Over the Balcony, for example, is a black comedy centering on three nationalist women living in Divis flats on the Falls Road on the eve of the anniversary of Internment and who are entirely surrounded by the Troubles. *Weddins, Weeins, and Wakes*,[8] by contrast, concerns itself primarily with women's communal activities in one section of the Protestant community. Both plays incorporate aspects of sectarian life in Northern Ireland: *Somewhere Over the Balcony* (whose title obviously suggests an ironic contrast with the hopeful "Somewhere Over the Rainbow") is, in fact, entirely set in the midst of the Troubles with countless British helicopters flying about and people being "lifted" (detained for questioning) by the British Army. A local wedding becomes the central event of the play when the wedding party is trapped in the chapel and besieged by three hundred British troops because the groom is a wanted man. Similarly, *Weddins, Weeins, and Wakes* includes a wedding between a local girl and a reluctant loyalist bridegroom who seems to be "up to no good," as well as a hilarious improvised representation of an Orange march, during which "Grandad" dies and is brought home in a "wheely" bin. In both plays, however, these strictly sectarian events are backdrops to the personal aspect of the plays: they become just another part of the plays' activities. But regardless of whether her drama is set in the Protestant or Catholic community, and regardless of how exclusively the events of the play reflect the traditions and concerns of that particular community, the emphasis in Jones's work is on the strengths, weaknesses, and foibles of the people who continue to go about their daily lives and, principally, in the relationship between women and their communities.

THE UNIONIST GAP:
THE SILENCE OF UNIONIST WOMEN WRITERS

With the exception of work by novelist Linda Anderson and playwrights Christina Reid and Marie Jones (either as solo playwright or as scriptwriter for Charabanc), however, one of the most noticeable aspects of contempo-

---

8. *Weddins', Weeins, and Wakes* was one of Charabanc's early plays and was reworked by Jones in late 2001 and performed throughout Ireland.

rary writing by women from Northern Ireland is the absence of an imagina-tively articulated Protestant or unionist woman's voice. Where it does appear, unionist ideology is most often represented as masculinist—women being either absent or complicit by their silence. Contemporary northern women writers who have emerged from a Protestant/unionist background, such as Linda Anderson, seem less interested in defending a particular political position than in investigating the actual politics as they affect women's lives. This perspective certainly seems to fit more comfortably with the way in which so many of the writers discussed here are of a gen-eration that no longer wants to maintain the status quo of bigotry and sectarianism—a conviction reflected in the writing of women from both traditions who refuse to perpetuate their respective society's mythologies.

As mentioned before, Linda Anderson's first novel, *To Stay Alive* (1984), is most often thought of as a dark and fatalistic representation of Northern Ireland's political present and future. Focusing as it does on a couple from within the nationalist community, however, the novel can only be analyzed as an example of a defensible Protestant position if it is assumed that the darkness and fatalism is the direct result of holding a nationalist position. But such a reading could be achieved only by a deliberately manipulative interpretation of the text. Her second novel, *Cuckoo* (1986), however, is lo-cated in London and might be seen as a rejection of Northern Ireland alto-gether, were it not for the fact that the protagonist is a woman whose entire present and future life—emotionally, politically, and sexually—is defined by her Northern Irish past. For Anderson, then, it seems more feasible that rather than rejecting either a Protestant or Northern Irish background, she is rejecting a narrow unionist ideology that calls for women to play a si-lenced, subsidiary role in both public and private life: "Loyalist women, like their men, are supposed to be loyal to the throne . . . but in addition they must be loyal to the male head of the household—the proper wife, the working companion, the helpmate, the silent support and drive. And loyal-ism means containing the intense frustrations which arise from meeting these expectations" (Ruth Moore 1994, 14). Certainly in the contemporary period, unionist women's imaginative voices are most evident at the com-munity level, both in terms of writing groups and in the production of drama. Perhaps unionist women have not been liberated in relation to their own cultural politics in the way that nationalist women in Northern Ireland, or women in the Irish Republic, have been.

But, in contrast to nationalist history and representation in Northern Ireland, for example, unionist Northern Ireland is tied closely to notions of modernity, industrialization, and myths of endeavor. Maurice Goldring shows that at the beginning of the twentieth century, Belfast was at the height of its commercial and industrial power, principally in the fields of shipbuilding, engineering, and linen, and it was immensely proud to be a young city in much the same way that American cities like Chicago were. An excerpt from a 1902 guide to the city reveals this sense of newness and denial of origins: "Belfast as a town has no ancient history and does not lay claim to remote origins like so many towns in Ireland. Its record is simply one of industrial progress" (Goldring 1991, 34). The same guide also emphasizes a wonderfully harmonious division of labor in Northern Ireland: shipbuilding and engineering for boys and men, linen and ropeworks for girls and women. But Goldring tells us that while it is not unusual for women's involvement in the workforce to be celebrated in this way, the image is totally inaccurate because, in general, the wives and daughters of skilled Protestant workers did not go out to work: those women who were in paid employment were either unmarried or the wives of unskilled and underpaid laborers—in other words, Catholics (35).

Liam O'Dowd has pointed out that Ulster unionists, unlike Irish nationalists, never actively sought a separate sovereign state in order to accomplish specific economic, political, or cultural goals: "From the outset, the state [Ulster] was not perceived as a positive initiating agent, but rather as a bulwark against Catholicism and nationalism. Its intellectuals, as part of either a British or Ulster framework, had no language to revive and no sustained critique of foreign oppression" (1991, 170).

Padraig O'Malley, among others, has also postulated that in Ireland Protestantism is, largely, religious while Catholicism is political (1984, 7). This could explain why nationalists in Northern Ireland have been prepared to follow the teachings of the Catholic Church in all matters except those relating to the use of violence for political ends. That the IRA has been formally condemned by the Catholic Church many times since 1931 further supports the hypothesis that in Northern Ireland at least "the national question transcends questions of faith and morals" (5).

But O'Malley has also pointed out that Ireland's sectarianism, today most evident in Northern Ireland, has two sets of starting points. The Catholic one is 1170 when Norman warriors speaking Norman French came from England with the approval of Henry II and at the invitation of the Irish chief Dermot MacMurrough. The Protestant starting point is 1641 when the remnants of the old Gaelic Catholic aristocracy rose up to reclaim confiscated lands and massacred large numbers of the Protestant minority before being defeated. This uprising confirmed the worst fears of the Protestant minority and gave birth to the fear of massacre, which, in turn, reinforced the myth of siege so evident in Northern Ireland today.

This siege mentality—articulated regularly since the 1960s by Ian Paisley—remains a strong strain in contemporary Protestant politics in Northern Ireland. Following the announcement of peace talks in 1994, for example, Paisley responded to a question concerning unionist policies for the future of Northern Ireland by stating that "when you are defending something, you don't have to develop policies of change: you just have to stand firm" (BBC News, 12 February 1994). This sense of defensiveness is based on solid historical evidence that Ulster unionism never undertook a fight for independence, self-rule, or nationalism. Many historians argue, in fact, that unionism never represented, nor ever could represent or align itself with any form of active nationalism (even in relation to Britishness) but is, rather, a form of antinationalism based on its relationship with Ireland and on the fact that the majority of unionists did not support partition in 1922.

But, again according to O'Malley, there are two myths of siege in Northern Ireland, "two psychological preconceptions of suppression": "Protestants, who account for a little more than one quarter of the island's population, see themselves as a minority in all of Ireland; Catholics, who account for a little more than one third of Northern Ireland's population, see themselves as a minority in Northern Ireland" (O'Malley 1984, 7).

David Taylor claims that the modern manifestation of the unionist siege mentality in Northern Ireland ultimately sees every group and institution beyond the realm of traditional Protestantism as a negative factor:

> Modernist ecumenical churches become enemies because they are moving towards accommodation with the Catholic Church; the population of Southern Ireland is feared because they are anti-Protestant and favour a United Ireland; and the British Government is distrusted for consistently turning its back on Ulster, and for favouring any political solution rather than devolved government with Protestant majority rule, which Paisley and his followers favour. (1984, 64)

In a different, though related, context, Barry Sloan examines the legacy of Calvinism in creating the particular kind of Protestant state identifiable today in Northern Ireland, both in political and literary spheres (2000). One of the most distinctive features of Calvinism, according to Sloan, is its attempt to produce a coherent world that combines all aspects of individual and social life. In this way, Calvinism addresses not only the individual's faith and the practice and organization of religion but extends to matters of conduct, morality, citizenship, and government. It points to one of the most important differences between the Protestantism of Luther and that of Calvin: "whereas the German Reformation (Luther) was primarily the restoration of true worship and the office of ministry, Calvin sought the restoration of the whole life, in home, school, state and society" (Henry Van Till cited in Sloan, 9). Calvin's attitude to art and artists is said to be a matter of inference rather than dogma, but it is clear that the work of art and artists must never be in competition with the creativity of God—including the word of God—and Calvin was explicit in his condemnation of art that might encourage idolatry as much as in his condemnation of ornate decoration, ritual, and the use of liturgy as dangerously Catholic in tendency. The old jokes about the austerity of the Presbyterian Church, then, including the simplest and hardest of pews, have an historical basis. Nothing should detract from the worship of God.

This organic relationship between the life and soul in Calvinism is illustrated by Maurice Goldring's description of life in nineteenth-century to a more contemporary Belfast, where Protestant men coming into the Protestant city were turned into skilled shipyard workers and assisted in provided housing near the yards in East Belfast: "The best way to find a job was through personal contacts, and many people were quite literally born into jobs" (1991, 71). The family connection, the handing down of jobs from father to son, the fact that most workers lived near their places of employment, meant that the connection between work and home was almost indistinguishable:

> The reverse was also the case: if home and the street were a continuation of work, then the workplace also witnessed activities which in other cities are associated with the home; religion was an integral part of the life of the yards, and George Preston ran a Bible class at Harland and Wolff every lunch hour. Another preacher was smiled on by management as he persuaded his followers to return wood, paint, brass and other items they had stolen from the yard. Ian Paisley, it is worth remembering, started his preaching career in a small chapel for shipyard workers just outside Harland and Wolff's gates. (Goldring 1991, 72)

There exists in Northern Ireland, then, a patriarchal ideology that can match anything from the republic, and that is most apparent in the extreme version of Protestantism that has developed there. This brings to mind northern playwright Christina Reid's characterization, "The public faces of the Protestant and Catholic paramilitaries are men . . . the people who talk about religion and the Church are men. The politicians are men . . . Ian Paisley and the Pope are basically in total agreement over what a woman's role in the home should be" (Herbert 1990).

Unionist politicians such as Ian Paisley reveal no sense of being out of sync with the modern world in their fundamentalist view of family morality and the role of women. Paisley has said:

> I am sure that none of us would take up an argument against the Christian's responsibility in the home. I believe that the husband is the head of the wife and the home. I believe that the father should be prophet, priest and king in his home. As king, he should exercise rulership. As prophet, he should exercise rulership. As prophet, he should establish a family altar

in the home and see that the family each day gathers around that altar in prayer. As priest he should intercede for, and on behalf of, his family. (Beale 1986, 266)

In 2001, at the conclusion of the Northern Irish elections, Nigel Dodds, the Democratic Unionist Party candidate for North Belfast, said in his election speech that he wanted to "thank my wife, Dianne, for working so hard for me" and added, as an afterthought, "not only my wife, my partner" (BBC, Northern Ireland).

Rhonda Paisley (daughter of Ian), while explicitly endorsing a unionist position politically, leaves no doubt about the fact that unionist women remain the minority of minorities when it comes to representation: "there exists very little room for feminism within the ranks of Unionism . . . Feminism and Unionism remain miles apart. To say anything else is to fool ourselves, and there is no evidence to argue otherwise—our representation is not growing" (1992, 33). Ruth Moore believes that while Protestant women's experiences are similar to those of other women—in that they are expected to be heterosexual, to marry and have children, "to care, to cater and to serve"—they differ in one important way:

the domination of loyalist ideology in everyday life extends also into the expectations of women. Protestant women are supposed to be either "the proper wife" or "The Orange Lily" . . . Loyalist women, like their men, are supposed to be loyal to the throne . . . but in addition they must be loyal to the male head of the household—the proper wife, the working companion, the helpmate, the silent support and drive. And loyalism means containing the intense frustrations which arise from meeting these expectations. (1994, 14)

Moore also points out that the perception of Northern Irish Protestants as:

outdated and reactionary is so well established that the very idea of a radical Protestant probably seems novel. . . . Yet there are radical Protestants in Northern Ireland. There are Protestant feminists, Protestant socialists, even Protestant republicans . . . all of them people who . . . challenge the idea that the Protestant community is a single, united, homogeneous group. (12)

Nevertheless, the particular brand of Protestantism that continues to dominate in Northern Ireland places little value on either the creative arts or on "women's worlds." Within such a setting, the idea of becoming a writer for most (unionist) women would evidently be akin to selling one's soul to the devil. But in light of the effects of the women's movement both in the Irish Republic and in nationalist communities in Northern Ireland, particularly in allowing women to articulate through their writing issues of concern to them and their community, it becomes clear that it is Protestant women in the north who currently constitute one of the most silenced groups on the island. A feminist political stance that permits them to artic-ulate issues relating to gender without feeling that they are betraying their cultural and ethnic loyalties has not yet come their way.

Further, while the entire political economy of the family and domestic-ity in general rests on a division of labor that militates against women be-coming writers, the working-class unionist women of Northern Ireland have been silenced even more by a level of national and international polit-ical distaste for anything they might have to say as a result of the way in which Northern Protestantism is represented—in much the same way as, say, white South Africa. This has resulted in a disturbing absence not only of published writing from unionist women but of critical analyses of their relationship to Northern Irish society:

The literature on women and collective action reflects the political agenda of the past 20 years focussing largely on the impact of the conflict on women's collective action and on the tension between the feminists in the republican and feminist movements. A major gap in the literature re-mains how women in Protestant and/or loyalist communities have and currently experience the conflict, the nature and extent of their collective action and organisation and whether the same factors underlie this as apply to the Catholic and/or republican communities. (Montgomery and Davies 1990, 37–38)

In an article on "Ulster's Family Feminists," Amanda Mitchison says that while community-based activities by women in Northern Ireland are becoming increasingly common, few inroads have been made into the entrenched conservatism of mass housing estates and rural areas, where traditional sexual politics and men's responsibilities in the home are hardly questioned (1988, 27). Mitchison believes, in fact, that Catholic women in Northern Ireland have marginally more freedom than Protestants since Catholic culture has a tradition of voluntary community work and also since within a disenfranchized society, rebellion comes more naturally:

> And while the role of women in the loyalist movement appears to have remained subsidary and relatively unchanged, Republicans have responded to pressure from women in the movement and from the British left wing. Sinn Féin set up a women's department in 1981, and two years later adopted a positive discrimination policy. In 1984, the movement finally came out for the acceptance of contraception and divorce. Sinn Féin policy is no longer "totally opposed to abortion," but just "opposed to abortion." (27)

Mitchison also acknowledges, however, that any gains for women within the nationalist community need to be balanced against the extent to which the Troubles have reinforced traditional family networks. This has not only discouraged the development of women's independence but has obscured the ways in which Northern Ireland's militarization has meant that nonpolitical and domestic violence has gone relatively unchecked in both Protestant and Catholic communities (25).

Around two thousand community-based women's groups are currently operating throughout Ireland, of which about five hundred are based in the north. Most are centered in working-class communities. In the republic, these include various ethnic or Traveller communities, but in the north, they tend to be limited to the two primary religious/political communities. The rise of women's groups in Ireland seems clearly linked to the changes that have taken place in the women's movement throughout the 1970s and 1980s and represents one of the ways in which feminism functions to accommodate the needs of particular groups or classes of women: "Prior to the 1980s most women in working class communities spent their time isolated in their homes looking after their families. . . . However, since [then] many women in the community have been striving to change their own lives and the lives of their sisters through education, personal and community development" (Kathleen Maher 1996, 6).

Curiously, there seem to have been somewhat fewer community-based *writing* groups in Northern Ireland during the 1980s, yet today the position is reversed—a reflection, perhaps, of the need for northern women to use more subversive ways of creatively expressing themselves in the light of "larger" political issues and sectarianism. As a result, community writing groups are more evident in the north than they are in the Irish Republic, where women's community activity has tended to focus more on issues of health, immigration, racism, and violence against women.

What is quite evident in contemporary women's writing from Northern Ireland, however, is that, like their counterparts in the republic, northern women writers have consistently integrated feminist issues—via conditions relating to women's lives—into nationalist discourse in an effort to force it onto the political agenda. There is little doubt that, in the process, nationalist women have been more successful in harnessing and using the conditions created by the second wave to creatively articulate their position as women of a particular place and time. It remains to be seen whether unionist women will ever be able to do the same.

3 Surveying the New Minefield

EARLIER VERSIONS of this book were more straightforwardly celebratory in relation to women's fiction of the contemporary period. But growing claims that feminism is now dead or, worse, so "fragmented" that it has become politically impotent, as well as the decline and shifts in women's publishing activities, contributed to a reassessment of what it was I wanted to celebrate: to limit myself to writing only about a body of work that appeared during a particular phase of Irish history could risk confirming that such a phase existed in isolation from what went before, during, and after—something that is clearly nonsense when Irish women's writing of the contemporary period is viewed as just one, albeit extraordinary, feature of an ongoing, strong, and discursive feminist agenda in Ireland. And so, the project became modified to take account of a number of things. First, contemporary Irish women's writing is part of a much larger historical and political process than many current discussions would lead us to believe. Second, while the political left—from which the second wave emerged—has fragmented, it is more useful to consider feminism in its current shape as having, instead, diversified and spread its influence far and wide. Finally, if we are to survive the current onslaught of debates about distinctions between practice and theory, academia and community, politics and society, literature and popular culture, then we need to remind ourselves that feminism—including that practiced at an institutional level—must rigorously retain a commitment to principles of interdisciplinarity (however hard it might be to achieve in reality), to antielitism, and to activism, in all its forms, if it is to remain a challenge to the status quo.

Elizabeth Wilson has argued that the increasing divisions evident within the contemporary feminist movement can be traced directly to the gradual replacement of socialist feminist themes by radical/cultural ones during the 1980s. During this period, according to Wilson, radical feminist debates began to privilege issues such as male violence, lesbianism, and pornography over peace and race, to which, traditionally, socialist women gave more emphasis (1988, 117). This is also the view of Paulina Palmer, who agrees that such divisions are also often based on differences directly related to a rift between "academic" and "popular" feminism in which academic feminists have become more interested in psychoanalytic and socialist feminist perspectives while women's fiction reveals a radical feminist bent in which topics related to the female experience are still privileged: woman-identified relationships, lesbian motherhood, and relations between mothers and daughters, to name a few (1989b, 3–4).

But the alleged problems of institutionalized feminism have also manifested themselves in claims that the category of political "woman" became, during the 1980s, that of theorized "gender," a process that witnessed politics and theory follow divergent paths, and that continues to risk the depoliticization of feminism:

> Finally, (so the story goes), the turn to gender in the 1980s was a definitive break with politics and so enabled this field to come into its own, for gender is a seemingly neutral term devoid of immediate ideological purpose. The emergence of women's history as a field of scholarship involves, in this rendition, an evolution from feminism to women to gender; that is from politics to specialized history to analysis. (Scott 1988, 235)

The main problem with this alleged dichotomy and, in fact, with the use of the terms "political" and "theoretical" themselves is that they imply that theory plays no part in political activities at all or, worse, that anything "political" is likely to be anti-intellectual, or even essentialist. This has particular implications for Irish feminism and its practices, including creative practices, which have too often been represented as "activist," theoretically backward, and entirely reliant on internationally generated theories.

The now familiar claim by minority groups that, at the precise time they establish a means of having their voices heard, the rules of listening change is echoed in the field of contemporary women's writing in both nationalist and feminist contexts. In relation to the former, postmodernist pluralism now privileges the heterogeneous nature of nationness yet fails to acknowledge that the world still consists of many, especially colonial, nations who see nationalism as a *potentially* mobilizing ideology. In feminist theory, gender debates that challenge essentialized notions of "woman," have, by implication, placed the whole idea of studying women writers under question.

Poststructuralist critiques of identity have enabled women of color, for example, to theorize the split or multiple subject of feminism, but these critiques have equally created an anxiety among other feminists that such a theory "deprives women of the right to be included in a humanist universality at precisely the point when they are beginning to become subjects in their own right" (Rajan 1993, 10). Anxiety about such deprivation is by no means limited to women of color, of course, but extends to those who have been marginalized and silenced by any number of oppressions, including hegemonic critical practices. In this final chapter, I will survey a number of theoretical crises as they relate to Irish women's writing and show how this work—which, on the one hand, exists outside any conventional definition of marginalized literature yet, on the other, is among the most marginalized in the contemporary period—has slipped through the cracks of the major theory debates.

SIGNS OR SUBJECTS?

The fact that the level of interest in Irish women's writing has been steadily growing in recent years would provide an optimistic outlook regarding future critical work were it not that such interest has come at a time of "crisis of the subject," which Rosemary Hennessy names as the foremost issue for feminism to resolve in the future (1993, xi).

In *Real and Imagined Women*, Rajeswari Rajan similarly pinpoints the gains and losses of the theoretical "unfixing" of the subject undertaken by poststructuralist critics that has most effectively deconstructed and, thus, challenged entrenched understandings of the "real." Poststructuralist-exposed notions of essentialism—particularly as they apply to women in cultural and literary contexts—have allowed a feminist analysis of the political construction and regulation of the category *woman*. Additionally, this problematization of the subject has created an apprehension that "without an ontologically grounded feminist subject there can be no politics" (Rajan 1993, 10). This is the position argued by many feminist critics, including Constance Penley:

> In order to be either a movement or a discipline, feminism must presuppose the category "woman." . . . It is politically necessary to claim that there is a class or group of humans ("women") that is universally oppressed (by "men," "patriarchy," etc.) because no movement can constitute itself without notions of identity and commonality. (1986, 143–44)

By contrast, other critics argue that a "return to real women" (Riley 1988, 148) would simply accentuate differences rather than challenge them.

Such poststructuralist (especially French) feminist theoretical debates have had a similar influence in Ireland as elsewhere in that there has been a recent reassessment of how useful they are to cultural practices in countries that do not have an emphasis on the abstract and philosophical, or in those places, like Ireland, where history has not necessarily been designated a place in the past.

Janet Todd points out that although French feminist theory was originally closely connected to the 1968 social and political revolution, many of its practitioners, in particular Kristeva—described as "arguably the most apolitical and anti-feminist" of them all (Todd 1988, 73)—became increasingly uneasy at any kind of political or historical alignment on the basis that it represented an acknowledgment and acceptance of the very power game which had marginalized her in the first place (54). While Todd acknowledges that there are deep distinctions among the French theorists, which makes any summary of their views intellectually unwise, she does assert:

> that in the main they united in disapproving of intellectual modes claiming to reveal an empirical reality or an unproblematized history, and they were dubious of any efforts at scrutinizing the surface manifestations of women's oppression; instead the usually hidden body, the unconscious, the deep structures of culture and language, were their data. (51)

But Todd also believes that feminist literary history, especially, must find an engagement with history necessary since there are undeniable "external points of reference, however problematized, both in the past writer and in the critic. . . . Materiality cannot be always and entirely subsumed into the subject, history into psychoanalysis, epistemology into sexuality, or what Lacan mocked as the 'reality principle' of Freudian theory into the sign and the symbolic" (136–37).

Elizabeth Wilson takes the argument against poststructuralist criticism even further by reasoning that its emphasis in feminist criticism has contributed to a decline in those sections of the feminist movement concerned with women's material conditions by privileging what she calls "a limited concept of woman as sign" (1988, 70) in which there is no such thing as a

> "unitary" woman—we are all bundles of contradictory atoms and impulses. The idea of the unitary self is a fiction. Leading on from this there is no such thing as "women's oppression" in any unitary sense. This may be logically correct in the perfect world of Mind: it is politically dubious, to put it mildly, when the Tory government is starting to argue that women should be in the home as a cloak for their spending cuts and unemployment. (1988, 70)

Similarly, Michèle Barrett argues that deconstruction reflects an inherently antipolitical conservatism that is to be avoided by feminist critics at all costs. She questions whether the project to deconstruct the category of "woman" could ever provide the basis for a feminist politics since, if there are no women to be oppressed, "then on what criteria do we struggle, and against what?" (1980, 96).

Lynne Segal targets the psychoanalytic approach to feminism as one that reduces women to mere subjects "who are denied autonomy, trapped within the operations of linguistic structures and laws" (1987, 131). And Donna Landry and Gerald MacLean hypothesize that one effect of the appropriation of psychoanalysis by feminism is likely to be the "reinscription of the family romance." Since psychoanalysis cannot confront the political, the result will be that women will be confined "forever 'on the couch' " (1993, 168).

Rajan, too, exposes a conflict between the problematization of the political construction and deployment of the "real" in poststructuralist theory, which appears to "forbid recourse to a 'real body' or a 'real sex' and the feminist conviction that such recourse is necessary to articulate moral and political opposition to violence, rape and other forms of oppression if we are not to end up in positions of moral relativism and political complicity" (1993, 11).

An important feature of so much poststructuralist theory relates to the reluctance of its critics to engage with history, apparently in an effort to deny its very existence. Yet, as Terry Eagleton argues, "narrative continuities do not merely orchestrate into momentary cohesion a cacophony of historical noises. For these *are* real historical continuities, and it is a dismal index of our theoretical befuddlement that one needs to assert anything so obvious" (1981, 73).

While poststructuralist feminist theories have been more often considered inappropriate or not particularly useful by Irish feminist critics, this does not mean they have been ignored. In 1983, for instance, Ailbhe Smyth published a substantial, annotated, selective bibliography, which was born, she explains, of "personal need" and frustration at the lack of accessible up-to-date information on the "profusion of books, articles, journals, etc., emerging from, around and even against the Women's Movement in France" (1997b, 203). At the same time, she argued that the image of French feminism filtering through to English-speaking feminists was somewhat lopsided: "French feminists are as convinced as their English-speaking sisters that 'the personal is political' and, accordingly, have exploded into action, speech and print, breaking the silence which shrouded their experiences, feelings and ideas" (203). With hindsight, this implies that whatever use early French feminist theory may have been to Irish feminism ultimately became diluted, obscured, or selectively appropriated by the few international stars who made it their own.

Perhaps, then, it would be more accurate to say that Irish feminist critics have been selective in their use of theory for reasons directly connected to the development of Irish feminism, which, as mentioned, has followed a different path than in other Western countries. It is also difficult, as a result of Irish nationalism, to talk of common feminist ground between Ireland

and, say, England or the United States; to do so is to continue to undermine what has been achieved within Ireland itself:

> Not only are women usually excluded from Irish historical representation, but the situation is also complicated by the fact that the most recent wave of feminism in Ireland has relied heavily on authors and ideas from other countries, especially North America. Hence, not only do dominant versions of Irish history marginalize feminism in Ireland, but the impact of feminist writing from other countries has also problematized the relationship between Irish women and their national history. (Mullin 1991, 40)

ANTAGONISMS: FEMINISM AND POSTCOLONIALISM

Given Ireland's position as Britain's earliest, longest held, and most intransigent colony, it seemed possible at one time that postcolonial theory would provide the most useful critical perspective to supplement feminism in a productive reading of women's writing within a national/ist context. That both critical schools have developed models that often intersect—in the areas of oppression and exclusion, for instance, and in creating alternative versions of master narratives—seemed to offer potential for Irish women's fiction to be discussed within the interrelated theoretical frameworks of gender and nationalism. However, given that both feminism and postcolonialism are embroiled in the contentious debates at the center of identity politics, as well as the fact that postcolonialism in Northern Ireland has increasingly become aligned with antirevisionism (or, even, pronationalism), indicates that at both the global and national levels, any usefulness in contributing to readings of Irish women's writing has given way to a territorial competition between the two schools for critical/intellectual space.

A few critics, such as Gayatri Chakravorty Spivak, Barbara Johnson, Kumari Jayawardena, and Nira Yuval-Davis, do address issues of both gender and nationalism in their work. Generally, however, they do so by means of a "marginalized as third world" perspective, which, again, leaves little room for a discussion of Irish women who, although not third world, have been marginalized: through double colonization in a national context as a result of Ireland's colonial history, and as women by an oppressive cultural imperialism resulting from the adoption of a rigid patriarchy within all forms of Irish nationalism. In the Republic of Ireland, this oppression has functioned historically as an important element in establishing a national identity following independence. In Northern Ireland, it serves to maintain the status quo of paternalism and inherited structures of imperialism. Bronwen Levy has argued that the incorporation of certain elements of some feminisms into postcolonial theory yields another form of "empire-building—when the work of writers like Gayatri Chakravorty Spivak or Trinh T. Minh-ha is claimed unproblematically for it [postcolonialism]. These writers, who develop accounts of differences within cultures as well as between them, contribute to postcolonial theory without being contained by it" (Levy 1993, 263).

Yet Spivak herself has argued that while literature should not be ignored in the production of cultural representation, feminist criticism simply reproduces the axioms of imperialism by privileging the "literature of the female subject in Europe and Anglo-America" and, thus, establishing the "high feminist norm" (1985, 243). Her work reveals a consistent focus on privileging issues of (overgeneralized) race over those of gender or class.

This antagonism between one brand of feminism and postcolonialism is most often manifested in a theoretical clash of interests whereby, on the one hand, feminism is seen to be critically insensitive to the effects of imperialism on colonized cultures, while, on the other, postcolonialism is seen to be equally insensitive to the effect of gender on cultural analyses. But neither is the clash confined to a liberal/radical feminist focus on gender, since there also exists a conflict between socialist feminism and postcolonialism arising from the latter's frequent occlusion of class. Ironically, it has been the critical work undertaken in recent years within both feminist and postcolonial studies in particular that has irrevocably exposed the processes by which the marginality of women and minority cultures is maintained by dominant or hegemonic discourses.

But there exists an additional theoretical antagonism that also has implications for the analysis of women's cultural practices in Ireland, and that is the increasing differences between schools of revisionism and postcolonialism, although proponents would not necessarily endorse such straightforward terms.[1] Both theories are equally controversial in terms of their applicability to an Irish context, but since both are related to nationalism and sovereignty, they tend to be interpreted quite differently in the independent Republic of Ireland than in the British province of Northern Ireland.

A crude and oversimplified version of the dispute would go something like this:[2] revisionists would claim that while Ireland's national mythology was a crucial part of its journey toward independence, the country is now in a position to "move on," as it were—to take its place in a politically sophisticated Europe of the twenty-first century. To do so, the hurts of the past need to be put aside as having been dealt with, and a rereading and rewriting of the national mythology undertaken to allow for a more politically sophisticated, "objective" version of Irish history to emerge.[3] By contrast, postcolonialists would see such revision as little more than a betrayal of Ireland's right to have the wrongs of the past addressed.[4] This betrayal brings with it not only a denial of that past, but a sense of being denied a step in the decolonization process whereby the inequities and injustices of a colonial history are dealt with, not through an intellectualized process of demythologizing (which is what revisionism is often seen to be doing), but

1. R. F. Foster's *Modern Ireland, 1600–1972* (1989) is considered to be one of the most influential of the modern sources of historical revisionism in Ireland. Yet Foster has often called for a rethinking of the term since it has become so overused and meaningless (see, for example, R. F. Foster 1986, 1993a). The debate between the two schools has also now entered many disciplines and fields of study and has become as central to literary and cultural studies as to history.

2. This oversimplified description should not be taken to mean that it is always a clear-cut debate between two opposing politics: many revisionists have strong nationalist sympathies, and, similarly, many proponents of postcolonialism as a framework for analysis argue for the parameters of the debate to be extended. For an overview of the complexity involved in the debate, see Declan Kiberd's essay "Imagining Irish Studies" in Kiberd 1995a.

3. For different aspects of this argument see, for example, Liam Kennedy 1996; Cairns and Richards 1988; Seamus Deane 1986a; Curtin, Kelly, and O'Dowd 1984.

4. For the differences in the way postcolonial parameters have been set, compare Spivak 1986 and Donaldson 1988 with Balzano 1996 and de Brún 1988.

through addressing—politically, economically, and socially—the material effects of colonization on the society.[5] On this side of the argument, principally in Northern Ireland, there is also the fear that to skip such a process of decolonization will politically favor those who would like the wrongs of the past simply to disappear.

In Ireland, the revisionist movement has had a major effect on challenging hegemonic discursive practices that for so long (re)circulated longstanding and powerful images of Ireland as an oppressed and victimized nation: the rebirth of modern Irish nationalism as a romantic and romanticized story of feminine liberation (passive Ireland) from a masculine imperialist oppressor (active Britain). Although native to Ireland for centuries, the tradition of personifying Ireland's political identity as female offered itself as a ready-made weapon to nineteenth-century British imperialism. No further evidence was required for Ireland's need of strong leadership than the work of historians like Ernest Renan and writer Matthew Arnold, who, as cultural commentators of their day, analyzed the temperament of the Celt as emotional, excitable, passive, and unquestionably feminine, thereby adopting existing patriarchal binaries of active/passive, culture/nature, possessor/possessed to justify Britain's colonial exploits in Ireland. This stereotype was consistently reinforced throughout the nineteenth century in British newspapers and journals.

The literary glorification of Ireland as female has served two distinct ideological purposes: first, in relation to English cultural imperialism, it has imprisoned the entire Irish race in a debilitating stereotype, and, second, it has enabled Irish men to confine Irish women in a straitjacket of purity and passivity (Butler-Cullingford 1990, 1). In her study of women's place in nationalist movements, Sheila Rowbotham concludes that women's roles have been pivotal in male constructions of a national tradition that presented definitions of what should be conserved and what should be made anew, but the progress of the nation was invested with different meanings for women than for men (1992, 62). Further, "nationalism and antiimperialism pulled women into public action because they were needed by the nation. Their emancipation was less an individual right than a public

5. See, for example, Eagleton, Jameson, and Said 1990; Eagleton 1998; Ward 1991.

duty" (75). Rowbotham also believes, however, that the modernizing elements in nationalism, such as greater educational opportunities for women, were linked to women's emancipation in a special dynamic in which the main focus was on transforming public aspects of the lives of privileged women and creating a new realm of reformed domesticity in which "the new woman in the home was to complement rather than challenge the nationalist man in the family" (62).

Elizabeth Butler-Cullingford has further hypothesized that the native response to the British "feminization" of Ireland was an inversion, rather than a deconstruction, of the stereotype in which Irish masculinity was emphasized, producing what Ashis Nandy calls "hyper-masculinity" (cited in Butler-Cullingford 1990, 6). Inevitably in a country whose writers played such a vital role in the struggle for independence, this inversion is pervasive in the writing of the period. Nationalists such as Patrick Pearse, whose claim that "to serve and suffer as women do is to be the highest thing" (Pearse 1968, 31), simply reinforced the fact that "images of women that originated as the projections of male anxieties and aggression are used as evidence of the need to control and subordinate the whole female sex" (Butler-Cullingford 1990, 2). And as a result, "the man who is trying to prove his hyper-masculinity naturally demands that his woman be hyper-feminine: which in the Irish Catholic context meant an intensification of the already heavy emphasis on virginity and motherhood, and a denial of autonomous female desire" (Butler-Cullingford 1990, 6). Or, as Gerardine Meaney explains, women in such situations become "guarantors of their men's status, bearers of national honour and the scapegoats of national identity. They are not merely transformed into symbols of the nation. They become the territory over which power is exercised" (1991, 7).

In his study of national fictions in Irish cinema, Kevin Rockett maintains that Irish historiography falls within three formulations: "green" nationalism, bourgeois/radical revisionism, and the search for a revolutionary theory. He posits that the dominant strand in Ireland until the 1960s was nationalist history that, when linked with a conservative Catholic ideology, excluded other discourses relating to sexuality, interpersonal relations, divorce, contraception, abortion, and capital/labor conflicts. The conflation of nation and woman during this early nationalist phase of Irish history meant that if women rejected the association, they were being unpatriotic. By 1958, however, when the internationalization of the Irish economy began, nationalist and Catholic discourses had begun to lose some of their power. According to Rockett, bourgeois revisionist history was firmly established by 1965 and, in taking further the work of economic historian Louis Cullen, served to counter and undermine the emotive symbols of "green" nationalism with empirical work on the organization of trade and agriculture (Rockett 1980, 115–16).

But whether revisionism is seen as an attempt to "demolish the nationalist mythology that had been in place for over fifty years, roughly from 1916 to 1966" (Deane 1986b, 6), or as a legitimization of colonial rule in Ireland (Ward 1991, 21), one of the most disappointing aspects of the revisionist exercise has been the way it, too, has failed to include women or any real sense of gendered history within what began as a radical attempt to write a new, more objective version of Irish history. This failure may be one reason why feminists in Ireland often seem to have a closer alliance with postcolonialism than with revisionism: both feminists and postcolonialists feel, for different reasons, that "malestream" history has left them out of the equation yet again, and that there are parts of their history they want to have recorded and dealt with before they can move on.

At the same time, the increasing construction of revisionism as antithetical to postcolonialism has both general significance in an Irish context, given Ireland's colonial history, and very particular significance in relation to Northern Ireland, where a challenge to British imperialism via a postcolonial critique is often interpreted to imply a straightforward pronationalist stance. Often there is also a clear distinction made between revisionism as part of an academic historiography and an increasingly pejorative view of postcolonialism as aligned with popular republicanism and neocolonialism. Liam Kennedy, for instance, considers that such neocolonialism is a perspective "espoused by ultra-nationalists, among others" and names Gerry Adams, president of Sinn Féin, as an example (1996, 173).

On the other hand, Irish feminist historian Margaret Ward maintains that revisionist discourse merely legitimized the appearance of an intellectual border between north and south, which, in turn, permitted the "troublesome six counties" to be shut off from the rest of Ireland. The political consequence of this "was an implicit assumption that if the British presence in Ireland was less malignant than formerly considered, the struggle of the nationalist minority in Northern Ireland could be dismissed as an atavistic impulse, to be ignored if not condemned by a progressive new generation." The resultant tendency within the practice of much Irish revisionist history, Ward declares, is to accept that the postnationalist age has arrived and, thus, women's struggle for emancipation can now be "documented without undue stress being placed upon the age-old story of the British imperial presence in Ireland" (Ward 1995a, 128). Sadly, it is precisely this "intellectual border" that virtually precludes the existence of an active cross-border women's movement in Ireland today.

My main interest in the differing views relates to their often problematic relationship to gender as an equally valid political category of analysis, but one that, as a result of specific historical developments in Ireland, has had to rely upon other critical theories to supplement feminism in a productive reading of women and their cultural practices in a nationalist context. The result has been that gender often gets either overlooked or appropriated by the binaries that have become central to contemporary Irish politics.

These binaries hold particular importance for the critical discussion of women and their cultural practices in Ireland since, falling outside any clearly defined parameters in the study of either gender or culture, such women remain largely absent from theoretical debates concerning the place of feminist cultural practices in the contexts of both postcolonialism and nationalism. Such arbitrary battle lines drawn between issues of culture and gender are more often attributable to internal theoretical disputes in critical schools that could themselves be accused of empire building. More importantly, these theoretical disagreements have serious implications for the future of a politically active feminist movement in Ireland and particularly in Northern Ireland, where the related issues of imperialism and nationalism continue to be the major stumbling blocks between women of the nationalist and unionist communities, and between women's groups in Northern Ireland and in the Irish Republic.

WHO SPEAKS? IDENTITY AND DIFFERENCE

At the same time, feminist theories of identity—defined by Sandra Harding as "working to emancipate one's group instead of humanity" (1991, 144)—have not been particularly helpful either in developing a productive model of feminist critique in Ireland, where, ironically, questions of identity have a particular urgency for feminist politics in the light of internal divisions between "reformist and radical perspectives, socialist and radical feminists, nationalists and non-aligned women" (A. Smyth 1988a, 332).

The "politics of experience" framework, which was challenged in the 1980s by black and other marginalized women on the basis that it represented a hegemonic "whiteness," has been replaced by a "politics of difference" framework, which too often simply inverts that which it challenged through rules such as *"White* writers can choose to write whatever they like; *minority* writers are forced into the position of speaking for their minority whether they want to or not" (Fee 1989, 15; emphasis added). The distinction implies that "white" and "minority" are mutually exclusive terms.

Similarly, it is possible to find numerous examples of marginalized writers expressing the difficulty of writing "under Western eyes" without too much attention being paid to those cultures that are both Western and marginalized. Despite Roddy Doyle's albeit lighthearted attempt to construct the Irish as the blacks of Europe, there is a sense in which both postcolonial and minority feminist "politics of difference" theories privilege a racial opposition based on a black/white dichotomy from which Ireland is excluded and that confirms Mary John's assertion that "feminism is a politics before it is an epistemology. It is therefore not only a question of 'what is being said' but 'who speaks for whom' " (1989, 63).

But, as mentioned earlier, the difficulty of discussing Ireland or Irish writing as marginalized and "different" is problematized generally as a result of geographical, cultural, and canonical assumptions: Ireland is geographically part of western Europe, it is racially white, economically capitalist, and many of its men writers are studied throughout the world as valued contributors to a "universal" canon of English literature, all of which works to maintain Ireland's exclusion from contemporary theoretical debates about marginality and difference.

Any attempt to analyze Irish women's writing within a "politics of difference" framework, then, requires an acknowledgment that such discussion of difference is not an attempt to set it apart from the larger, political body of feminism, women's writing or even cultural studies. Equally important is an acknowledgment that such writing is the product of specific cultural and material conditions:

> the subordination of context to text in the search for white or black "images of women," and of text to context . . . is a "con," or a trick assumption, which in fact distorts the relationship of a literary work to its sociocultural production. By deconstructing the terms that have heretofore grounded the debate, however, both feminists and sympathetic critics could forge an extremely powerful and subversive strategy of reading both contextually *and* textually, ideologically *and* semiotically. (Donaldson 1988, 55)

DIRTY WORDS: ACCESSIBLE REALISM

By no means limited to Ireland, though crucial to it, is a further significant feature of such theory debates associated, at the most fundamental level, with the fact that the majority of women writers have and continue to write in the mode of realism. Barthes's critique of realism as the manifestation of a literary ideology that conceals the socially relative or constructed nature of language, as well as the emergence of deconstruction as the antithesis of realism, has meant that the genre has become somewhat stigmatized, especially within certain sections of the critical and academic communities. But the fact remains that the vast majority of women writers, including those in Ireland, have used realism as their preferred choice of genre. This continued use of a literary genre that is seen by many as not only conservative but patriarchal has caused additional problems for the critical analysis of Irish women's writing, even during its most recent radical periods.

Although undergoing something of a revival in the work of critics such as Rita Felski, realism has been considered, in recent times, quite passé within a poststructuralist and, thus, ahistorical orthodoxy that avers that experimental writing is more subversive and potentially more politically radical than realist texts. But, as Felski points out, the significance of the social function of literature—as opposed to its self-referential and metalinguistic function—in relation to a relatively broad-based women's movement, is necessarily important to an emancipatory feminist politics (1989, 7). This significance has been obscured, however

> by the assertion that experimental writing constitutes the only truly "subversive" or "feminine" textual practice and that more conventional forms such as realism are complicit with patriarchal systems of representation, a position which maps onto gender what are in fact class questions and thus avoids any examination of the potentially elitist implications of its own position. (7)

But Felski also declares that the two most influential strands of contemporary feminist literary theory, namely French and Anglo-American, offer a reenactment of an ongoing dispute between what she describes as "instrumental" and "aesthetic" theories of the text, including many points of comparison to the earlier debate between realism and modernism within Marxist aesthetics of the 1930s (3). This privileging of experimentalism (or castigation for its absence) can be found in many critical analyses of contemporary Irish writing.

In his introduction to *The Penguin Book of Irish Fiction* (1999), for instance, Colm Toibin says that "while there has been stylistic innovation in the work of, say, Anne Enright and Roddy Doyle and Patrick McCabe and Aiden Matthews, a playing with tone, an ability to write sentences like no one had ever written them before, most of the work being produced in Ireland now is formally conservative." Toibin indicates that in contemporary Scottish writing—which he identifies as the inheritor of Sterne, Swift, Joyce, Beckett, and Flann O'Brien—"books are written, as in Ireland in the old days, to replace a country" (xxxii). He continues:

> Some clues about what might replace this can be seen in the works of several women writers, most notably K. Arnold Price whose account of a marriage in *The New Perspective* could equally be set in contemporary Scandinavia, or Deirdre Madden, whose novel *Remembering Light and Stone* concentrates on the experiences of an Irishwoman in Italy, or Emma

Donoghue whose dramatizations of sexual politics have set a new tone in
Irish fiction, or Anne Enright who has taken up and refined the legacy of
Stern and Flann O'Brien and placed it in a Dublin which, for the first time
in its long life in fiction, has become post-Freudian, post-feminist and, of
course (three cheers!) post-nationalist. (xxxii–iii)

While such arguments are seductive in their ostensible gender
egalitarianism—"we're all equal now as writers"—they are only a step away
from a much older liberal humanist argument that would see value only in
those texts that "transcend the provincial contexts of their initial production and deal with moral preoccupations relevant to people of all times and
places" (Sebastian Barry 1986, 11). Or, as the conventional literary wisdom
of A. Norman Jeffares would argue, "good writing is something which transcends borders, whether local or national, whether of the mind or of the
spirit" (1965, vxiii).

Within current definitions of realism, it has been too easy for those opposed to it to see it as "escapist" or "romantic" and, thus, dismiss its political
potential, which clearly goes far beyond an Irish context into links between
the lives of Irish women and those of women elsewhere. For example, realism, as a tool of what Terry Eagleton calls the "ideology of Literature"
(1983, 20) is conventionally associated with bourgeois realism (and ideology), which views Literature as a reflection of individual experience and,
thus, liberal humanism. Its effectiveness in endorsing such a position relies
on the identification with "real" characters by a reader who is drawn into a
series of events based on a classic narrative structure of equilibrium-
disruption-restored equilibrium.

In her defense of Irish realist film, Barbara O'Connor says that while
Lacan's psychoanalytic theories, Althusserian theories of the subject, and
Freud's theories of ego development have been insightful, a major weakness
is in their monolithic and universal character: "Since there is rarely a distinction made between the 'subject' spectator [reader] addressed by the . . .
text and the audience as a social group there is the danger of falling into a
theoretical cul-de-sac where the object of analysis is the ahistorical, asocial
concept of reader/spectator or 'woman' " (1984, 80). Further, limited definitions of realism oversimplify what has been, historically, a much more com-

plex and diverse genre: social realism, socialist realism, magic realism, confessional realism, and even naturalism have been used by many writers for purposes other than the presentation of an ostensibly straightforward reflection of "reality" unmediated by language.

But above all else, books and stories that tell of identifiable people in specific historic, cultural, and class-based situations have proved their popularity and longevity with an increasingly aware reading public. Even a straightforward commercial connection between the emergence of second wave feminism and the economics of publishing does not satisfactorily explain this popularity and longevity. Publishers have almost certainly exploited the commercialization of feminism via autobiographical realist women's novels that encourage identification and are accessible to a large reading audience. But this cannot explain the prevalence of realist forms in feminist fiction, "a trend intimately related to the centrality of the notion of personal change to the politics of feminism . . . clearly, autobiographical feminist writing fulfils important cultural needs" (Felski 1989, 80). As such, feminist literature does not necessarily reveal a given female identity but is involved in the construction of this self as a cultural reality: "The literary text needs to be seen as one important site for the struggle over meaning through the formulation of narratives which articulate women's changing concerns and self-perceptions. Writing should be grasped in this context as a social practice which *creates* meaning rather than merely communicating it" (Felski 1989, 78).

In the hands of contemporary Irish women writers, realism is used primarily as a mode of writing that permits an accurate, though not necessarily "natural," re/presentation of various aspects of women's lives in Ireland today. This usage is in keeping with the theory that "literary texts are assumed to be ideological in the sense that they cannot give us a knowledge of the social formation; but they do give us something of equal importance in analyzing culture, an imaginary representation of real relations" (Marxist-Feminist Literature Collective 1978, 27).

For Rajan, this concept of "representation" is useful precisely because it can serve a mediating function between two theoretical positions: being neither foundationalist (privileging "reality") nor superstructural (privileging "culture") while not denying the real, or essentializing it "as some pre-given metaphysical ground for representation." This makes it productive for feminism to engage with as a domain with its own substantial political reality and effects: "Our understanding of the problems of 'real' women cannot lie outside the 'imagined' constructs in and through which 'women' emerge as subjects. Negotiating with these mediations and simulacra we seek to arrive at an understanding of the issues at stake" (Rajan 1993, 10).

Realist texts, by their very nature, and by the fact that they are more likely to be read by a larger number of women, have a much greater potential to maintain links between feminism and the lives of women than does experimental writing, thus endorsing Ann Snitow's view that realist texts rely on the existence of a "female community [that] provides women writers with that audience eager to recognize itself" (1980, 161). Irish writer Mary Dorcey sums up the importance of this sense of audience as a "voice" characteristic of women and the way they relate to one another:

> the voice of one woman or more talking to, telling a story to, one or more women. It is the very root of my desire to write this talking of women that I heard all about from my earliest years . . . I write in a speaking voice which presupposes a listener and invites the reader into a dialogue. It makes the reader an active force in the telling of the tale or poem in the way that women's conversation does, whereas men "think aloud" at others. (Nuala Archer 1990, 24)

But what happens when realism is used to endorse an oppositional position? The natural, seamless world in which the reader is situated as subject is disrupted in favor of a world in which the reader is still subject, but it is a disrupted, contradictory, and fragmented world. In particular, when women with agency of one sort or another are placed at the center of a realist text and that realism maintains its "naturalness" and clear "reflection" of the world, then the reader becomes subject at the center of a narrative that is also contradictory and disrupted: she sees herself (or at least a re/presentation of herself) amidst the disarray. Put simply, if the reader as subject identifies with a central protagonist who is struggling with the contradictions and inequalities of women's lives, then there is a good chance that the reader will struggle with those issues as well.

As Rajan has pointed out, the not entirely fortuitous convergence of political (that is, feminist, postcolonial, black) and theoretical (that is, post-structuralist, postmodernist) criticisms on a critique of essentialism has had important consequences for the understanding of subjectivity whereby the displacement of the individual (bourgeois white male) subject of Western humanism, whose totalizing centrality had elided questions of class, gender, and racial differences, has created a vacant space. The existence of this vacant space allows for the potentially radical installation of a resisting subject: "one who will be capable of the agency and enabling selfhood of the 'active' earlier subject, while at the same time acknowledging the politics of difference. The cleared site of the subject must provide the grounds of (new) gendered subjectivities that will enact more contingent, varied and flexible modes of resistance" (Rajan 1993, 11).

I am asserting, then, that in an Irish feminist context, realism, far from being stagnant or unadventurous, has been both radical and politically enabling since an important part of the political enterprise for contemporary women writers has been in re/presenting and, where necessary, challenging aspects of their society. There is very little evidence in the work of such writers to suggest that realism is being used simply to entertain or provide escape. On the contrary, it is more often used to hold up to readers aspects of Irish society that need to be made visible. As a result, contemporary Irish women's writing retains a strong orientation of political connection between the work and the reader.

Moreover, there is little evidence in contemporary Irish women's writing to suggest any clear distinction between politics as being something that exists in the "real" world and a fictional world, separate and removed from the issues. On the contrary, the two concepts are closely, though not always overtly, connected: at times the connection is through nothing more than implicit reader identification with a central female protagonist; sometimes, however, the connection is more explicit through a central protagonist who confronts the politics of Irish life via a realist plot that is entirely accessible to an Irish reader, demanding either identification or rejection.

The writing discussed here, as a body of political and politicized work, exists, then, as one very important link between the theories and practices of feminism, not least because it provides an important challenge to the temporal distancing that much mainstream academic literary criticism conventionally prefers. But unless a more concerted effort is made to resist the imposition of dichotomous labels like academic/popular, political/theoretical, or literary/popular, then this writing will almost certainly be left to suffer the process of depoliticization imposed by mainstream criticism's application of retrospectively applied literary value.

Within Ireland, women's fiction of the contemporary period has been both radical and subversive, terms more often associated with Irish men's writing. For while such terms fit comfortably in discussions of writers as diverse in time and genre as Swift, Wilde, Joyce, Yeats, O'Casey, Behan, and Beckett, they are rarely, if ever, associated with Irish women writers in mainstream literary criticism. Yet in the nineteenth and early twentieth centuries in particular, Irish (men's) writing was at its most radical and subversive in response to imperial stereotyping or in its attempts to construct an Irish cultural identity that was different from that imposed by England. At the same time, women's *political* activity has also been at its most intense during periods of anti-imperialism. In contrast to this convention-breaking political role, the conventional understanding of the role of women *writers* has been as conservative, supportive, and domestic: most often, in fact, confined either to the genre categories of Big House or Anglo-Irish fiction, or, alternatively, seen as having been appropriated into a "larger" political or humanist cause.

DEFINING "GREATNESS": THE MALE LITERARY TRADITION

In the introduction to her 1984 anthology, *Woman's Part*, Janet Madden-Simpson states that Irish women have not written "great" literature in the way that "Yeats, Joyce or Beckett have produced it . . . female writers have generally worked within the confines of literary convention, have not experimented in startlingly obvious ways and have, perhaps, been too accepting of sociological and historical limitations" (Madden-Simpson 1984, 6).

Similarly, in what has become a controversial essay, Nuala O'Faolain claimed in 1985 that in modern Ireland "there has been no woman writer of the very highest ambition—no Emily Dickenson, no Dorothy Richardson, no Christina Stead" (1985, 128).

O'Faolain's argument rests on the fact that the "great" literature of Ireland has been produced by men, none of whom have been realists, yet realism is the primary vehicle of women writers who feel compelled to speak to and about women's lives in Ireland. O'Faolain goes on to assert that "the ideal feminist novel would be known by other women to tell the truth about the individual and about the condition. It would demand super-realism," and yet "a womanly novel has to be, but theoretically cannot be, a realist novel" (131).

Such ruminations, whatever their accuracy, imply that the absence of an undefined "great" Irish woman writer was of some concern to Irish critics like Madden-Simpson and O'Faolain during the mid-1980s—a time when the body of contemporary Irish women's writing was in its infancy. Yet the critical interest in women's writing generally was part of a wider, and less diversified movement.

Even more unsettling, however, is the appearance of an article by Eve Patten in 1990, which acknowledges that "Ireland's constitution remains unchanged; so, then, does the urgent need experienced by women to put it all down in writing . . . confessional realism is a necessity, not a choice." Patten goes much further than either Madden-Simpson or O'Faolain by explicitly contrasting Irish women's writing with that produced in Europe: "If feminism in Ireland lags behind its Continental counterpart by as much as sixty years, as one commentator has suggested, how long will the powerful grip on writing continue to define, and to fossilise, the fiction which frequently becomes its vehicle?" (Patten 1990, 1–2).

Patten fails to provide any source for the claim concerning the retardation in Irish feminism, or even an identification of where, geographically, the specific "Continental counterpart" might be located. Of more importance is that all the examples cited reveal a Gabriel Conroy–like gaze toward a mythical center of European feminism as a benchmark or standard against which Irish writing and feminism falls short: an attitude that is commonly found in Irish feminist criticism of the 1980s, in particular.

One of the earliest and most influential critiques of confessional realism was Rosalind Coward's " 'This Novel Changes Lives': Are Women's Novels Feminist Novels?" (1980), in which she proposes that "speaking about sexuality, a preoccupation with sexuality, is not in and of itself progressive. Feminists have been involved for too long now in the analysis of images and ideologies to be conned into thinking that accounts of sexuality are progressive just because they take women's sexuality as their central concern" (233). Coward goes on to relate these comments to pornography and its negative effect on women's lives. But, written at a time when feminism was entering a new theoretical stage, Coward's comments more closely reflect the beginnings of a shift in Anglo-American feminist discourses that would ultimately see certain strands of feminism become more aligned with the New Right than they might otherwise have liked—in their antipornography stance, for example. The point is, however, that while these changes were taking place in the international arena, within Ireland confessional realism was not only extremely popular but represented a very progressive aspect of Irish women's writing.

There are a number of possible answers to the question of why Ireland has produced no "great" woman or feminist writer, some of which are particular to conditions within Ireland and others that are relevant to women writers elsewhere. The most obvious answer perhaps is that Ireland's long and impressive tradition of "great" men writers has been so outstanding that its achievements are simply unassailable. Or it could be that the Irish nationalist response to the nineteenth-century imperialist construction of Celtic Ireland as defenseless and victimized woman, which created female literary figures of legendary proportions, has made the task of convincingly or realistically portraying women's lives impossible for Irish women writers.

Within a wider context, of course, Irish women writers have shared with those from a number of other countries the difficulties of trying to forge a place in what has been for so long a phallocentric literary tradition, and while it could be argued that women writers from many other countries have overcome such limitations,[6] perhaps the timing of economic, social,

6. According to Nuala O'Faolain, for instance, there has been no condition applicable to Ireland from which women writers from other places have not been able to escape. She maintains Katherine Mansfield ably escaped her provincialism; Margaret Atwood and

and educational oppressions in relation to Irish women have been different from those elsewhere. Whatever the reasons, and there are many that could be argued convincingly, their validity entirely rests on an implicit acceptance of the concept of "greatness" itself, a concept that, when interrogated, reveals a value-laden bias in favor of those very dogmas that have traditionally worked to the detriment of marginalized writers, both men and women.

"Great" writers are judged by criteria that are not absolute but are ideologically inflected and at the mercy of cultural and political hegemonies. Of more concern is that this expectation of "greatness" should continue to come from feminist critics who, it might have been hoped, would recognize that the critical treatment of women's writing in relation to men's—or in relation to other women's for that matter—is directly analogous to that of marginalized writers in relation to the dominant discourses of traditional literary criticism. Ironically, it has been primarily the critical work undertaken by feminist and "cultural" critics that has exposed how the process of selecting "great" writers on the basis of race, class, or gender has historically been an aspect of the power relations between dominant and marginalized groups through which writers are appropriated and politically neutralized. For feminist critics to fail to recognize and question such a process, then, means that they risk placing women's writing in the same position as Irish men's writing has traditionally been placed in relation to the English canon as a whole.

Ireland's honored place, for example, in the English literary canon has consistently obscured the position of Irish literature as a minority discourse by virtue of Ireland's political marginality to England. Irish writers, like those from elsewhere, have written and continued to write from within particular historical, cultural, and material conditions, yet historically they

---

Marge Piercy escaped disaffected provincialism; Lady Gregory and Doris Lessing escaped the trap of being caught between ideologies during the First and Second World Wars, respectively. "In the English-speaking world, no woman in any country has an absolute defence, in socio-political terms, for silence. Even in police states, even outside literacy, women have made imaginative statements of great power. Neo-colonialism cannot, in this, be our defence" (1985, 129).

have depended for appraisal on the dominant discourses of principally Anglo/American literary criticisms. The criteria for selecting "great" writers within such criticisms more often than not rely on the absolute denial of difference: initially by simply not recognizing difference at all or, in a more recent shift, by reconfiguring critical space so that the concept of "difference" no longer exists.

A further unfortunate yet integral aspect of such a hierarchical process, which has the power to valorize one body of writing over another, has been the creation of what might be called a subcanon of Irish writing within the English literary canon. In this construction, Irish writers are unproblematically grouped together on the basis of common nationality, a situation that inevitably and necessarily denies the very important differences that may exist between them. The most obvious example of authors that end up in the same Irish category in spite of the great many other differences in their work are W. B. Yeats and James Joyce. Such groupings rarely allow for a discussion of these writers as more anomalous than representative within a national literary canon. The emphasis on Yeats as one of the greatest modern poets, for example, overlooks the resistance within Ireland to the methods used by the Irish literary revival, of which he was the most prominent figure, in creating new images of Irish identity. And while James Joyce undoubtedly altered existing notions of the novel, it is rarely acknowledged that his influence on Irish writing as a whole was minimal.

Joyce is valued in the English literary canon not as an Irish writer but as one of, if not the greatest exponents of modernism. His position was achieved, primarily, as a result of the experimentalism of *Ulysses* as opposed to the ostensibly straightforward realism of *Dubliners*. Yet David Lloyd has shown how *Ulysses* was recalcitrant both to the emergent nationalism *and* to the imperial state formation precisely because it refused the homogeneity of "style" required for national citizenship (1993, 2). It is difficult to imagine Joyce's experimentalism arising outside of his Irish context. In a similar way, Yeats's international status as a great modern poet incorporates very little of the ambiguity associated with his Irish/Anglo-Irish identity.

Samuel Beckett's plays continue to be valued for their "universal" themes of humankind's alienation and for his contribution to the Theater of the Absurd, rather than for anything they may reveal about the Irish identity and its particular alienation. True, Beckett spent most of his literary career in self-imposed exile in Europe, but so did Joyce. Is the difference simply that Beckett resisted using Ireland as a subject and consistently attempted to "transcend" national limitations, while for Joyce those limitations were something of an obsession? Do such questions really matter since both writers have secured apparently privileged places within both national and international canons of "great" literature? But what of Irish realist writers like William Carleton, Sean O'Faolain, and Patrick Kavanagh, or the satirist Flann O'Brien? Is it simply that they were only good enough as writers to secure places within a national canon, but not "great" enough to make the big time? To believe so is naively to accept the premise that great writers, whether men or women, are born and not created.

"Greatness," then, can be seen as a deceptively simple and potentially disempowering term that, particularly when allocated by a hegemonic body, should be treated with great suspicion if not resisted altogether. For just as the nationality of such "great" writers as Joyce and Yeats has never really been central to their acceptance, neither has the gender of those literary women selected to bear the same title of "greatness," confirming Lilian Robinson's comparison of the canon to a "gentleman's agreement" whereby class and gender bias is disguised within the civility/gentility of canonization (1992, 106).

All of this is not to say, of course, that Irish feminist criticism has or should entirely abandon the concept of literary value or achievement by Irish women writers, an allegation made in 1988 by Katie Donovan in her essay, "Irish Women Writers, Marginalized by Whom?" in which she convincingly, though selectively, discusses various Irish women and men writers to reveal similarities in their work. Donovan argues strongly against the category "woman writer" on the basis that it not only further marginalizes women's writing but that those critics who focus on such writing form a "converted audience" (1988, 5), thereby limiting their ability to critique the material in an open and balanced way (although the resulting way is left entirely unexplained). As Patricia Boyle Haberstroh has argued, Donovan's argument "makes for easy distinctions between woman and feminist, feminist and good critic, and feminist and mainstream publishing houses, distinctions which are both arbitrary and oversimplified" (1992, 184).

A similar lack of engagement exists in some discussions concerning the place of Irish women writers in literary canons. It is often implied in these discussion that the literary success of such writers can be allied to the literary success of Irish men writers, and there is no real interrogation of the ways in which marginalized writers often become appropriated through the whole process of canon formation.

By the standards of an external, theoretically sophisticated and somewhat hegemonic critical world, Irish women's writing can seem unadventurous and even static as a result of a number of dominant features: an emphasis on political and historical events, a focus on women in a nationalist context, and a prevalence of realism as the preferred literary genre. Yet all of these features imply that contemporary Irish women's fiction has been and continues to be grounded in the concrete reality of day-to-day Ireland, especially as it is lived by "real" women, a situation that has largely precluded this body of work from critical analyses that favor the abstract, experimental, and linguistic.

In one of the earliest and most influential studies of Irish women's writing, *Woman's Part: An Anthology of Short Fiction by and about Irish Women, 1890–1960*, Janet Madden-Simpson, referring to the writing of women during and since the Irish literary revival, declares that they are often mistakenly considered writers of popular and sentimental verse and fiction as a result of their leaning toward realistic, even "social problem" fiction (1984, 11). Even when undertaking nationalistic myths or romance, such women's writing was apt to include a good dose of down-to-earth details about the day-to-day lives of women, indicating that even when orthodox attitudes about women's place and function were being transmitted, the writers were as intimately aware of the difficulties of being a woman as were those who approached their subjects from a more "crusading and analytical angle": "this common awareness is a bond which to some extent makes most Irish female writing feminist; that is, in the sense that the reader is almost without exception expected to identify with the heroines and to participate in their stories" (11). Realism has dominated the fiction produced by contemporary Irish women writers, as has the short story, and continues to represent the most radical literary genre and one of the most effective links between feminism (as a philosophical and political movement) and the lives of women in Ireland today.

While English and American feminist critics were undertaking analyses of "images of women" in fiction, Irish feminists were frustrated by the long tradition of strong, but often legendary, heroic women who appear throughout Irish literature written by men: heroic, fictional women like Yeats's Cathleen Ni Houlihan, Joyce's Molly Bloom, Synge's Pegeen Mike, and O'Casey's Juno. Irish literature contains, on the whole, exemplars that are not only difficult to live up to but even more difficult to destroy. Put simply, the images of women in Irish fiction by men are basically so powerful, albeit mythical, that they can only be countered by realistic figures; however, while such realistic figures (basically ordinary, fallible women) achieve the necessary confrontation with those created by men, they have tended to draw disapproval from feminist critics. Edna O'Brien, for instance, has often been castigated by feminist critics for creating defeated women or women whose lives revolve entirely around a man, despite the fact that O'Brien created some of the most realistic—and thus brutal— images of what life in rural Ireland was like for women during the 1940s, 1950s, and 1960s. In doing so, O'Brien's early stories not only provide readers with a narrative that engages the imagination but exist as sociological documents.

The development of two Irish literary traditions, then, identified by genre and gender, has resulted in an extraordinarily biased and restricted representation, not only of Irish literature but of Irish life, particularly as experienced by women. In the hands of men writers, Irish women achieved a legendary fictional status, which has belied the often-brutal reality of their everyday lives. But legendary and powerful fictional women hold very limited potential as figures of identification for a significant proportion of a population that was for so long, and in some cases is still, denied many basic rights and held in place by the collusion of churches and states.

Criticism that seems more interested in what is happening elsewhere, rather than with seeing those external events in relation to Ireland, has not been particularly useful to Irish feminism or Irish women's writing. The external focus tends to undermine the bulk of feminist criticism within Ireland, which does more frequently take into account the specifics of cultural practices and production. Rosalind Coward's rejection of confessional realism on the basis that it is no longer progressive may indeed have been valid for English or American feminists in 1985; but, given the slightly later development of feminism in Ireland, and its own culturally specific contexts, it is also possible that in Ireland in 1990 there was still a need to ensure that "somewhere in the historical canon in Ireland somebody had to be more frank about the actual sexual lives of women in this country" (Evelyn Conlon in Pelan 1995, 123).

STRIKING A BALANCE

Confronted with the vast array of complex historical feminist and cultural theory debates, it becomes clear that anyone undertaking a study of women's writing today faces a whole new minefield to be traversed. Calls for the acknowledgment of difference by women of color, third world women, and lesbians, to name a few, have revealed the once politically mobilizing category of *woman* to be a potentially essentialized and increasingly hegemonic one that can ignore other forms of oppression. At the same time, there is the danger that too great an emphasis on difference and plurality will inevitably lead to such a diffusion of feminist perspective that its ability as a politically empowering movement will be totally eroded. Clearly, then, a crucial element in current gender theory debates is an attempt to theorize a relationship between the political and the symbolic in a way that avoids reductionism and what Rita Felski calls "inadequate homologies" between literary structures and social and political structures (1989, 8). As Rosemary Hennessy concludes, "the challenge is to find ways to anchor feminist analysis in our recognition of the continued brutal force certain social totalities like patriarchy and racism still exercise, at the same time acknowledging that the social construction of 'woman' is never monolithic" (1993, xi). This critical/theoretical minefield manifests itself most immediately in the problem of finding a way to discuss Irish women's writing and feminism in a way that avoids totalizing or essentializing women but, at the same time, recognizes the place of such work and writing within a wider framework of women's writing and feminist analysis generally: finding a way, in other words, to walk the fine critical line between constructing yet another grand narrative based on gender alone and entirely deconstructing women's writing as an integral part of an enabling ideology through an emphasis on difference and plurality.

The imaginative writing produced by contemporary Irish women over the past thirty years, in all its forms, is one very important strand of feminist publishing to appropriate and use aspects of feminist discourse to re/present more complex images of Ireland and its women than those images that had become so deeply entrenched. In the Republic of Ireland, this appropriation has allowed a challenge to outmoded, nationally privileged images of women in an attempt to replace them with an updated, re-imag(in)ing of women through fictional representations of radical feminist politics. In Northern Ireland, women writers have been less concerned with themes of lesbianism, domestic violence, and relationships between mothers and daughters—prevalent in much feminist writing from America, Britain, and the Republic of Ireland—than they have been with issues of class, ethnicity, and the creative recording of the ways in which women and men in that society have dealt with the violence and sectarianism that have surrounded them for so long. These different thematic emphases clearly relate to the social and political contexts in which the women have written. To a large extent, much of this writing in both Northern Ireland and the Irish Republic has been directly concerned with addressing and challenging male histories and nationalist mythologies.

The conventional, institutionalized conservatism of the Republic of Ireland prior to, say, the mid-1970s reflects an older, lost, mythical identity against which the creative arts, and women's writing in particular, significantly contributed revised notions of identity in order to bring about a more diverse, modern Ireland. In this reimaging, an obsession with the "enemy" of colonial oppression, evident in much modern Irish men's writing, was replaced by issues of sexism, the breakdown of the nuclear family, unemployment, crime, drug addiction, rape, domestic violence, and other "modern" issues. The republic's institutionalized and increasingly revis(ion)ed mythology has continued to play an important role in the lives of the nationalist communities in Northern Ireland, however, in which an older, transferred nationalist mythology has represented a potentially mobilizing ideology. Yet the writing produced by women from the Northern communities shows that, while unable or unwilling wholly to disengage from such nationalist politics, they have been able, to varying degrees, to mediate issues of gender, class, *and* nationality while retaining a prioritized commitment to women's issues achieved primarily through placing women central to their fiction, poetry, and drama, and by merging feminist and nationalist discourses, thus altering our understanding of both.

Generally speaking, then, it is within the body of contemporary Irish women's writing that a realistic re/presentation of the diversity and complexity of Irish identity exists, thereby undermining, in the Republic of Ireland, an entrenched idea of a unified Irish cultural or national identity based on an equally essentialized notion of what it means to be "Irish." In Northern Ireland, this has meant challenging an imposed and dichotomous view of what it means to be female and Northern Irish by introducing the category of gender into existing, entrenched binaries of identity. In attempting to redefine what it means to be an Irish or Northern Irish woman today, such writers form a crucial component in the feminist project of producing alternative visions of the Irish past that can compete with the dominant historical constructions sponsored by the state and the popular media (Mullin 1991, 46).

Women in the Irish Republic have produced an immensely rich and prolific body of work, and even though much of it is now out of print, it has still contributed substantially to shifts in the ways Irish women are represented and talked about. During the same period, women in Northen Ireland produced a distinct body of work revealing considerable achievements there too in mediating the fine line between gender and other dominant features of identity formation, even though their work has been much less influential in changing either the representation of northern women or the general way of life in that region.

Women in the Irish Republic have made extraordinary inroads in both the political and cultural spheres; women in Northern Ireland have progressed more slowly, their gains always being contingent on the fragility of northern politics and the nature of their relationship to their communities. In the context of Northern Ireland, it has been nationalist women who have best found a way to balance gender issues with those of nationalist politics.

With just a few exceptions, northern unionist women have so far largely failed to find a way out from under the immensely powerful weight of patriarchy to articulate creatively the intersection of gender and unionism. The most productive view of these varying levels of "achievement" by Irish women, however, is to see them as diverse *feminisms*. Unless we recognize the differences as being relative only in relation to the local and contingent, rather than in relation to some distant "international" ideal, then we are going to continue to deprive certain women of a voice: unionist women in Northern Ireland, for example, or women of the Traveller community and other minority groups throughout Ireland.

Yet there are also important points of comparison between women's writing from Northern Ireland and from the Irish Republic: a remarkable similarity in thematic focus, for instance, and the dominance of realism as the favored genre, popular with northern women writers for precisely the same reasons as for those from the Irish Republic. There are a great many short stories written over other fictional forms. And there is an emphasis on central women protagonists who are represented as being integral members of their community as opposed to aberrant observers or outsiders.

The women's writing discussed throughout this book forms an integral component of a multi- and interdisciplinary movement in which such creative practices exist comfortably alongside other forms of women's activism. Many women writers since the mid-1990s—creative and other—have returned to individual concerns in their writing, some no longer write, some have retained a commitment to leftist politics but have moved beyond issues relevant only to Ireland, and some have become part of the very literary establishment they once challenged.

What I have attempted to do here is record aspects of what has been a productive and important period in Irish women's literary history: a period of high productivity that reveals a remarkable level of collective political consciousness and that was largely facilitated by the second wave, during which historically defined images and representations have been and, to a lesser degree, continue to be challenged and undermined by contemporary Irish women's writing as an example of feminist oppositional discourse. But having achieved a great deal over the previous thirty-year period—to which women's writing contributed substantially—feminism in Ireland is now functionally quite different from what it was even ten years ago: a significant part of feminist activity today involves a form of institutionalized vigilance to resist the erosion or depoliticization of those women's issues that have already entered the mainstream of social and political life, while topics of ethnicity and (anti)racism have overtaken feminism with a sense of urgency.

Certainly, we could be forgiven for thinking that everything has been fought for and won judging by much Irish women's writing that has appeared in very recent years, including the chicklit genre mentinoed earlier. But I think these significant and recent changes in Irish feminist writing and publishing activity are attributable to a number of factors that resonate throughout feminist activities everywhere: the changes evident in the women's movement today, for instance, including shifts toward post- and third-wave feminism; the severe restraints experienced through conservative economic rationalist policies, which have had a debilitating effect on the publishing industry and on the expansion of women's studies programs at an institutional level; the paralysis created by dominant gender and cultural theory debates that have questioned the sense of studying "women" writers at all; the "women-blaming discourses" and alleged tyranny of political correctness over free speech and common sense (Griffin et al. 1994, 2); and the escalating division between the practice and theory of feminism. All these current issues point to a need for a sustained examination of what has and has not yet been achieved to protect the attainments and consider fresh strategies.

WORKS CITED

SELECTED READINGS

INDEX

Works Cited

"The Adultery" and Other Stories and Poems. 1982. Maxwell House Winners 3. Dublin: Arlen House.

Alyn, Marjory. 1984. *The Sound of Anthems.* London: Hodder & Stoughton.

Anderson, Benedict. 1991. *Imagined Communities.* London: Verso.

Anderson, Linda. 1984. *To Stay Alive.* London: Bodley Head. Published in the United States as *We Can't All Be Heroes, You Know.* New York: Ticknor and Fields, 1985.

———. 1986. *Cuckoo.* London: Bodley Head.

Archer, J. R. 1986. "Necessary Ambiguity: Nationalism and Myth in Ireland." *Eire-Ireland* 21, no. 2: 23–37.

Archer, Nuala. 1986. *Midland Review* 3 (Winter). Contemporary Irish Women's Writing issue.

———. 1990. "The Spaces between the Words." Interview with Mary Dorcey. *Women's Review of Books* 8: 21–24.

Aston, Elaine. 1995. *An Introduction to Feminism and Theatre.* London: Routledge.

The Attic Guide-Book and Diary. 1994. Dublin: Attic Press.

Balzano, Wanda. 1996. "Irishness: Feminist and Post-Colonial." In *The Post-Colonial Question: Common Skies, Divided Horizons,* ed. Iain Chambers and Lidia Curti. London: Routledge.

Bardwell, Leland. 1970. *The Mad Cyclist.* Dublin: New Writers Press.

Bardwell, Leland. 1984. *The House.* Kerry: Brandon.

———. 1987. *Different Kinds of Love.* Dublin: Attic Press.

———. 1989. *There We Have Been.* Dublin: Attic Press.

Barr, Fiona. 1979. "The Wall Reader." In *The Wall Reader and Other Stories,* by Eavan Boland, Fiona Barr, and Others. Dublin: Arlen House.

———. 1980. *Women's Oppression Today: Problems in Marxist Feminist Analysis.* London: Verso.

Barry, Sebastian, ed. 1986. *The Inherited Boundaries: Younger Poets of the Republic of Ireland.* Portlaoise: Dolmen Press.

Barry, Ursula. 1986. *Lifting the Lid: Handbook of Facts and Information on Ireland.* Dublin: Attic Press.

———. 1987. "Women in Ireland." *Women's Studies International Forum* 11, no. 4: 317–22.

Bates, H. E. 1972. *The Modern Short Story.* Boston: Writer.

Batsleer, Janet, Tony Davies, Rebecca O'Rourke, and Chris Weedon. 1985. *Rewriting English: Cultural Politics of Gender and Class.* London: Methuen.

Battersby, Eileen. 2002. "Stalked by an Agenda." *Irish Times* 5 Oct.: 10.

Beale, Jenny. 1986. *Women in Ireland: Voices of Change.* London: Macmillan Education.

Beckett, Mary. 1980. *A Belfast Woman.* Dublin: Poolbeg Press.

———. 1985. "Under Control." In *The Female Line: Northern Irish Women Writers,* ed. Ruth Hooley [Carr]. Belfast: Northern Ireland Women's Rights Movement.

———. 1987. *Give Them Stones.* London: Bloomsbury.

Benstock, Shari. 1982. "The Masculine World of Jennifer Johnston." In *Twentieth Century Women Novelists,* ed. Thomas Staley, 191–217. London: Macmillan.

Bergmann, Laurel. 1994. "Where to From Here? Contemporary New Zealand Women's Fiction." *Hecate* 20, no. 2: 217–25.

Blackwood, Caroline. 1974. *For All That I Found There.* London: Duckworth.

Boland, Eavan. 1989. *Selected Poems.* Dublin: Women's Education Bureau in conjunction with Carcanet Press.

Bork, Shirley. 1985. "The Palm House." In *The Female Line: Northern Irish Women Writers,* ed. Ruth Hooley [Carr]. Belfast: Northern Ireland Women's Rights Movement.

Bourke, Angela, Siobhán Kilfeather, Maria Luddy, Margaret MacCurtain, Gerardine Meaney, Máirín Ní Dhonnchadha, Mary O'Dowd, and Clair Wills, eds. 2002. *The Field Day Anthology of Irish Writing Volumes 4 and 5: Irish Women's Writing and Traditions.* Cork: Cork Univ. Press in Association with Field Day.

Boylan, Clare. 1989a. *Concerning Virgins.* London: Hamish Hamilton.

———. 1989b. "A Particular Calling." In *Concerning Virgins,* by Clare Boylan, 154–70. London: Hamish Hamilton.

Brophy, Catherine. 1985. *The Liberation of Margaret McCabe.* Dublin: Wolfhound Press.

———. 1991. *Dark Paradise.* Dublin: Wolfhound.

Burke, Helen Lucy. 1980. *A Season for Mothers.* Dublin: Poolbeg.

————. 1987. *The People and the Poor Law in Nineteenth-Century Ireland.* Dublin: Women's Education Bureau.

Butler-Cullingford, Elizabeth. 1990. " 'Thinking of her . . . as . . . Ireland': Yeats, Pearse, and Heaney." *Textual Practice* 4, no. 1: 1–21.

Cairns, David, and Shaun Richards. 1988. *Writing Ireland: Colonialism, Nationalism, and Culture.* Manchester: Manchester Univ. Press.

————. 1991. "Tropes and Traps: Aspects of 'Woman' and Nationality in Twentieth-century Irish Drama." In *Gender in Irish Writing,* ed. Toni O'Brien Johnson and David Cairns, 128–42. Buckingham: Open Univ. Press.

Callaghan, Mary Rose. 1990. *The Awkward Girl.* Dublin: Attic Press.

Casey, Daniel J., and Linda M. Casey, eds. 1990. *Stories by Contemporary Irish Women.* Syracuse: Syracuse Univ. Press.

Cinderella on the Ball: Fairytales for Feminists. 1991. Dublin: Attic Press.

Claffey, Anne, Róisín Conroy, Linda Kavanagh, Mary Paul Keane, Catherine Mac-Conville, and Sue Russell. 1985. "Rapunzel's Revenge." In *Rapunzel's Revenge: Fairy Tales for Feminists.* Dublin: Attic Press.

Clancy, Tom. 1987. *Patriot Games.* London: William Collins.

Clark, Clara. 1979. *Coping Alone.* Dublin: Arlen House.

Cloud, Darrah. n.d. *The Stick Wife.* Unpublished. Performed 1987.

Comhairle. Social Policy Series. 2002. *Supporting Carers: A Social Policy Report.* Dublin: Comhairle.

Conlon, Evelyn. 1987. *My Head Is Opening.* Dublin: Attic Press.

————. 1993. *Taking Scarlet as a Real Colour.* Belfast: Blackstaff Press.

Coulter, Carol. 1993. *The Hidden Tradition: Feminism, Women, and Nationalism in Ireland.* Cork: Cork Univ. Press.

Coward, Rosalind. 1980. " 'This Novel Changes Lives': Are Women's Novels Feminist Novels? A Response to Rebecca O'Rourke's Article 'Summer Reading.' " *Feminist Review* 5: 53–64.

Cullen, Linda. 1990. *The Kiss.* Dublin: Attic Press.

Cullen, Mary. 1985. "How Radical Was Irish Feminism, 1860–1920?" In *Radicals, Rebels, and Establishments,* ed. P. J. Corish. Belfast: Appletree.

————, ed. 1987. *Girls Don't Do Honours: Irish Women in Education in the Nineteenth and Twentieth Centuries.* Dublin: Women's Education Bureau.

————. 1992. "Sex Is a Political Issue." *Irish Reporter* 8, no. 4: 3–5.

Cullimore, Claudine. 2001. *Lola Comes Home.* London: Penguin.

Cummins, Mary. 1994. "Lesbians Still Loath to Come Out." *Irish Times* 8 Feb.: 27.

Curtin, Chris, Mary Kelly, and Liam O'Dowd, eds. 1984. *Culture and Ideology in Ireland.* Galway: Galway Univ. Press.

Daly, Ita. 1987. *A Singular Attraction.* London: Black Swan.

———. 1989. *Dangerous Fictions.* London: Bloomsbury.

Daly, Mary. 1989. *Women and Poverty.* Dublin: Attic Press.

D'Arcy, Margaretta. 1981. *Tell Them Everything: A Sojourn in the Prison of Her Majesty Queen Elizabeth II at Ard Macha (Armagh).* Dublin: Pluto Press.

Deane, Seamus. 1985. *Celtic Revivals: Essays in Modern Irish Literature 1880–1980.* London: Faber and Faber.

———. 1986. *A Short History of Irish Literature.* London: Hutchinson.

———, ed. 1991. *Field Day Anthology of Irish Writing.* 3 vols. London: Faber and Faber.

Deane, Seamus, and Seamus Heaney, Richard Kearney, Declan Kiberd, and Tom Paulin, eds. 1986. *Ireland's Field Day.* Notre Dame: Univ. of Notre Dame Press.

De Brun, Bairbre. 1988. "Women and Imperialism in Ireland." *Women's Studies International Forum* 11, no. 4: 323–28.

Departures 5: Of Ordinary Lives and Stones. Vol. 5 (1993).

DeSalvo, Louise, Kathleen Walsh D'Arcy, and Katherine Hogan, eds. 1989. *Territories of the Voice: Contemporary Stories by Irish Women Writers.* Boston: Beacon Press.

Devlin, Anne. 1986a. "Naming the Names." In *The Way-Paver.* London: Faber and Faber.

———. 1986b. *Ourselves Alone, with The Long March, and A Woman Calling.* London: Faber and Faber.

Devlin, Bobby. 1985. *An Interlude with Seagulls: Memories of a Long Kesh Internee.* London: Information on Ireland.

Devlin, Polly. 1979. *The Vogue History of Photography.* London: Thames and Hudson.

———. 1983a. *All of Us There.* London: Weidenfeld and Nicholson.

———. 1983b. *The Far Side of the Lough: Stories from an Irish Childhood.* London: Gollancz.

———. 1990. *Dora, or the Shifts of the Heart.* London: Chatto and Windus.

Devlin McAliskey, Bernadette. 1994. "The Irish Struggle Today." *Against the Current* March/April: 36–41.

Donaldson, Laura E. 1988. "The Miranda Complex: Colonialism and the Question of Feminist Reading." *Diacritics* 18: 65–77.

Donoghue, Emma. 1993a. *I Know My Own Heart.* Toronto: Playwrights Co-op.

———. 1993b. *Passions between Women: British Lesbian Culture 1668–1801.* Dublin: Scarlett Press.

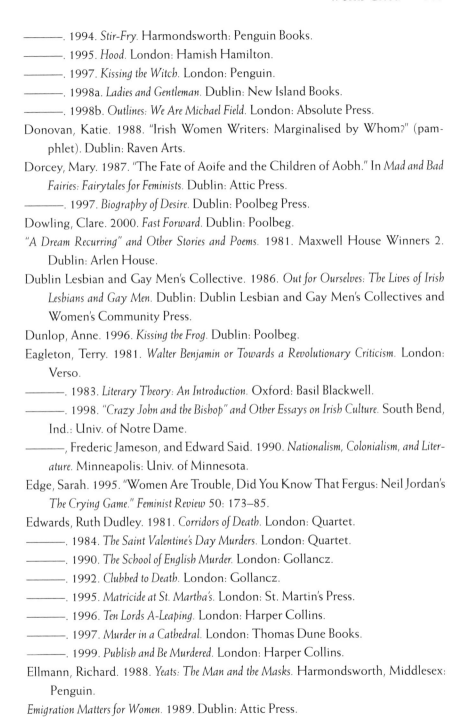

———. 1994. *Stir-Fry.* Harmondsworth: Penguin Books.

———. 1995. *Hood.* London: Hamish Hamilton.

———. 1997. *Kissing the Witch.* London: Penguin.

———. 1998a. *Ladies and Gentleman.* Dublin: New Island Books.

———. 1998b. *Outlines: We Are Michael Field.* London: Absolute Press.

Donovan, Katie. 1988. "Irish Women Writers: Marginalised by Whom?" (pamphlet). Dublin: Raven Arts.

Dorcey, Mary. 1987. "The Fate of Aoife and the Children of Aobh." In *Mad and Bad Fairies: Fairytales for Feminists.* Dublin: Attic Press.

———. 1997. *Biography of Desire.* Dublin: Poolbeg Press.

Dowling, Clare. 2000. *Fast Forward.* Dublin: Poolbeg.

"A Dream Recurring" and Other Stories and Poems. 1981. Maxwell House Winners 2. Dublin: Arlen House.

Dublin Lesbian and Gay Men's Collective. 1986. *Out for Ourselves: The Lives of Irish Lesbians and Gay Men.* Dublin: Dublin Lesbian and Gay Men's Collectives and Women's Community Press.

Dunlop, Anne. 1996. *Kissing the Frog.* Dublin: Poolbeg.

Eagleton, Terry. 1981. *Walter Benjamin or Towards a Revolutionary Criticism.* London: Verso.

———. 1983. *Literary Theory: An Introduction.* Oxford: Basil Blackwell.

———. 1998. *"Crazy John and the Bishop" and Other Essays on Irish Culture.* South Bend, Ind.: Univ. of Notre Dame.

———, Frederic Jameson, and Edward Said. 1990. *Nationalism, Colonialism, and Literature.* Minneapolis: Univ. of Minnesota.

Edge, Sarah. 1995. "Women Are Trouble, Did You Know That Fergus: Neil Jordan's *The Crying Game.*" *Feminist Review* 50: 173–85.

Edwards, Ruth Dudley. 1981. *Corridors of Death.* London: Quartet.

———. 1984. *The Saint Valentine's Day Murders.* London: Quartet.

———. 1990. *The School of English Murder.* London: Gollancz.

———. 1992. *Clubbed to Death.* London: Gollancz.

———. 1995. *Matricide at St. Martha's.* London: St. Martin's Press.

———. 1996. *Ten Lords A-Leaping.* London: Harper Collins.

———. 1997. *Murder in a Cathedral.* London: Thomas Dune Books.

———. 1999. *Publish and Be Murdered.* London: Harper Collins.

Ellmann, Richard. 1988. *Yeats: The Man and the Masks.* Harmondsworth, Middlesex: Penguin.

Emigration Matters for Women. 1989. Dublin: Attic Press.

Encyclopaedia Britannica Year Book. 1994. Chicago: Encyclopaedia Britannica.

An End . . . and a Beginning. Calendar. 1979. Dublin: Irish Feminist Information.

Enright, Anne. 1992. *The Portable Virgin.* London: Minerva.

Fairweather, Eileen, Roisin McDonough, and Melanie McFadyean, eds. 1984. *Only the Rivers Run Free. Northern Ireland: The Women's War.* London: Pluto Press.

Fee, Margery. 1989. "Why C. K. Stead Didn't Like Keri Hulme's *The Bone People.* Who Can Write Other?" *Australia and New Zealand Studies in Canada* (Spring): 10–27.

Felski, Rita. 1989. *Beyond Feminist Aesthetics: Feminist Literature and Social Change.* Cambridge, MA: Harvard Univ. Press.

Ferreira, Patricia. 1993. "Claiming and Transforming an 'Entirely Gentlemanly Artifact': Ireland's Attic Press." *Canadian Journal of Irish Studies* 19, no. 1: 97–109.

Fields, Rona M. 1976. *Society Under Siege.* Philadelphia: Temple Univ. Press.

Finney, Patricia. 1977. *A Shadow of Gulls.* London: Collins.

———. 1979. *The Crow Goddess.* London: Fontana.

Flitton, Sheila. 1991. *Notions.* London: Emperor Publishing.

Foster, R. F. 1986. "We're All Revisionists Now." *Irish Review* 1, no. 1: 1–5.

———. 1989. *Modern Ireland 1600–1972.* Harmondsworth: Penguin.

Freeman, Jo. 1983. *Social Movements of the Sixties and Seventies.* London: Longman.

Gibbons, Luke. 1983. "Lies That Tell the Truth: Maeve, History, and Irish Cinema." *The Crane Bag* 7, no. 1: 149–54.

Gilbert, Helen, ed. 2001. *Postcolonial Plays: An Anthology.* London: Routledge.

Glover, Sue. 1995. *Bondagers.* In *Made In Scotland: An Anthology of New Scottish Plays,* ed. Ian Brown and Mark Fisher. London: Methuen.

Goldring, Maurice. 1991. *Belfast: From Loyalty to Rebellion.* London: Lawrence and Wishart.

Graves, Robert, ed. 1963. *Selected Poems of Robert Frost.* New York: Rinehart.

Haberstroh, Patricia Boyle. 1992. "Literary Politics: Mainstream and Margin." *Canadian Journal of Irish Studies* 18, no. 1: 181–91.

———. 1996. *Women Creating Women: Contemporary Irish Women Poets.* Syracuse: Syracuse Univ. Press.

Harding, Sandra. 1991. *Whose Science? Whose Knowledge? Thinking from Women's Lives.* Milton Keynes: Open Univ. Press.

Hayes, Alan. 1999. "Big Women, Little Women: Toward a History of Second Wave Commercial Feminist Publishing in Ireland." *Women's Studies Review* 6: 139–50.

Hennessy, Rosemary. 1993. *Materialist Feminism and the Politics of Discourse.* New York: Routledge.

Herbert, Michael. 1990. "Across the Great Divide." *Irish Post* 22 Sept.: 4.

Hill, Niki. 1992. *Death Grows on You.* London: Paladin.

Hooley [Carr], Ruth, ed. 1985. *The Female Line: Northern Irish Women Writers.* Belfast: Northern Ireland Women's Rights Movement.

Hopkins, Alannah. 1982. *A Joke Goes a Long Way in the Country.* London: Hamish Hamilton.

———. 1985. *The Out-Haul.* London: Hamish Hamilton.

Hughes, Eamonn. 1991. *Culture and Politics in Northern Ireland 1960–1990.* Milton Keynes: Open Univ. Press.

If You Can Talk You Can Write. 1983. Dublin: Irish Feminist Information.

Innes, C. L. 1993. *Woman and Nation in Irish Literature and Society 1880–1935.* New York: Harvester Wheatsheaf.

Irish Book Publishing Survey. 1998. http://www.irelandseye.com/cle/report.htm.

Irish Feminist Review. 1984. Dublin: Women's Community Press.

Irish Girls About Town. 2002. London: Pocket/Townhouse.

Irish Women's Guide Book and Diary. 1979. Dublin: Irish Feminist Information.

Irish Women's Guide Book and Diary. Dublin: Attic Press, 1980–1997.

Jeffares, A. Norman. 1965. *Commonwealth Literature: Unity and Diversity in a Common Culture,* ed. John Press. London: Heinemann.

John, Brian. 1979. "Ireland Mythologized." *Mosaic* 12, no. 3: 181–87.

John, Mary E. 1989. "Postcolonial Feminists in the Western Intellectual Field." *Inscriptions* 5. 49–73.

Johnston, Jennifer. 1972. *The Captains and the Kings.* London: Hamish Hamilton.

———. 1973. *The Gates.* London: Hamish Hamilton.

———. 1974. *How Many Miles to Babylon?* London: Hamish Hamilton.

———. 1977. *Shadows on Our Skin.* London: Hamish Hamilton.

———. 1979. *The Old Jest.* London: Hamish Hamilton.

Jones, Marie. *Weddins', Weeins, and Wakes.* Unpublished text. Performances 1989 and 2001.

———. 1990. "The Hamster Wheel." In *The Crack In The Emerald.* London: Nick Hern Books.

———. 1999. *Women on the Verge of HRT.* London: Samuel French.

———. 2001. *Somewhere Over the Balcony.* In *Postcolonial Plays: An Anthology,* ed. Helen Gilbert. London: Routledge.

Jones, Mary. 1985. *Resistance*. Belfast: Blackstaff Press.

K. Arnold Price. 1980. *The New Perspective*. Dublin: Poolbeg.

Kearney, Richard. 1980. "The IRA Strategy of Failure." *The Crane Bag* 4, no. 2: 699–707.

Kelly, Maeve. 1976. *A Life of Her Own*. Dublin: Poolbeg Press.*

———. 1985. *Necessary Treasons*. London: Michael Joseph.

———. 1991. *Orange Horses*. London: Michael Joseph.

———. 1993. *Alice in Thunderland: A Feminist Fairytale*. Dublin: Attic Press.

Kelly, Rita. 1981. "En Famille." In *"A Dream Recurring" and Other Stories and Poems*. 1981. Maxwell House Winners 2. Dublin: Arlen House.

———. 1986. *"The Whispering Arch" and Other Stories*. Dublin: Arlen House.

Kennedy, Jan. 1985. "June 23rd." In *The Female Line: Northern Irish Women Writers*, ed. Ruth Hooley [Carr]. Belfast: Northern Ireland Women's Rights Movement.

Kennedy, Liam. 1996. *Colonialism, Religion, and Nationalism in Ireland*. Belfast: Institute of Irish Studies.

Kennedy, Stanislaus. 1983. *But Where Can I Go? Homeless Women in Dublin*. Dublin: Arlen House.

Kenny, Mary. 1978. *Woman X Two: How to Cope with a Double Life*. London: Sidgewick and Jackson.

———. 1981. *Why Christianity Works*. London: Joseph.

———. 1986. *Abortion: the Whole Story*. London: Quartet.

———. 1989. *A Mood for Love*. New York: Quartet.

Keyes, Marian. 1995. *Watermelon*. New York: Avon Books.

———. 1996. *Lucy Sullivan Is Getting Married*. Dublin: Poolbeg.

Kiberd, Declan. 1984. "Inventing Irelands." *The Crane Bag* 8, no. 1: 11–23.

———. 1995. *Inventing Ireland: The Literature of the Modern Nation*. London: Jonathan Cape.

Kiely, Benedict. 1979. *Proxopera: A Tale of Modern Ireland*. London: Quartet Books.

Landry, Donna, and Gerald MacLean. 1993. *Materialist Feminisms*. Cambridge, MA: Blackwell.

Lawrence, Karen. 1992. *Decolonizing Tradition: New Views of Twentieth Century "British" Canons* Urbana: Univ. of Illinois Press.

Leland, Mary. 1985. *The Killeen*. London: Hamish Hamilton.

Lentin, Ronit. 1982. *Conversations with Palestinian Women*. Jerusalem: Mifras.

———. 1989. *Night Train to Mother*. Dublin: Attic Press.

———. 1997. *Gender and Catastrophe*. London: Zed Books.

————. 2000. *Israel and Daughters of the Shoah: Reoccupying the Territories of Silence*. New York: Berghahn Books.

Lentin, Ronit, and Geraldine Niland. 1979. *Who's Minding the Children?* Dublin: Arlen House.

Lentin, Ronit, and Nahla Abdo, eds. 2002. *Women and the Politics of Military Confrontation: Palestinian and Israeli Gendered Narratives of Disclocation*. New York: Berghahn Books.

Lentin, Ronit, ed. 2004. *Re-presenting the Shoah for the Twenty-first Century*. New York: Berghahn Books.

Levine, June. 1982. *Sisters*. Dublin: Ward River Press.

————. 1992. *A Season of Weddings*. Dublin: New Island Books.

Levine, June, and Lyn Madden. 1987. *Lyn: A Story of Prostitution*. Dublin: Attic Press.

Levy, Bronwen. 1993. "A Wide Brown Land for a Speaking Subject? Women and the New Republicanism." *Southern Review* 26, no. 2: 262–69.

Lloyd, David. 1993. *Anomolous States: Irish Writing and the Post-Colonial Moment*. Durham: Duke Univ. Press.

MacCurtain, Margaret, and Donncha O'Corráin, eds. 1978. *Women in Irish Society: The Historical Dimension*. Dublin: Arlen House.

MacLaverty, Bernard. 1983. *Cal*. London: Jonathan Cape.

Mad and Bad Fairies: Fairytales for Feminists. 1987. Dublin: Attic Press.

Madden, Deirdre. 1986. *Hidden Symptoms*. Boston: Atlantic Monthly Press.

————. 1992. *Remembering Light and Stone*. London: Faber and Faber.

Madden-Simpson, Janet. 1984. *Woman's Part: An Anthology of Short Fiction by and about Irish Women, 1890–1960*. Dublin: Arlen House.

Maher, Kathleen. 1996. "Straight Talking: Feminist Community Activism." In *Feminism, Politics, Community*, ed. Ailbhe Smyth. WERRC Annual Conference Papers. Dublin: UCD: 28–33.

Maher, Mary. 1992a. *The Devil's Card*. London: St Martin's Press.

————. 1992b. "Hi Ho, It's off to Strike We Go." In *Ride on Rapunzel: Fairytales for Feminists*. Dublin: Attic Press.

Manning, Kitty. 1990. *The Between People*. Dublin: Attic Press.

Martin, Carol. 1989. "Charabanc Theatre Company: 'Quare Women 'Sleggin' and Geggin' the Standards of Northern Ireland by 'Tappin' the People." *Drama Review* 31, no. 2: 92.

Martin, Janet. 1977. *The Essential Guide for Women in Ireland*. Galway: Arlen House.

Marxist-Feminist Literature Collective. 1978. "Women's Writing: *Jane Eyre, Shirley, Villette, Aurora Leigh*." *Ideology and Consciousness* 3: 27–48.

Maxwell, D. E. S. 1982. "Semantic Scruples: A Rhetoric for Politics in the North." In *Literature and the Changing Ireland*, ed. Peter Connolly. Gerrards Cross: Colin Smythe.

McCann, Eamonn. 1994. "Worth Fighting For." *Socialist Review* 175: 17–19.

McEnaney, Frances. 1985. "The Cage." In *The Female Line: Northern Irish Women Writers*, ed. Ruth Hooley [Carr]. Belfast: Northern Ireland Women's Rights Movement.

McKenna, Jill. 1985. "The Reprisal." In *The Female Line: Northern Irish Women Writers*, ed. Ruth Hooley [Carr]. Belfast: Northern Ireland Women's Rights Movement.

McWilliams, Monica. 1991. "Women in Northern Ireland: An Overview." In *Culture and Politics in Northern Ireland 1960–1990*, ed. Eamonn Hughes, 81–100. Milton Keynes: Open Univ. Press.

Meaney, Gerardine. 1991. *Sex and Nation: Women in Irish Culture and Politics.* Dublin: LIP Pamphlet, Attic Press.

Missing Pieces: Women in Irish History. 1983. Dublin: Irish Feminist Information Publications with Women's Community Press.

Mitchell, Julie. 1988. *Sunday Afternoons.* London: Penguin.

Mitchison, Amanda. 1988. "Ulster's Family Feminists." *New Society* 19 Feb. 24–29.

Molloy, Frances. 1985a. "An Irish Fairy Tale." In *The Female Line: Northern Irish Women Writers*, ed. Ruth Hooley [Carr]. Belfast: Northern Ireland Women's Rights Movement.

————. 1985b. *No Mate for the Magpie.* London: Virago.

Montgomery, Pamela, and Celia Davies. 1990. *Women's Lives in Northern Ireland Today: A Guide to Reading.* Coleraine: Univ. of Ulster.

Moore, Brian. 1990. *Lies of Silence.* London: Bloomsbury.

Moore, Carole, and Sue Ashby. n.d. *A Wife, a Dog, and a Maple Tree.* Unpublished play text. Performed 1995.

Moore, Ruth. 1994. "Kissing King Billy Goodbye." *New Internationalist* May: 12–14.

More Missing Pieces: Women in Irish History. 1985. Dublin: Attic Press.

Ms. Muffett and Others: Feminist Fairytales. 1986. Dublin: Attic Press.

Mullarney, Máire. 1983. *Anything School Can Do You Can Do Better.* Dublin: Arlen House.

Mullin, Molly. 1991. "Representations of History, Irish Feminism, and the Politics of Difference." *Feminist Studies* 17, no. 1: 29–49.

Murphy, Brenda. 1989. "A Curse." In *Territories of the Voice: Contemporary Stories by Irish Women Writers*, ed. Louuise DeSalvo, Kathleen Walsh D'Arcy, and Katherine Hogan. Boston: Beacon Press.

Murray, Melissa. 1987. *Changelings.* Dublin: Attic Press.

Nandy, Ashis. 1983. *The Intimate Enemy: Loss and Recovery of Self under Colonialism.* Oxford: Oxford Univ. Press.

Ní Chuilleanáin, Eiléan, ed. 1985. *Irish Women: Image and Achievement.* Dublin: Arlen House.

Ní Dhuibhne, Éilís. 1990a. *The Bray House.* Dublin: Attic Press.

———. 1990b. *The Uncommon Cormorant.* Dublin: Poolbeg Press.

———. 1991. *Hugo and the Sunshine Girl.* Dublin: Poolbeg Press.

O'Connor, Barbara. 1984. "Aspects of Representation of Women in Irish Film." *The Crane Bag* 8, no. 2: 79–83.

O'Donoghue, Noreen, and Sue Richardson. 1983. *Pure Murder: A Book about Drug Use.* Dublin: Women's Community Press.

O'Dowd, Liam. 1987. "Church, State, and Women: The Aftermath of Partition.' " In *Gender in Irish Society,* ed. Chris Curtin, Pauline Jackson, and Barbara O'Connor. Galway: Galway Univ. Press.

———. 1991. "Intellectuals and Political Culture: A Unionist-Nationalist Comparison." In *Culture and Politics in Northern Ireland 1960–1990,* ed. Eamonn Hughes. Milton Keynes: Open Univ. Press.

O'Faolain, Nuala. 1985. "Irish Women and Writing in Modern Ireland." In *Irish Women: Image and Achievement,* ed. Eiléan Ní Chuilleanáin. Dublin: Arlen House.

O'Flanagan, Sheila. 2002. *He's Got to Go.* London: Headline.

O'Malley, Padraig. 1984. *The Uncivil Wars: Ireland Today.* Belfast: Blackstaff Press.

ó Murchadha, Felix. 1993. "Violence, Reconciliation, Pluralism: A Critique of Irish Nationalism." *Canadian Journal of Irish Studies* 19, no. 2: 1–12.

O'Neill, Joan. 1990. *Daisy Chain War.* Dublin: Attic Press.

Owens, Rosemary Cullen. 1984. *Did Your Granny Have a Hammer? A History of the Irish Women's Suffrage Movement 1876–1922.* Dublin: Attic Press.

Paisley, Rhonda. 1992. "Feminism, Unionism, and 'the Brotherhood.' " *Irish Reporter* 8, no. 4: 32–33.

Palmer, Paulina. 1989. *Contemporary Women's Fiction: Narrative Practice and Feminist Theory.* Jackson: Univ. Press of Mississippi.

Passages 2: Short Stories by Modern Irish Authors. N.d. Belfast: Caldo Publications.

Patten, Eve. 1990. "Women and Fiction: 1985–1990." *Krino* 8, no. 9: 1–7.

Pearse, Patrick. 1968. *Short Stories,* ed. Desmond Maguire. Cork: Mercier.

Pelan, Rebecca. 1995. "It's What Happens after You're Born That Gets It Knocked Out of You. . . ." Interview with Evelyn Conlon. *Hecate* 21, no. 1: 111–23.

Penley, Constance. 1986. "Teaching in Your Sleep: Feminism and Psychoanalysis." In *Theory in the Classroom,* ed. Cary Nelson. Urbana: Univ. of Illinois Press.

Plummer, Ken. 1995. *Telling Sexual Stories: Power, Change, and Social Worlds.* London: Routledge.

Prone, Terry. 1985. *The Scattering of Mrs Blake and Related Matters.* Dublin: Arlen House.

Purcell, Deirdre. 1991. *A Place of Stones.* Dublin: Townhouse.

———. 1992. *That Childhood Country.* Dublin: Townhouse.

Quinn, John, ed. 1987. *A Portrait of the Artist as a Young Girl.* London: Methuen.

Rajan, Rajeswari Sunder. 1993. *Real and Imagined Women: Gender, Culture, and Postcolonialism.* London: Routledge.

Rapunzel's Revenge: Fairytales for Feminists. 1985. Dublin: Attic Press.

Reid, Christina. 1972. *Joyriders.* New Playwrights' Network.

———. 1986. *The Last of a Dyin' Race. Best Radio Plays.* London: Methuen.

———. 1987. *Tea in a China Cup.* London: Methuen.

———. 1989a. *The Belle of the Belfast City.* London: Methuen.

———. 1989b. *Did You Hear the One About the Irishman?* London: Methuen.

Reilly, Anne-Marie. 1985. "Leaving." In *The Female Line: Northern Irish Women Writers,* ed. Ruth Hooley [Carr]. Belfast: Northern Ireland Women's Rights Movement.

Richards, Maura. 1982. *Interlude.* Dublin: Ward River Press.

Ride on Rapunzel: Fairytales for Feminists. 1992. Dublin: Attic Press.

Riley, Denise. 1988. *Am I That Name?* London: Macmillan.

Robinson, Lilian S. 1992. "Canon Fathers and Myth Universe." In *Decolonizing Tradition: New Views of Twentieth Century 'British.' Literary Canons,* ed. Karen R. Lawrence. Urbana: Univ. of Illinois Press.

Rockett, Kevin. 1980. *Film and Ireland: A Chronicle.* Dublin: A Sense of Ireland.

Rolston, Bill, ed. 1991. *The Media and Northern Ireland.* London: Macmillan.

Rose, Catherine. 1975. *The Female Experience: The Story of the Women's Movement in Ireland.* Dublin: Arlen House.

Rowbotham, Sheila. 1992. *Women in Movement: Feminism and Social Action.* New York: Routledge.

Russell, Sue. 1992. "Goldilocks Finds a Home." In *Ride on Rapunzel: Fairytales for Feminists.* Dublin: Attic Press.

Ryan, Mary. 1990. *Whispers in the Wind.* Dublin: Attic Press.

Scott, Bonnie Kime. 1988. "Feminist Theory and Women in Irish Writing." In *The Uses of the Past: Essays on Irish Culture,* ed. Audrey S. Eyler and Robert F. Garratt. Newark: Univ. of Delaware Press: 55–63.

Segal, Lynne. 1987. *Is the Future Female? Troubled Thoughts on Contemporary Feminism.* London: Virago.

Sekine, Masaru, ed. 1985. *Irish Writers and Society at Large.* Gerrards Cross: Colin Smythe.

Seymour, Gerald. 1980. *Harry's Game.* Glasgow: William Collins.

Sheridan, F. D. 1980. *Captives.* Dublin: Co-Op Books.

Singled Out: Single Mothers in Ireland. 1983. Dublin: Irish Feminist Information.

Sloan, Barry. 2000. *Writers and Protestantism in the North of Ireland: Heirs to a Damnation.* Dublin: Irish Academic Press.

Smyth, Ailbhe. 1983. *Women's Rights in Ireland: A Practical Guide.* Dublin: Ward River Press.

———. 1988a. "The Contemporary Women's Movement in the Republic of Ireland." *Women's Studies International Forum* 11, no. 4: 331–41.

———. 1988b. "States of Emerge.n.c.e." *Trouble and Strife* 14: 46–52.

———. 1988c."Women's Worlds and the Worlds of Irish Women." Editorial. *Women's Studies International Forum* 11, no. 4: 273–75.

———. 1997a. "Contemporary French Feminism: An Annotated Shortlist of Recent Works." *Hecate* 11, no. 1 & 2: 203–36.

———. 1997b. "Feminism: Personal, Political, Unqualified (or Ex-Colonized Girls Know More)". *Irish Journal of Feminist Studies* 2, no. 1: 37–54.

Snitow, Ann. 1980. "The Front Line: Notes on Sex in Novels by Women, 1967–1979." In *Women, Sex, and Sexuality*, ed. Catherine R. Stimpson and Ethel Spector. Chicago: Univ. of Chicago Press.

Speers, Neill. n.d. *Cauterised.* Unpublished play.

Spivak, Gayatri Chakravorty. 1985. "Imperialism and Sexual Difference." *Oxford Literary Review* 8, no. 1–2: 225–40.

———. 1986. "Three Women's Texts and a Critique of Imperialism." *Critical Enquiry* 12: 243–61.

———. 1987. *In Other Worlds: Essays in Cultural Politics.* London: Methuen.

Strong, Eithne. 1981. *Patterns.* Dublin: Poolbeg Press.

———. 1990. "The Bride of Christ." In *Territories of the Voice: Contemporary Stories by Irish Women Writers*, ed. Louise DeSalvo, Kathleen Walsh D'Arcy, and Katherine Hogan. Boston: Beacon Press. 41–45.

Surviving Sexual Abuse. 1990. Dublin: Attic Press.

Sweeping Beauties: Fairytales for Feminists. 1989. Dublin: Attic Press.

Taylor, David. 1984. "Ian Paisley and the Ideology of Ulster Protestantism." In *Culture and Ideology in Ireland*, ed. Chris Curtin, Mary Kelly, and Liam O'Dowd. Galway: Galway Univ. Press.

Todd, Janet. 1988. *Feminist Literary History: A Defence.* London: Polity Press.

Toibin, Colm. 1999. *The Penguin Book of Irish Fiction*. Harmondsworth, Middlesex: Penguin.

Tovey, Hilary. 1989. *Why Irish: Language and Ethnicity in Ireland*. Dublin.

Treacy, Maura. 1977. *"Sixpence in Her Shoe" and Other Stories*. Dublin: Poolbeg Press.

————. 1981. *Scenes from a Country Wedding*. Dublin: Poolbeg Press.

Tuohy, Frank. 1985. "Five Fierce Ladies." In *Irish Writers and Society at Large*, ed. Masaru Sekine, 199–206. Gerrards Cross, England: Colin Smythe.

Walker, Mary. 1981. "Cherubim." In *"A Dream Recurring" and Other Stories and Poems*. 1981. Maxwell House Winners 2. Dublin: Arlen House.

"The Wall Reader" and Other Stories. 1979. First Maxwell House Winners. Dublin: Arlen House/Women's Press.

Walsh, Caroline, ed. 1993. *Virgins and Hyacinths: An Attic Book of Fiction*. Dublin: Attic Press.

Walshe, Dolores. 1993. *Where the Trees Weep*. Dublin: Wolfhound Press.

Ward, Margaret. 1983. *Unmanageable Revolutionaries: Women and Irish Nationalism*. London: Pluto Press.

————. 1987. "Feminism in the North of Ireland: A Reflection." *H.U./The Honest Ulsterman* 83: 59–70.

————. 1995. "Conflicting Interests: The British and Irish Suffrage Movements." *Feminist Review* 50: 127–47.

Weekes, Ann Owens. 1993. *Unveiling Treasures: The Attic Guide to The Published Works of Irish Women Literary Writers*. Dublin: Attic Press.

Whelehan, Imelda. 1995. *Modern Feminist Thought: From the Second Wave to "Post-Feminism."* Edinburgh: Edinburgh Univ. Press.

Who Owns Ireland, Who Owns You? 1984. Dublin: Attic Press.

Whyte, J. H. 1980. *Church and State in Modern Ireland 1923–1979*. New Jersey: Gill and Macmillan.

Wills, Clair. 1993. *Improprieties: Politics and Sexuality in Northern Irish Poetry*. Oxford: Clarendon Press.

Wilson, Elizabeth. 1988. "Say It Like It Is: Women and Confessional Writing." In *Sweet Dreams: Sexuality, Gender, and Popular Fiction*, ed. Susannah Radstone. London: Lawrence and Wishart.

Woods, Una. 1984. *The Dark Hole Days*. Belfast: Blackstaff Press.

Write Up Your Street: An Anthology of Community Writing. 1985. Dublin: Women's Community Press.

Selected Readings

Abel, Elizabeth. 1990. "Race, Class, and Psychoanalysis." In *Conflicts in Feminism*, ed. Marianne Hirsch and Evelyn Fox Keller, 184–204. London: Routledge.

Abel, Elizabeth, ed. 1980. *Writing and Sexual Difference*. Chicago: Univ. of Chicago Press.

Alexander, Yonah, and Alan O'Day, eds. 1984. *Terrorism in Ireland*. London: Croom Helm.

Anderson, Linda. 1991. "A Lack of Alternatives." *H.U./The Honest Ulsterman* 91: 92–3.

———. 1992. "The Death of Men." *H.U./The Honest Ulsterman*: 91.

Anderson, Linda, ed. 1990. *Plotting Change: Contemporary Women's Fiction*. London: Edward Arnold.

Andrews, Elmer. 1988. *The Poetry of Seamus Heaney*. London: Macmillan.

Ardagh, John. 1995. *Ireland and the Irish: Portrait of a Changing Society*. London: Penguin Books.

Aretxaga, Begona. 1997. *Shattering Silence: Women, Nationalism, and Political Subjectivity in Northern Ireland*. Princeton: Princeton Univ. Press.

Arnsberg, Conrad M., and Solon T. Kimball. 1986. *Family and Community in Ireland*. Gloucester, Mass.: Peter Smith.

Arthur, P. 1984. *Government and Politics of Northern Ireland*. London: Longman.

Arthur, P., and Keith Jeffery. 1988. *Northern Ireland Since 1968*. Oxford: Basil Blackwell.

Aughey, Arthur, and Duncan Morrow. 1996. *Northern Ireland Politics*. New York: Longman.

Austin, Gayle. 1990. *Feminist Theories for Dramatic Criticism*. Ann Arbor: Univ. of Michigan Press.

Averill, Deborah M. 1982. *The Irish Short Story from George Moore to Frank O'Connor*. Washington, D.C.: Univ. Press of America.

Bardon, Jonathan. 1992. *A History of Ulster*. Belfast: Blackstaff Press.

Bardwell, Leland. 1977. *Girl on a Bicycle*. Dublin: Co-Op Books.

———. 1981. *That London Winter.* Dublin: Co-Op Books.

———. 1984. *The Fly and the Bed Bug.* Dublin: Beaver Row Press.

———. 1989. *Borderlines: Poems by South-Ulster Youth.* Monaghan: County Monaghan Vocational Education Committee.

———. 1991. *Dostoevsky's Grave.* Dublin: Dedalus Press.

———. 2000. *The White Beach: New and Selected Poems.* Galway: Salmon Publishing.

———. 2002. *Mother to a Stranger.* Belfast: Blackstaff Press.

Barker, Francis, ed. 1986. *Literature, Politics, and Theory.* London: Methuen.

Barnes, Clive. 2001. "Keeping Up with Jones." *New York Post* 2 Apr.

Barrett, Michèle. 1979. *Ideology and Cultural Production.* London: Croom Helm.

Barr, Fiona. 1982. "Feminism and the Definition of Cultural Politics." In *Feminism, Culture and Politics,* ed. Rosalind Brunt and Caroline Rowan, 37–58. London: Lawrence and Wishart.

———. 1985. Ideology and the Cultural Production of Gender." In *Feminist Criticism and Social Change: Sex, Class, and Race in Literature,* ed. Judith Newton and Deborah Rosenfelt. London: Methuen.

———. 1987. "The Concept of Difference." *Feminist Review* 26: 29–42.

———. 1992a. *Destabilizing Theory: Contemporary Feminist Debates.* London: Polity Press.

———. 1992b. *The Politics of Truth: From Marx to Foucault.* London: Polity Press.

———. 1999. *Imagination in Theory: Culture, Writing, Words, and Things.* New York: New York Univ. Press.

Barry, Peter. 1995. *Beginning Theory.* Manchester, U.K.: Manchester Univ. Press.

Barry, Ursula. 1986. *Lifting the Lid: Handbook of Facts and Information on Ireland.* Dublin: Attic Press.

———. 1987. "Women in Ireland." *Women's Studies International Forum* 11, no. 4: 317–22.

Bates, H. E. 1972. *The Modern Short Story.* Boston: Writer.

Beauvoir, Simone de. 1974. *The Second Sex.* New York: Vintage Press.

Beckett, J. C. 1976. *The Anglo-Irish Tradition.* London: Faber and Faber.

Beckett, Mary. 1989. *Orla Was Six.* Dublin: Poolbeg Press.

———. 1990. *A Literary Woman.* London: Bloomsbury.

———. 1991. *Orla at School.* Dublin: Poolbeg Press.

———. 1992. *A Family Tree.* Dublin: Poolbeg Press.

Belfrage, Sally. 1987. *The Crack: A Belfast Year.* London: Andre Deutsch. Published in the United States as *Living with War: A Belfast Year.* New York: Viking.

Bell, Desmond. 1985. "Contemporary Cultural Studies in Ireland and the 'Problem' of Protestant Ideology." *The Crane Bag* 9, no. 2: 91–95.

Bell, Sam Hanna. 1972. *The Theatre in Ulster.* Dublin: Gill and Macmillan.

Benhabib, Seyla, and Drucilla Cornell, eds. 1987. *Feminism as Critique: On the Politics of Gender.* Minneapolis: Univ. of Minnesota Press.

Bennett, Ronan. 1998. "Don't Mention the War: Culture in Northern Ireland." In *Rethinking Northern Ireland,* ed. D. Miller. London: Longman.

Bensyl, Stacia. 2000. "Swings and Roundabouts: An Interview with Emma Donoghue." *Irish Studies Review* 8, no. 1: 73–81.

Benton, Sarah. 1995. "Women Disarmed: The Militarization of Politics in Ireland, 1913–23." *Feminist Review* 50: 148–72.

Berger, Iris, Elsa Barkley Brown, and Nancy A. Hewitt. 1992. "Intersections and Collision Courses: Women, Blacks, and Workers Confront Gender, Race, and Class." *Feminist Studies* 18, no. 2: 283–94.

Betterton, R., ed. 1987. *Looking On: Images of Femininity in the Visual Arts and Media.* London: Pandora.

Bew, P., P. Gibbon, and H. Patterson. 1979. *The State of Northern Ireland, 1921–1972: Political Forces and Social Classes.* Manchester: Manchester Univ. Press.

Bew, Paul, and Gordon Gillespie. 1993. *Northern Ireland: A Chronology of the Troubles, 1968–1993.* Dublin: Gill and Macmillan.

Bhabha, Jacqueline, ed. 1985. *Worlds Apart: Women under Immigration and Nationality Law.* London: Pluto Press.

Blackstock, Charity. 1974. "Jennifer Johnston." *Books and Bookmen* 19, no. 7: 93.

Blackwood, Caroline. 1976. *The Stepdaughter.* London: Duckworth.

———. 1977. *Great Granny Webster.* London: Duckworth.

———. 1981. *The Fate of Mary Rose.* London: Cape.

———. 1983. *Good Night Sweet Ladies.* London: Heinemann.

———. 1984. *Corrigan.* London: Heinemann.

———. 1985. *On the Perimeter.* Harmondsworth, Middlesex: Penguin.

———. 1995. *The Last of the Duchess.* London: Random House.

Bloom, William. 1990. *Personal Identity, National Identity and International Relations.* New York: Cambridge Univ. Press.

Boland, Eavan. 1989. *A Kind of Scar: The Woman Poet in a National Tradition.* LiP Pamphlet. Dublin: Attic Press.

———. 1992. "Outside History." *PN Review* 17, no. 1: 24.

———. 1994. *In a Time of Violence.* Manchester: Carcanet Press.

———. 1995a. "Guest Introduction: The Minds and Voices of Modern Irish Women." In *Irish Women's Voices, Past and Present,* ed. Joan Hoff and Moureen Coulter. Bloomington: Indiana Univ. Press.

———. 1995b. *Object Lessons: The Life of the Woman and the Poet in Our Time.* Manchester: Carcanet Press.

———. 1998. *The Lost Land.* Manchester: Carcanet Press.

———. 2003a. *Against Love Poetry.* London: Norton.

———. 2003b. *The Three Irish Poets.* Manchester: Carcanet Press.

Eavon Boland, Fiona Barr, and Others. 1979. *The Wall Reader and Other Stories.* Dublin: Arlen House.

Boone, Joseph A., and Michael Cadden, eds. 1990. *Engendering Men: The Question of Male Feminist Criticism.* London: Routledge.

Boylan, Clare. 1983. *Holy Pictures.* London: Hamish Hamilton.

———. 1984. *Last Resorts.* London: Hamish Hamilton.

———. 1985. *A Nail on the Head.* Harmondsworth, Middlesex: Penguin.

———. 1989. *Black Baby.* London: Hamish Hamilton.

———. 1992. *Home Rule.* London: Hamish Hamilton.

———. 1996. *Literary Companion to Cats.* Rbhp Trade Group.

———. 1998. *Room for a Single Lady.* Tunbridge Wells: Abacus.

———. 2000. *Beloved Stranger.* Tunbridge Wells: Abacus.

———. 2003. *Emma Brown.* London: Little, Brown.

Boylan, Henry. [1978] 1998. *A Dictionary of Irish Biography.* Dublin: Gill and Macmillan.

Brady, Anne M., with Brian Cleeve, eds. 1985. *A Biographical Dictionary of Irish Writers.* Mullingar: Lilliput Press.

Brady, Ciarán, ed. 1994. *Interpreting Irish History: The Debate on Historical Revisionism.* Dublin: Irish Academic Press.

Bradley, Anthony, ed. 1989. *Contemporary Irish Poetry.* Rev. ed. Berkeley: Univ. of California Press.

Bradley, Anthony, and Maryann Gialanella Valiulis, eds. 1997. *Gender and Sexuality in Modern Ireland.* Amherst: Univ. of Massachusetts.

Bramsbäck, Birgit, and Martin Croghan, eds. 1988. *Anglo-Irish and Irish Literature, Aspects of Language and Culture* Papers from the 1986 IASAIL Conference. Stockholm: Almqvist & Wiksell.

Brennan, Teresa, ed. 1989. *Between Feminism and Psychoanalysis.* London: Routledge.

Brewster, Scott, Virginia Crossman, Fiona Becket, and David Alderson, eds. 1999. *Ireland in Proximity: History, Gender, Space.* London: Routledge.

Bridgewood, C. 1986. "Family Romances: The Contemporary Family Saga." In *The Progress of Romance: The Politics of Popular Fiction*, ed. J. Radford, 167–93. London: Routledge and Kegan Paul.

Brophy, James D., and Raymond J. Porter, eds. 1983. *Contemporary Irish Writing*. Boston: Twayne.

———. 1989. *New Irish Writing*. New York: Twayne.

Brown, Elsa Barkley. 1992. " 'What Has Happened Here': The Politics of Difference in Women's History and Feminist Politics." *Feminist Studies* 18, no. 2: 295–312.

Brown, Terence. 1985a. *Ireland: A Social and Cultural History, 1922 to the Present*. Ithaca: Cornell Univ. Press.

———. 1985b. "Irish Ideology." *The Crane Bag* 9, no. 1: 90–91.

———. 1988. *Ireland's Literature: Selected Essays*. Dublin: Lilliput Press.

Brown, Terence, and Nicholas Grene, eds. 1989. *Tradition and Influence in Anglo-Irish Poetry*. Basingstoke, UK: Macmillan.

Brunt, Rosalind, and Caroline Rowan, eds. 1982. *Feminism, Culture, and Politics*. London: Lawrence and Wishart.

Buckland, P. 1972. *Ulster Unionism and the Origins of Northern Ireland 1886–1922*. Dublin: Gill and Macmillan.

Buckley, Suzann, and Pamela Lonergan. 1984. "Women and the Troubles, 1969–1980." In *Terrorism in Ireland*, ed. Yonah Alexander and Alan O'Day, 75–87. London: Croon Helm.

Bulbeck, Chilla. 1998. *Re-Orienting Western Feminisms: Women's Diversity in a Postcolonial World*. Cambridge: Cambridge Univ. Press.

Burke, Helen Lucy. 1979. *Close Connections*. Dublin: Poolbeg.

Burleigh, David. 1985. "Dead and Gone: The Fiction of Jennifer Johnston and Julia O'Faolain." In *Irish Writers and Society at Large*, ed. Masaru Sekine, 1–15. Gerrards Cross: Colin Smythe.

Butler-Cullingford, Elizabeth. 1981. *Yeats, Ireland, and Fascism*. New York: New York Univ. Press.

———. 1989. "Labor and Memory in the Love Poetry of W. B. Yeats." In *Essays for Richard Ellmann*, ed. Susan Dick, 204–19. Gerrards Cross: Colin Smythe.

Butler, Hubert. 1996. *Independent Spirit: Essays*. New York: Farrar, Straus and Giroux.

Byrne, Anne, and Madeleine Leonard, eds. 1997. *Women and Irish Society: A Sociological Reader*. Belfast: Beyond the Pale.

Byrne, Ophelia. 1997. *The Stage in Ulster from the Eighteenth Century*. Belfast: Linen Hall Library.

Byrne, Terry. 1997. *Power in the Eye: An Introduction to Contemporary Irish Film.* Lanham, MD: Scarecrow Press.

Cahalan, James M. 1971. *Great Hatred, Little Room: The Irish Historical Novel.* Syracuse: Syracuse Univ. Press.

———. 1988. *The Irish Novel: A Critical History.* Boston: Twayne.

———. 1999. *Double Visions: Women and Men in Modern and Contemporary Irish Fiction.* Syracuse: Syracuse Univ. Press.

Cahill, Susan, and Thomas Cahill. 1973. *A Literary Guide to Ireland.* New York: Scribner's.

Calhoun, C. 1993. "Nationalism and Ethnicity." *Annual Review of Sociology* 19: 211–39.

Callaghan, Louise C. 1999. *The Puzzle-Heart.* Galway: Salmon.

Callaghan, Mary Rose. 1982. *Mothers.* Dublin: Arlen House.

———. 1985. *Confessions of a Prodigal Daughter.* London: Marion Boyars.

———. 1989. *Kitty O'Shea: A Life of Katherine Parnell.* London: Pandora Press.

Callaghan, Mary Rose. 1990. *Has Anyone Seen Heather?* Dublin: Attic Press (Bright Sparks).

———. 1996. *Emigrant Dreams.* Dublin: Poolbeg.

———. 1997. *I Met a Man Who Wasn't There.* London: Marion Boyars.

———. 2001. *The Visitor's Book.* Dublin: Brandon.

Candy, Catherine. 1994. "Relocating Feminisms, Nationalisms, and Imperialisms: Ireland, India, and Margaret Cousin's Sexual Politics." *Women's History Review* 3, no. 4.

Carlson, Julia. 1990. *Banned in Ireland: Censorship and the Irish Writer.* Athens: Univ. of Georgia Press.

Caroll, Berenice A. 1976. *Liberating Women's History.* Champaign: Univ. of Illinois Press.

Carpenter, Andrew, and Peter Fallon, eds. 1990. *The Penguin Book of Contemporary Irish Poetry.* London, New York: Penguin.

Carr, Ruth [Hooley]. 1995. *The Fine Art of Loving.* Nottingham: Arrow Press.

———. 1996a. *Making It.* Nottingham: Arrow Press.

———. 1996b. *Word of Mouth.* Belfast: Blackstaff Press.

———. 1999. *There Is a House.* Donegal: Summer Palace Press.

Carty, Ciaran, and Dermot Bolger, eds. 1995. *The Hennessy Book of Irish Fiction.* Dublin: New Island Books.

Case, Sue-Ellen. 1988. *Feminism and Theatre.* Basingstoke: Macmillan.

Casey, Juanita. 1966. *Hath the Rain a Father?* London: Phoenix House.

————. 1968. *Horse by the River.* Dublin: Dolmen Press.

————. 1969. *Horse by the River and Other Poems.* Dublin: Dolmen.

————. 1971. *The Horse of Selene.* Dublin: Dolmen Press.

————. 1974. *The Circus.* Dublin: Dolmen Press.

————. 1985. *Eternity Smith.* Dublin: Dolmen Press.

Central Statistics Office. 2000. *That Was Then, This Is Now: Change in Ireland.* Cork: CSO.

Claffy, Una. 1973. *The Women Who Won: Women of the Twenty-seventh Dáil.* Dublin: Attic Press.

Clark, Clara, and Eileen Evason. 1983. *Women and Social Policy, North and South. Submission to the New Ireland Forum.* Dublin: Stationery Office.

Clarke, A. P. 1994. *The Way of the Bees: An Ovarian Yarn.* Dublin: Attic Press.

Clear, Catríona. 2000. *Women of the House: Women's Household Work in Ireland, 1922–1961.* Dublin: Irish Academic Press.

Cockburn, Cynthia. 1998. *The Space between Us: Negotiating Gender and National Identities in Conflict.* London: Zed Books.

Coleborne, Bryan. 1994. "To Retrieve the Underlay: Northern Ireland in Some Contemporary Political Fiction." *Irish-Australian Studies: Papers Delivered at the Seventh Irish-Australian Conference,* ed. Rebecca Pelan, 120–31. Sydney: Crossing Press.

Collins, Kevin. 1990. *The Cultural Conquest of Ireland.* Dublin: Mercier.

Condren, Mary. 1989. *The Serpent and the Goddess: Women, Religion and Power in Celtic Ireland.* San Francisco: Harper and Row.

Conlon, Evelyn. 1982. *Where Did I Come From?* Dublin: Ardbui.

————. 1986. "Millions Like Us." *Graph:* 4–6.

————. 1989. *Stars in the Daytime.* Dublin: Attic Press.

————. 1990. "Boys Talk." *Graph:* 2–3.

————. 1995. *A Glassful of Letters.* Belfast: Blackstaff Press.

————. 2000. *Telling: New and Selected Stories.* Belfast: Blackstaff Press.

Conlon, Evelyn, and Hans-Christian Oeser, eds. 2002. *Cutting the Night in Two: Short Stories by Irish Women Writers.* Dublin: New Island.

————. 2003. *Skin of Dreams.* Dublin: Brandon.

Connolly, Brid, and Anne B. Ryan, eds. 1999. *Gender and Education in Ireland,* vol. 2. Maynooth: MACE.

Connolly, Claire. 1998. "Postcolonial Ireland, Hyperreal Europe." *The European English Messenger* 7, no. 1: 76–79.

————. 2001. "Theorising Ireland." *Irish Studies Review* 9, no. 3: 301–15.

Connolly, Clara. 1993. "Culture or Citizenship? Notes from the 'Gender and Colonialism' Conference, Galway, Ireland, May 1992." *Feminist Review* 44: 104–11.

———. 1995. "Ourselves Alone? Clár na mBan Conference Report." *Feminist Review* 50: 118–27.

Connolly, Linda. 1996. "The Women's Movement in Ireland: A Social Movement Analysis 1970–1995." *Irish Journal of Feminist Studies* 1, no. 1: 43–77.

———. 1997. "From Revolution to Devolution: The Contemporary Women's Movement." In *Women and Irish Society: A Sociological Reader*, ed. Anne Byrne and Madeleine Leonard. Belfast: Beyond the Pale.

———. 1999a. "Don't Blame Women: An Exploration of Current Challenges Facing Feminist Academics." *Gender and Education in Ireland*, vol. 2, ed. Brid Connolly and Anne B. Ryan, 109–20. Maynooth: MACE.

———.1999b. "Feminist Politics and the Peace Process." *Capital and Class* 69: 145–60.

Connolly, Peter, ed. 1982. *Literature and the Changing Ireland*. Gerrards Cross: Colin Smythe.

Conrad, Kathryn. 1996. "Occupied Country: The Negotiation of Lesbianism in Irish Feminist Narrative." *Eire-Ireland* 31, no. 1–2: 83–100.

Cooke, Emma. 1981. *Female Forms*. Dublin: Poolbeg Press.

———. 1982. *A Single Sensation*. Dublin: Poolbeg Press.

———. 1985. *Eve's Apple*. Blackstaff Press.

———. 1994. *Wedlocked*. Dublin: Poolbeg.

Coote, A., and B. Campbell. 1982. *Sweet Freedom: The Struggle for Women's Liberation*. London: Pan Books.

Corcoran, Neil, ed. 1991. *The Chosen Ground: Essays on the Contemporary Poetry of Northern Ireland*. Brigend, Wales: Seren.

———. 1997. *After Yeats and Joyce: Reading Modern Irish Literature*. Oxford: Oxford Univ. Press.

Corish, P. J., ed. 1985. *Radicals, Rebels and Establishments*. Belfast: Appletree Press.

Costello, Mary. 1992. *Titanic Town*. London: Methuen.

Cott, Nancy. 1987. *The Grounding of Modern Feminism*. New Haven: Yale Univ. Press.

Coulter, Carol. 1990. *Ireland: Between the First and the Third Worlds*. Dublin: Attic Press, LiP Pamphlet.

———. 1992. "The Blinkered West: The Heritage of the Enlightenment." *Irish Reporter* 8, no. 4: 25–28.

———. 1994. *Web of Punishment: An Investigation*. Dublin: Attic Press.

———. 1995. "Feminism, Nationalism, and the Heritage of the Enlightenment."

In *Gender and Colonialism*, ed. Timothy P. Foley, Lionel Pilkington, Séan Ryder, and Elizabeth Tilley. Galway: Galway Univ. Press.

————. 1998. "Feminism and Nationalism in Ireland." In *Rethinking Northern Ireland*, ed. David Miller. London: Longman Addison Wesley.

Coulter, Colin. 1999. *Contemporary Northern Irish Society: An Introduction*. London: Pluto.

Coward, Rosalind. 1984. *Female Desire: Women's Sexuality Today*. London: Granada Publishing.

Craig, Patricia, ed. 1992. *The Rattle of the North: An Anthology of Ulster Prose*. Belfast: Blackstaff Press.

————. 2002. *The Oxford Book of Travel Stories*. Oxford: Oxford Univ. Press.

Craig, Patricia, and Mary Cadogan, eds. 2003a. *'You're a Brick, Angela': The Girls' Story, 1839–1985*. London: Girls Gone By.

————. 2003b. *The Oxford Book of Ireland*. Oxford: Oxford Univ. Press.

Cregagh Writing Group. 1991. *Echoes from the East*. Belfast: Greenway Women's Press.

————. 1992. *Write to the Core*. Belfast: Greenway Women's Press.

Crickley, Anastasia. 1992. "The Double Burden: Feminism and Ethnicity." *Irish Reporter* 8, no. 4: 9–10.

Crone, Joni. 1988. "Lesbian Feminism in Ireland." *Women's Studies International Forum* 11, no. 4: 343–47.

Cronin, Anthony. 1982. *Heritage Now: Irish Literature in English Language*. Dingle: Brandon; New York: St. Martin's.

Cronin, John. 1980. *The Anglo-Irish Novel*. 2 vols. New York: Barnes & Noble Books.

————. 1992. *Irish Fiction: 1900–1940*. Belfast: Appletree.

Cronin, Michael, and Cormac ó Cuilleanáin, eds. 2003. *The Languages of Ireland*. Dublin: Four Courts Press.

Cullen Owens, Rosemary. 1984. *Smashing Times: A History of the Irish Women's Suffrage Movement 1889–1922*. Dublin: Attic Press.

Curtin, Chris, Pauline Jackson, and Barbara O'Connor, eds. 1987. *Gender in Irish Society*. Galway: Galway Univ. Press.

Curtis, Liz. 1984. *Ireland: The Propaganda War: The British Media and the Battle for Hearts and Minds*. London: Pluto Press.

Curtis, L. P. 1971. *Apes and Angels: The Irishman in Victorian Caricature*. Washington: Smithsonian Institute Press.

Daly, Ita. 1980. *The Lady With the Red Shoes*. Dublin: Poolbeg Press.

————. 1986. *Ellen*. London: Cape.

————. 1989. *Candy on the Dart*. Dublin: Poolbeg Press.

————. 1996. *Unholy Ghosts*. London: Bloomsbury.

————, and Bea Willey (illustrator). 2001. *Irish Myths and Legends*. Oxford: Oxford Univ. Press.

Daly, Mary. 1973. *Beyond God the Father: Toward a Philosophy of Women's Liberation*. Boston: Beacon.

————. 1975. *The Church and the Second Sex*. New York: Harper Colophon.

————. 1978. *Gyn/Ecology: The Metaethics of Radical Feminism*. Boston: Beacon.

————. 1981. "Women in the Irish Workforce from Pre-industrial to Modern Times." *Saothar* 7: 74–82.

————. 1995. "Women in the Irish Free State 1922–1939: The Interaction between Economics and Ideology." In *Irish Women's Voices Past and Present*, ed. Joan Hoff and Moureen Coulter. Bloomington: Indiana Univ. Press.

Davies, Celia, and Eithne McLaughlin. 1991. *Women, Employment, and Social Policy in Northern Ireland: A Problem Postponed?* Belfast: Policy Research Institute.

Dawe, Gerald, and Edna Longley. 1985. *Across a Roaring Hill: the Protestant Imagination in Modern Ireland*. Belfast: Blackstaff.

————. 1991a. *How's The Poetry Going? Literary Politics and Ireland Today*. Belfast: Lagan.

————, ed. 1991b. *The New Younger Irish Poets*. Belfast: Blackstaff.

————. 1992/93. "False Faces" *Graph* 13: 19–20.

Deane, John F., ed. 1991. *Irish Poetry of Faith and Doubt: The Cold Heaven*. Dublin: Wolfhound.

Deane, Seamus. 1997. *Strange Country: Modernity and Nationhood Since 1790* New York: Oxford Univ. Press.

Delanty, Greg, and Nuala Ní Dhomhnaill, eds. 1995. *Jumping Off Shadows*. Cork: Cork Univ. Press.

Delmar, Rosalind. 1986. "Broken Agenda." *New Statesman* 112, no. 2887 (25 July).

Delphy, Christine. 1994. "Changing Women in a Changing Europe: Is 'Difference' the Future for Feminism?" *Women's Studies International Forum* 17, no. 2/3: 187–201.

Devlin, Anne. 1994. *After Easter*. London: Faber and Faber.

————. 1999. *"Titanic" Town*. London: Faber and Faber.

Devlin, Polly. 1997. *Only Sometimes Looking Sideways*. Dublin: O'Brien Press.

DiCenzo, Maria R. 1993. "Charabanc Theatre Company: Placing Women Center-Stage in Northern Ireland." *Theatre Journal* 45: 173–84.

Dillon, Eilís. 1973. *Across the Bitter Sea*. London: Hodder and Stoughton.

————. 1977. *Blood Relations*. London: Hodder and Stoughton.

Donoghue, Denis. 1986. *We Irish: Essays on Irish Literature and Society*. New York: Knopf.

Donoghue, Emma. 1997a. *Poems between Women*. New York: Columbia Univ. Press.

————. 1997b. *What Sappho Would Have Said: Four Centuries of Love Poems between Women*. London: Hamish Hamilton.

————. 2001. *Slammerkin*. London: Virago.

————. 2003. *The Woman Who Gave Birth to Rabbits: Stories*. London: Harcourt.

————. 2004. *Life Mask*. London: Virago.

Donoghue, Freda, Rick Wilford, and Robert Miller. 1997. "Feminist or Womanist? Feminism, the Women's Movement and Age Difference in Northern Ireland." *Irish Journal of Feminist Studies* 2, no. 2: 86–105.

Donovan, Josephine. 1975. *Feminist Literary Criticism: Explorations in Theory*. Lexington: Univ. of Kentucky Press.

Donovan, Katie, A. Norman Jeffares, and Brenda Kennelly, eds. 1995. *Ireland's Women: Writing Past and Present*. New York, London: Norton.

Dorcey, Mary. 1982. *Kindling*. London: Only Women Press.

————. 1989. *A Noise from the Woodshed*. London: Only Women Press.

————. 1991. *Moving into the Space Cleared by Our Mothers*. Galway: Salmon Publishing.

————. 1996. *The River That Carries Me*. Galway: Salmon Publishing.

————. 2002. *Like Joy in Season, Like Sorrow*. Galway: Salmon Publishing.

Dorgan, Theo, ed. 1996. *Irish Poetry Since Kavanagh*. Blackrock, Ireland: Four Courts Press.

Doyle, Rose. 1994. *Kimbay*. Dublin: Town House in association with Macmillan (London).

Drew, Eileen. 1991. "Part-time Working in Ireland: Meeting the Flexibility Needs of Women Workers or of Employers?" *Canadian Journal of Irish Studies* 18, no. 1: 95–109.

Duffaud, Briege. 1993. *A Wreath Upon the Dead*. Dublin: Poolbeg.

————. 1994. *Nothing Like Beirut*. Dublin: Poolbeg.

Duffy, Noel, and Theo Dorgan, eds. 1999, *Watching the River Flow: A Century in Irish Poetry*. Dublin: Poetry Ireland.

Dunn, Douglas, ed. 1975. *Two Decades of Irish Writing*. Manchester, UK: Carcanet.

Eager, Alan R. 1980. *A Guide to Irish Bibliographical Material: A Bibliography of Irish Bibliographies and Sources of Information*. Rev. ed. London: Library Association; Westport: Greenwood Press.

Eagleton, Mary, and David Pierce. 1979. *Attitudes to Class in the English Novel: From Walter Scott to David Storey.* London: Thames and Hudson.

———. 1986. *Feminist Literary Theory: A Reader.* Oxford: Basil Blackwell.

———. 1991. *Feminist Literary Criticism.* London: Longman.

———. 1996. *Working with Feminist Criticism.* Oxford: Blackwell.

———. 2003. *A Concise Companion to Feminist Theory.* Oxford: Blackwell.

Eagleton, Terry. 1978. *Criticism and Ideology.* London: Verso.

———. 1989. "The End of English." *Textual Practice* 1, no. 1: 1–10.

Echoes from the East: Cregagh Writing Group. 1991. Belfast: Greenway Women's Press.

Edge, Sarah. 1998. "Representing Gender and National Identity." In *Rethinking Northern Ireland,* ed. D. Miller. London: Longman.

Edwards, Ruth Dudley. 1973. *An Atlas of Irish History.* London: Methuen.

———. 1977. *Patrick Pearse: The Triumph of Failure.* London: Gollancz.

———. 1981. *James Connolly.* Dublin: Gill and Macmillan.

———. 1983. *Harold Macmillan: A Life in Pictures.* London: Macmillan.

———. 1987. *Victor Gollancz: A Biography.* London: Gollancz.

———. 2000. *The Faithful Time: The Loyalist Institutions.* London: Harper Collins.

———. 2001. *The Anglo-Irish Murders.* London: Harper Collins.

———. 2003. *Newspapermen: Hugh Cudlipp, Cecil Harmsworth King, and the Glory Days of Fleet Street.* London: Secker & Warburg.

———. 2004. *Carnage on the Committee.* London: Harper Collins.

Eisenstein, Hester, and Alice Jardine, eds. 1980. *The Future of Difference.* Boston: G. K. Hall.

———. 1984. *Contemporary Feminist Thought.* London: Unwin.

———. 1991. *Gender Shock: Practising Feminism on Two Continents.* Sydney: Allen and Unwin.

Ellmann, Mary. 1968. *Thinking about Women.* New York: Harcourt.

Enright, Anne. 1996. *The Wig My Father Wore.* London: Minerva.

———. 2001. *What Are You Like?* London: Vintage.

———. 2003. *The Pleasure of Eliza Lynch.* London: Vintage.

Etherton, Michael. 1989. *Contemporary Irish Dramatists.* Basingstoke, UK: Macmillan Education; New York: St. Martin's.

Evason, Eileen. 1982. *Hidden Violence.* Belfast: Farset Co-op Press.

———. 1991. *Against the Grain: The Contemporary Women's Movement in Northern Ireland.* Dublin: Attic Press.

Eyler, Audrey S., and Robert F. Garratt, eds. 1988. *The Uses of the Past: Essays on Irish Culture.* Newark: Delaware Univ. Press.

Fallis, Richard. 1977. *The Irish Renaissance.* New York: Syracuse Univ. Press.

Faludi, Susan. 1992. *Backlash: The Undeclared War Against Women.* London: Vintage.

Fanning, Charles, ed. 2002. *Selected Writings of John V. Kelleher on Ireland and Irish-America.* Carbondale: Univ. of Southern Illinois Press.

Farley, Pamela. 1980. "Lesbianism and the Social Function of the Taboo." In *The Future of Difference,* ed. Hester Eisenstein and Alice Jardine, 167–272. Boston: G. K. Hall.

Fearon, Kate. 1996. "Power, Politics, Positioning: Women in Northern Ireland." *Democratic Dialogue Report* 4 (Belfast).

———. 1999. *Women's Work: The Story of the Northern Ireland Women's Coalition.* Belfast: Blackstaff.

Felski, Rita. 1986. "The Novel of Self-Discovery: A Necessary Fiction." *Southern Review* 19, no. 2: 131–48.

———. 1995. *The Gender of Modernity.* Cambridge, MA: Harvard Univ. Press.

———. 2000. *Doing Time: Feminist Theory and Postmodern Culture.* New York: New York Univ. Press.

———. 2003. *Literature After Feminism.* Chicago: Univ. of Chicago Press.

Feminist Review. 1995. Special Issue. "The Irish Issue: The British Question." 50.

Fennell, Desmond. 1985. "How Not to See Ireland." *The Crane Bag* 9, no. 1: 92–93.

———. 1994. "Against Revisionism." In *Interpreting Irish History: The Debate on Historical Revisionism,* ed. Ciarán Brady, 181–90. Dublin: Irish Academic Press.

Ferguson, Kathleen. 1994. *The Maid's Tale.* Dublin: Torc Press.

Ferriter, Diarmaid. 1999. *A Nation of Extremes: The Pioneers in Twentieth Century Ireland.* Dublin: Irish Academic Press.

Field Day Theatre Company. 1985. *Ireland's Field Day.* London: Hutchinson.

Finneran, Richard, ed. 1983. *Recent Research in Anglo-Irish Writers.* New York: MLA.

Fitzgerald, Gretchen. 1992. *Repulsing Racism: Reflections on Racism and the Irish.* LiP Pamphlet. Dublin: Attic Press.

Fitzgerald, Jennifer. 1987. "Feminist Literary Criticism." *The Irish Review* 2: 100–104.

Fitzmaurice, Gabriel, ed. 1993. *Irish Poetry Now: Other Voices.* Dublin: Wolfhound.

Fitzpatrick, David. 1985. "Marriage in Post-Famine Ireland." In *Marriage in Ireland,* ed. Art Cosgrove. Dublin: College Press.

———. 1987. "The Modernisation of the Irish Female." In *Rural Ireland: Modernisation and Change 1600–1900,* ed. Patrick O'Flanagan, Kevin Whelan, and Paul Ferguson, 162–80. Cork: Cork Univ. Press.

———. 1991. "Women, Gender, and the Writing of Irish History." *Irish Historical Studies* 27, no. 107: 267–73.

Flackes, W. D., and Sydney Elliott. 1989. *Northern Ireland: A Political Directory 1968–88*. Belfast: Blackstaff Press.

Fogarty, Anne. 2000. "Uncanny Families: Neo-Gothic Motifs and the Theme of Social Change in Contemporary Irish Women's Fiction." *Irish University Review* 30, no. 1: 59–81.

Foley, Imelda. 2003. *The Girls in the Big Picture: Gender in Contemporary Ulster Theatre*. Belfast: Blackstaff Press.

Foley, Timothy, Lionel Pilkington, Séan Ryder, and Elizabeth Tilley, eds. 1995. *Gender and Colonialism*. Galway: Galway Univ. Press.

Foster, Aisling. 1993. *Safe in the Kitchen*. London: Hamish Hamilton.

Foster, John Wilson, ed. 1974. *Forces and Themes in Ulster Fiction*. Dublin: Gill and Macmillan.

———. 1987a. "Critical Forum: Feminism North and South, Fifteen Years On." *H.U./The Honest Ulsterman* 83: 39–70.

———. 1987b. *Fictions of the Irish Literary Revival: A Changeling Art*. Syracuse: Syracuse Univ. Press.

———. 1991. *Colonial Consequences: Essays in Irish Literature and Culture*. Dublin: Lilliput.

Foster, R. F. 1993a. "Anglo-Irish Relations and Northern Ireland." In *Northern Ireland and the Politics of Reconciliation*, ed. Dermot Keogh and Michael H. Haltzel. Cambridge: Cambridge Univ. Press.

———. 1993b. *Paddy and Mr. Punch: Connections in Irish and English History*. New York: Penguin.

Franklin, Sarah, Celia Lury, and Jackie Stacey, eds. 1991. *Off-Centre: Feminism and Cultural Studies*. London: Harper Collins.

Froula, Christine. 1983. "When Eve Reads Milton: Undoing the Canonical Economy." *Critical Inquiry* 10: 321–48.

Frye, Marilyn. 1983. *The Politics of Reality: Essays in Feminist Theory*. Trumansburg, NY: Crossing.

Gallagher, Sean. 1983. *Woman in Irish Legend, Life, and Literature*. Gerrards Cross: Colin Smythe.

Galligan, Yvonne. 1998. *Women and Contemporary Politics in Ireland: From the Margins to the Mainstream*. London: Pinter.

Gardiner, Frances. 1992. "Political Interest and Participation of Irish Women 1922–1992: The Unfinished Revolution." *Canadian Journal of Irish Studies* 18, no. 1: 15–39.

Gardiner, Judith Kegan. 1981. "On Female Identity and Writing by Women." *Critical Enquiry* 8: 347–61.

———. Elly Bulkin, Rena Grasso Patterson, and Annette Kolodny. 1982. "An Interchange on Feminist Criticism: On 'Dancing Through the Minefield.'" *Feminist Studies* 8, no. 3: 629–75.

Garratt, Robert. 1986. *Modern Irish Poetry: Tradition and Continuity from Yeats to Heaney.* Berkeley: Univ. of California Press.

Gibbons, Luke. 1996. *Transformations in Irish Culture.* Notre Dame, IN: Univ. of Notre Dame Press.

Gillespie, Michael Patrick. 2001. *James Joyce and the Fabrication of an Irish Identity.* Amsterdam: Rodopi.

Gasper, Phil. 1994. "Worth Fighting For." Interview with Eamonn McCann. *Socialist Review* 175: 17–19.

Gerrard, Nicci. 1989. *Into The Mainstream.* London: Pandora.

———. 2003. *Things We Knew Were True.* London: Michael Joseph.

Gilbert, Sandra, and Susan Gubar, eds. 1989. *No Man's Land: The Place of the Woman Writer in the Twentieth Century.* 2 vols. New Haven, Conn.: Yale Univ. Press.

Gilley, Sheridan, and Roger Swift. 1985. *The Irish in the Victorian City.* Beckenham, Kent: Croom Helm.

Gordon, Deborah A. 1995. "Feminism and Cultural Studies." *Feminist Studies* 21, no. 2: 363–77.

Graham, C. 1996. "Subalternity and Gender: Problems of Post-Colonial Irishness." *Journal of Gender Studies* 5, no. 3: 363–73.

Gray, Breda. 1999. "Longings and Belongings Gendered Spatialities of Irishness." *Irish Studies Review* 5, no. 3: 363–73.

———. 2000a. "Gendering the Irish Diaspora: Questions of Enrichment, Hybridization, and Return." *Women's Studies International Forum* 23, no. 2: 167–85.

Gray, Jane. 1995. "Gender Politics and Ireland." In *Irish Women's Voices: Past and Present,* ed. Joan Hoff and Moureen Coulter, 240–49. Bloomington: Indiana Univ. Press.

Greene, Gayle. 1991. *Changing the Story: Feminist Fiction and the Tradition.* Bloomington: Indiana Univ. Press.

Griffin, Gabriele, Marianne Hester, Shirin Rai, and Sasha Roseneil, eds. 1994. *Stirring It: Challenges for Feminism.* London: Taylor & Francis.

Gutwin, Catherine. 1991. "Innisfree, Beezie, and Me." *Canadian Journal of Irish Studies* 18, no. 1: 151–56.

Haberstroh, Patricia Boyle. 2001. *My Self, My Muse: Irish Women Poets Reflect on Love and Art.* Syracuse: Syracuse Univ. Press.

Hall, Wayne E. 1980. *Shadowy Heroes: Irish Literature of the 1890s.* Syracuse: Syracuse Univ. Press.

Hannon, Dennis J., and Nancy Means Wright. 1986. "Irish Women Poets: Breaking the Silence." *The Canadian Journal of Irish Studies* 12, no. 1: 53–58.

Haraway, Donna. 1990a. "A Manifesto For Cyborgs: Science, Technology, and Socialist Feminism in the 1980s." In *Feminism/Postmodernism*, ed. Linda Nicholson, 196–97. New York: Routledge.

———. 1990b. *Primate Visions: Gender, Race, and Nature in the World of Modern Science.* London: Routledge.

———. 1991. *Simians, Cyborgs, and Women: The Reinvention of Nature.* London: Free Association Books.

———. 1998. *Cyborg Babies: From Techno-sex to Techno-tots.* London: Routledge.

———. 2003a. *The Haraway Reader.* London: Routledge.

———. 2003b. *The Companion Species: Dogs, People, and Significant Otherness.* Chicago: Univ. of Chicago Press.

Harding, Sandra. 1986a. "The Instability of the Analytical Categories of Feminist Theory." *Signs* 11, no. 4: 645–64.

———. 1986b. *The Science Question in Feminism.* Ithaca: Cornell Univ. Press.

———. 1987. *Feminism and Methodology: Social Sciences Issues.* Bloomington: Indiana Univ. Press.

———. 1993. *The "Racial" Economy of Science: Toward a Democratic Future.* Bloomington: Indiana Univ. Press.

Hargreaves, Tamsin. 1988. "Women's Consciousness and Identity in Four Irish Women Novelists." In *Cultural Contexts and Literary Idioms in Contemporary Irish Literature*, ed. Michael Kenneally, 290–305. Gerrards Cross: Colin Smythe.

Harkness, David. 1996. *Ireland in the Twentieth Century: Divided Island.* London: Macmillan.

Harmon, Maurice. 1975. "Generations Apart: 1925–1975." In *The Irish Novel in Our Time*, ed. Patrick Rafroidi and Maurice Harmon. Lille: Publications de l'Universite de Lille III.

Harrington, John P., ed. 1991. *Modern Irish Drama.* New York: Norton.

———, and Elizabeth J. Mitchell, eds. 1999. *Politics and Performance in Contemporary Northern Ireland.* Amherst: Univ. of Massachusetts Press.

Harris, Claudia W. 1996. "Reinventing Women: Charabanc Theatre Company:

Recasting Northern Ireland's Story." In *The State of Play: Irish Theatre in the 'Nineties*, ed. Eberhard Bort. Trier: Wissenschaftlicher Verlag.

Harris, Rosemary. 1972. *Prejudice and Tolerance in Ulster: A Study of Neighbours and "Strangers" in a Border Community*. Totowa, NJ: Manchester Univ. Press.

Harte, Lynda, ed. 1992. *Making a Spectacle: Feminist Essays on Contemporary Women's Theatre*. Ann Arbor: Univ. of Michigan Press.

Harte, Liam, and Michael Parker, eds. 2000. *Contemporary Irish Fiction: Themes, Tropes, Theories*. New York: St. Martin's.

Hazard, Adams. 1987. "Canons: Literary Criteria/Power Criteria."*Critical Enquiry* 14: 748–64.

Hayes, Liz. 1990. "Working for Change: A Study of Three Women's Community Groups." *Report Research Series 8*. Dublin: Combat Poverty Agency.

Hearne, Dana. 1992. "The Irish Citizen 1914–1916: Nationalism, Feminism, and Militarism." *Canadian Journal of Irish Studies* 18, no. 1: 1–14.

Heaton, Caroline. 1988. "Women's Lives and Women's Writing." *British Book News*: 12–15.

Hennessey, Thomas. 1997. *A History of Northern Ireland, 1920–1996*. Dublin: Gill and Macmillan.

Henry, P. L., ed. 1991. *Dánta Ban: Poems of Irish Women, Early and Modern*. Cork: Mercier Press.

Herr, Cheryl. 1990. "The Erotics of Irishness." *Critical Enquiry* 17: 1–34.

———. 1991. *For the Land They Loved: Irish Political Melodramas, 1890–1925*. Syracuse: Syracuse Univ. Press.

Hesketh, Tom. 1990. *The Second Partitioning of Ireland*. Dublin: Brandsma Books.

Hewitt, Nancy A. 1992. "Compounding Differences." *Feminist Studies* 18, no. 2: 313–26.

Hickman, Mary J., and Bronwen Walter. 1995. "Deconstructing Whiteness: Irish Women in Britain." *Feminist Review* 50: 5–19.

Higgins, Rita Ann. 1988. *Goddess and Witch*. Galway: Salmon.

———. 1992. *Philomena's Revenge*. Galway: Salmon.

Hill, Niki, and Colin Turner (illustrator). 1994. *The Mournes: Paintings and Stories from Around the Mountains*. Donaghadee, Co. Down: Cottage Publications.

Hill, John, and Martin McLoone, Paul Hainsworth, eds. 1994. *Border Crossings: Film in Ireland, Britain, and Europe*. Belfast: Institute for Irish Studies.

Hirsch, Marianne, and Evelyn Fox Keller, eds. 1990. *Conflicts in Feminism*. London: Routledge.

Hobsbawn, E. 1990. *Nations and Nationalism Since 1780: Myth and Reality.* Cambridge: Cambridge Univ. Press.

Hoff, Joan, and Moureen Coulter, eds. 1995. *Irish Women's Voices: Past and Present.* Bloomington: Indiana Univ. Press.

Hogan, Robert. 1979. *Dictionary of Irish Literature.* Westport, Conn.: Greenwood Press; London: Macmillan (retitled *Macmillan Dictionary of Irish Literature*).

Holmes, Janice, and Diane Urquhart. 1994. *Coming into the Light: The Work and Politics of Women in Ulster 1840–1940.* Belfast: Institute of Irish Studies.

Hopkins, Alannah. 1989. *The Living Legend of Saint Patrick.* London: Grafton Books.

Hulme, Peter, and Francis Barker, eds. 1993. *Colonial Discourse/Post-Colonial Theory.* Manchester: Manchester Univ. Press.

Humm, Maggie. 1986. *Feminist Criticism: Women as Contemporary Critic.* Brighton: Harvester.

———. 1989. *The Dictionary of Feminist Theory.* Brighton: Harvester.

———. 1991. *Border Traffic: Strategies of Contemporary Women Writers.* Manchester: Manchester Univ. Press.

———. 1992. *Feminisms: A Reader.* London: Harvester Wheatsheaf.

———. 1997. *Feminism and Film.* Edinburgh: Edinburgh Univ. Press.

———. 2002. *Modernist Women and Visual Culture: Virginia Woolf, Vanessa Bell, Photography, and Cinema.* Edinburgh: Edinburgh Univ. Press.

Hussey, Gemma. 1993. *Ireland Today: Anatomy of a Changing State* Dublin: Townhouse.

Hutton, Sean, and Paul Stewart, eds. 1991. *Ireland's Histories: Aspects of State, Society and Ideology.* London: Routledge.

Imhof, Rüdiger, ed. 1990. *Contemporary Irish Novelists.* Tübingen: Gunter Narr.

Ingoldby, G. D. 1983. "Wiping a Waxed Floor with Men." *Fortnight* (Belfast) 191 (Feb.): 20.

Irish Reporter. 1992. Special Issue. "Stating Our Case: The Many Voices of Feminism." 8, no. 4.

Jackson, Ellen-Raisa. 1999. "Gender, Violence, and Hybridity: Reading the Postcolonial in Three Irish Novels." *Irish Studies Review* 7, no. 2: 221–31.

Jackson, Pauline. 1992. "Abortion Trials and Tribulations." *Canadian Journal of Irish Studies* 18, no. 1: 112–20.

Jackson, Stevi. 2001. "Why a Materialist Feminism Is (Still) Possible." *Women's Studies International Forum* 24, no. 3–4: 283–93.

Jacobson, Ruth. 2000. "Women and Peace in Northern Ireland: A Complicated Relationship." In *States of Conflict: Gender, Violence, and Resistance,* ed. Susie Jacobs, Ruth Jacobson, and Jen Marchbank. London: Zed Books.

Jayawardena, Kumari. 1986. *Feminism and Nationalism in the Third World.* London: Zed Books.

Johansson, Sheila Ryan. 1976. " 'Herstory' as History: A New Field or Another Fad?" In *Liberating Women's History,* ed. Berenice A. Carroll. Champaign: Univ. of Illinois Press.

Johnson, Barbara. 1980. *The Critical Difference: Essays in the Contemporary Rhetoric of Reading.* Baltimore: Johns Hopkins Univ. Press.

———. 1987. *A World of Difference.* Baltimore: Johns Hopkins Univ. Press.

Johnson, Toni O'Brien. 1988. "Questions for Irish Feminist Criticism." *Text and Context* 111: 25–28.

———, and David Cairns, eds. 1991. *Gender in Irish Writing.* Buckingham: Open Univ. Press.

Johnston, Dillon. 1997. *Irish Poetry after Joyce.* 2nd ed. Syracuse: Syracuse Univ. Press.

Johnston, Jennifer. 1981. *The Christmas Tree.* London: Hamish Hamilton.

———. 1984. *The Railway Station Man.* London: Hamish Hamilton.

———. 1987. *Fool's Sanctuary.* London: Hamish Hamilton.

———. 1988. *The Nightingale and Not the Lark.* Dublin: Raven Arts Press.

———. 1991. *The Invisible Worm.* London: Hamish Hamilton.

———. 2003. *Jennifer Johnston's Selected Short Plays.* Dublin: New Island Press.

Jones, Kathleen B. 1991. "The Trouble With Authority." *Differences: A Journal of Feminist Cultural Studies* 3, no. 1: 104–27.

Jones, Marie. 2000a. *A Night in November.* London: Nick Hern Books.

———. 2000b. *Stones in His Pockets.* London: Nick Hern Books.

K. Arnold Price. 1988. *The Captain's Paramours.* London: Hamish Hamilton.

Kaufman, Linda, ed. 1989. *Gender and Theory: Dialogues on Feminist Criticism.* Oxford: Basil Blackwell.

———. 1993. *American Feminist Thought at Century's End: A Reader.* Cambridge, MA: Blackwell.

Kearney, Richard. 1985. *The Irish Mind: Exploring Intellectual Traditions.* Dublin: Wolfhound Press.

———. 1997. *Postnationalist Ireland: Politics, Culture, Philosophy.* New York: Routledge.

———, ed. 1988. *Across the Frontiers : Ireland in the 1990s: Cultural, Political, Economic.* Totowa, N.J.: Barnes and Noble.

Kelleher, Margaret. 2001. "Writing Irish Women's Literary History." *Irish Studies Review* 9, no. 1: 5–14.

Kelly, A. A., ed. 1987. *Pillars of the House: An Anthology of Verse by Irish Women from 1690 to the Present.* Dublin: Wolfhound.

Kelly, Maeve. 1986. *Resolution*. Belfast: Blackstaff Press.

———. 1991. *Florrie's Girls*. Belfast: Blackstaff Press.

Kelly, Rita. 2001. *Kelly Reads Bewick: Rita Kelly, Poet, Interprets the Paintings of Pauline Bewick*. Galway: Arlen House.

Kenneally, James J. 1986. "Sexism, the Church, Irish Women." *Eire-Ireland*: 3–16.

Kenneally, Michael, ed. 1988. *Cultural Contexts and Literary Idioms in Contemporary Irish Literature*. Gerrards Cross: Colin Smythe.

———. 1992. *Irish Literature and Culture*. Gerrards Cross: Colin Smythe.

Kenny, Mary. 2000. *Goodbye to Catholic Ireland*. Dublin: New Island Books.

———. 2002. *Abortion: Debating Matters*. London: Hodder Arnold.

———. 2003. *Germany Calling: A Personal Biography of William Joyce—Lord Haw Haw*. Dublin: New Island Books.

Kiberd, Declan. 1979. *Synge and the Anglo-Irish Language*. London: Macmillan.

———. 1985. *Men and Feminism in Modern Literature*. London: Macmillan.

———. 1993. *Fare Well/Beir Beannacht*. Dublin: Attic Press.

———. 1995. "Insecurity, Local Piety, and Ulsterisation." *Fortnight* (21 Oct.): 11–22.

———. 2000. *Irish Classics*. Cambridge: Harvard Univ. Press.

Kiberd, Declan, and Gabriel Fitzmaurice, eds. 1991. *An Crann Faoi Bhláth/The Flowering Tree: Contemporary Irish Poetry with Verse Translations*. Dublin: Wolfhound.

Kilgore, Emilie S., ed. 1992. *Landmarks of Contemporary Women's Drama*. London: Methuen Drama.

Kinsella, Thomas. 1995. *The Dual Tradition: An Essay on Poetry and Politics in Ireland*. Manchester: Carcanet.

———, ed. 1986. *The New Oxford Book of Irish Verse*. Oxford: Oxford Univ. Press.

Kirk, G. S. 1971. *Myth: Its Meaning and Functions in Ancient and Other Cultures*. Cambridge: Cambridge Univ. Press.

Kirkpatrick, Kathryn. 2000. *Border Crossings: Irish Women Writers and National Identities*. Dublin: Wolfhound.

Krause, David. 1982. *The Profane Book of Irish Comedy*. Ithaca: Cornell Univ. Press.

———. 2002. *Revisionary Views: Some Counter-Statements About Irish Life and Literature*. Dublin: Maunsel.

Kreilkamp, Vera. 1998. *The Anglo-Irish Novel and the Big House*. Syracuse: Syracuse Univ. Press.

Larkin, Mary. 1993. *The Wasted Years*. London: Warner Books.

Lauretis, Teresa de. 1984. *Alice Doesn't: Feminism, Semiotics, Cinema*. London: Macmillan.

————. 1987. *Technologies of Gender: Essays on Theory, Film, and Fiction.* Bloomington: Indiana Univ. Press.

————. 1988. *The Feminist Studies, Critical Studies: The Women's Film of the 1940s.* London: Palgrave Macmillan.

————. 1985. *Cinematic Apparatus.* London: Palgrave Macmillan.

————. 1989. *Technologies of Gender: Essays on Theory, Film, and Fiction.* London: Palgrave Macmillan.

————. 1994. *The Practice of Love: Lesbian Sexuality and Perverse Desire.* Bloomington: Indiana Univ. Press.

————, ed. 1986. *Feminist Studies, Critical Studies.* Bloomington: Indiana Univ. Press.

Lee, Joseph J. 1978. "Women and the Church Since the Famine." In *Women in Irish Society: The Historical Dimension,* ed. Margaret MacCurtain and Donnachadh ó Corráin. Dublin: Arlen House.

————. 1989. *Ireland 1912–1985. Politics and Society.* Cambridge: Cambridge Univ. Press.

Leith, Linda. 1992. "Subverting the Sectarian Heritage: Recent Novels of Northern Ireland." *Canadian Journal of Irish Studies* 18, no. 2: 88–106.

Leland, Mary. 1987. *The Little Galloway Girls.* London: Hamish Hamilton.

————. 1991. *Approaching Priests.* London: Sinclair Stevenson.

————. 1995. *Changeling.* London: Sinclair Stevenson.

————. 1996. *Cork Cocraigh.* Cork: Collins Press.

————. 2000. *Lie of the Land: Journeys Through Literary Cork.* Cork: Cork Univ. Press.

Lentin, Ronit. 1975. *Stone of Claims.* Tel Aviv: Siman Kria.

————. 1977. *Like a Blindman.* Tel Aviv: Siman Kria.

————. 1985. *Tea with Mrs Klein.* Dublin: Wolfhound Press.

————. 1993. "Feminist Research Methodologies: A Separate Paradigm? Notes for a Debate." *Irish Journal of Sociology* 3: 119–38.

————. 1996. *Songs on the Death of Children.* Dublin: Poolbeg Press.

————. 1998. " 'Irishness,' the 1937 Constitution, and Citizenship: A Gender and Ethnicity View." *Irish Journal of Sociology* 8: 5–24.

Lentin, Ronit, ed. 1995. *In from the Shadows: The UL Women's Studies Collection.* Women's Studies Centre. Limerick: Univ. of Limerick.

Lentin, Ronit, and Robbie McVeigh, eds. 2002. *Racism and Anti-Racism in Ireland.* Belfast: Beyond the Pale Publications.

Leonard, Madeleine. 1992. "The Politics of Everyday Living in Belfast." *The Canadian Journal of Irish Studies* 18, no. 1: 83–94.

Lerner, Gerda. "Placing Women in History: A 1975 Perspective." In *Liberating Women's History*, ed. Berenice A. Carroll. Urbana: Univ. of Illinois Press, 1976.

———. 1986. *The Creation of Patriarchy*. New York: Oxford Univ. Press.

Lingard, Joan. 1970. *The Lord on Our Side*. London: Hodder and Stoughton.

———. 1984. *Sisters by Rite*. New York: St. Martin's Press.

Livesey, James, and Stuart Murray. 1997. "Post-Colonial Theory and Modern Irish Culture." *Irish Historical Studies* 30, no. 119: 452–61.

Lloyd, David. 1987. *Nationalism and Minor Literature: James Clarence Mangan and the Emergence of Irish Cultural Nationalism*. Berkeley: Univ. of California Press.

———. 1999. *Ireland After History*. Cork: Cork Univ. Press.

———. 2001. "Regarding Ireland in a Post-Colonial Frame." *Cultural Studies* 15, no. 1: 12–32.

Lojek, Helen. 1990. "Difference without Indifference: The Drama of Frank McGuinness and Anne Devlin." *Eire Ireland* 25: 56–68.

———. 1999. "Playing Politics with Belfast's Charabanc Theatre Company." In *Politics and Performance in Contemporary Northern Ireland*, ed. John P. Harrington and Elizabeth J. Mitchell. Amherst: Univ. of Massachusetts Press.

Longley, Edna. 1985. "Poetry and Politics in Northern Ireland." *The Crane Bag* 9, no. 1: 26–39.

———. 1986. *Poetry in the Wars*. Newcastle upon Tyne: Bloodaxe Books.

———. 1990. *From Cathleen to Anorexia: The Breakdown of Irelands*. Dublin: Attic Press, LiP Pamphlet.

———. 1994. *The Living Stream: Literature and Revisionism in Ireland*. Newcastle upon Tyne: Bloodaxe Books.

———, and Declan Kiberd. 2001. *Multi-Culturalism: The View from the Two Irelands*. Cork: Cork Univ. Press.

Loughran, Christina. 1985. "The Women's Movement in Northern Ireland: Between Republicanism and Feminism." *Fortnight*: 220.

———. 1986. "Armagh and Feminist Strategy." *Feminist Review* 23: 59–79.

Luddy, Maria, and Cliona Murphy, eds. 1989. *Women Surviving: Studies in Irish Women's History in the Nineteenth and Twentieth Centuries*. Dublin: Poolbeg Press.

Luddy, Maria. 1995. *Women in Ireland 1800–1918: A Documentary History*. Cork: Cork Univ. Press.

Lugones, Maria C., and Elizabeth V. Spelman. 1983. "Have We Got a Theory For You! Feminist Theory, Cultural Imperialism, and the Demand for 'the Woman's Voice.' " *Women's Studies International Forum* 6, no. 6: 573–81.

MacCurtain, Margaret. 1985. "The Historical Image." In *Irish Women: Image and Achievement*, ed. Eiléan Ní Chuilleanáin, 37–50. Dublin: Arlen House.

———. 1990. "Fullness of Life: Defining Female Spirituality in Twentieth-Century Ireland." In *Women Surviving: Studies in Irish Women's History in the Nineteenth and Twentieth Centuries*, ed. Maria Luddy and Clíona Murphy, 233–63. Dublin: Poolbeg.

———. 1995. "Late in the Field: Catholic Sisters in Twentieth Century Ireland and the New Religious History." In *Chattel, Servant, or Citizen: Women's Status in Church, State, and Society*, ed. Mary O'Dowd and Sabine Wichert. Belfast: Institute of Irish Studies: 34–44.

MacCurtain, Margaret, and Suellen Joy. 1994. *From Dublin to New Orleans: Nora and Alice's Journey to America, 1889.* Dublin: Attic Press.

MacCurtain, Margaret, and Mary O'Dowd. 1992. "An Agenda for Women's History in Ireland." *Irish Historical Studies* 28: 109.

MacKillop, James, ed. 1999. *Contemporary Irish Cinema: From "The Quiet Man" to "Dancing at Lughnasa."* Syracuse: Syracuse Univ. Press.

Madden, Deirdre. 1988. *The Birds of the Innocent Wood.* London: Faber and Faber.

———. 1994. *Nothing Is Black.* London: Faber and Faber.

———. 1996. *One by One in the Darkness.* London: Faber and Faber.

Madden-Simpson, Janet. 1986. "Womanwriting: The Arts of Textual Politics." *Midland Review* 3: 121–28.

Maher, Kathleen. 1992. "Doing It for Themselves." *Irish Reporter* 8, no. 4: 6–8.

Mahon, Bríd. 1994. *Devogilla.* Dublin: Poolbeg.

Mahon, Evelyn. 1987. "Women's Rights and Catholicism in Ireland." *New Left Review* 166: 53–77.

———. 1994. "Feminist Research: A Reply to Lentin." *Irish Journal of Sociology* 4: 165–69.

Mahony, Christina Hunt. 1998. *Contemporary Irish Literature: Transforming Tradition.* New York: St. Martin's.

Mahony, Rosemary. 1993. *Whoredom in Kimmage: Irish Women Coming of Age.* Boston: Houghton Mifflin.

Marcus, David, ed. 1976a. *Best Irish Short Stories.* London: Paul Elek.

———. 1976b. *New Irish Writing.* London: Quartet.

———. 1979. *Body and Soul.* Dublin: Poolbeg Press.

———. 1994. *The Midnight Court.* Dublin: Poolbeg Press.

———. 1996. *Phoenix: Irish Short Stories.* Dublin: Phoenix Press.

Marks, Elaine, and Isabelle de Courtivron, eds. 1981. *New French Feminisms: An Anthology.* Brighton: Harvester.

Martin, Augustine, ed. 1985. *The Genius of Irish Prose.* Dublin: Mercier.

Martin, Joy. 1989. *A Wrong to Sweeten.* London: Grafton Books.

———. 1990. *Ulick's Daughter.* London: Grafton Books.

———. 1990. *The Moon Is Red in April.* London: Grafton Books.

———. 1991. *A Heritage of Wrong.* London: Grafton Books.

———. 1993. *Image of Laura.* London: Harper Collins.

Mathews, P. J. 2000. *New Voices in Irish Criticism.* Dublin: Four Courts.

Maxwell, D. E. S. 1984. *A Critical History of Modern Irish Drama 1891–1980.* Cambridge: Cambridge Univ. Press.

———. 1990. "Northern Ireland's Political Drama." *Modern Drama* 33, no. 1: 1–13.

McAuley, Chrissie, ed. N.d. [1970?]. *Women in a War Zone: Twenty Years of Resistance.* Dublin: AP/RN Print.

McBreen, Joan, ed. 1999. *White Page, The/ An Bhligeog Bh'an: Twentieth Century Irish Women Poets.* Cliffs of Moher, Ireland: Salmon Press.

McCafferty, Nell. 1981. *In the Eyes of the Law.* Dublin: Ward River Press.

———. 1981. *The Armagh Women.* Dublin: Co-op Books.

———. 1984. *The Best of Nell: A Selection of Writings Over Fourteen Years.* Dublin: Attic Press.

———. 1985. *A Woman to Blame: The Kerry Babies Case.* Dublin: Attic Press.

———. 1987. *Goodnight Sisters: Selected Writings.* Dublin: Attic Press.

———. 1988. *Peggy Deery: A Derry Family at War.* Dublin: Attic Press.

———. 1991. "At the Edges of the Picture: The Media, Women, and the War in the North." In *The Media and Northern Ireland,* ed. Bill Rolston. London: Macmillan. 207–13.

———. 1995. *War and Peace: Twenty-Five Years On.* Dublin: Attic Press.

McCarthy, Conor. 2000. *Modernisation, Crisis, and Culture in Ireland, 1969–1992.* Dublin: Four Courts.

McClintock, Anne. 1993. "Family Feuds: Gender, Nationalism, and the Family." *Feminist Review* 44: 61–81.

McConnell, Michael. 2002. *Changed Utterly: Ireland and the New Irish Psyche.* Dublin: Liffey.

McCrory, Moy. 1988. *Bleeding Sinners.* London: Methuen.

McCurry, Jacqueline. 1991. " 'Our Lady Dispossessed': Female Ulster Poets and Sexual Politics." *Colby Quarterly* 27, no. 1: 4–8.

McDonagh, Rosaleen. 1999. "Nomadism, Ethnicity, and Disability: A Challenge for Irish Feminism." *f/m* 3: 30–31.

McDonald, Peter. 1997. *Mistaken Identities: Poetry and Northern Ireland* Oxford: Clarendon Press.

McGivern, Marie Therese, and Margaret Ward. 1980. "Images of Women in Northern Ireland." *The Crane Bag* 4, no. 1: 66–72.

McGurk, Brendan. 1996. "Commitment and Risk in Anne Devlin's *Ourselves Alone* and *After Easter.*" In *The State of Play: Irish Theatre in the 'Nineties,* ed. Eberhard Bort. Trier: Wissenschaftlicher Verlag.

McIlroy, Brian. "When the Ulster Protestant and Unionist Looks: Spectatorship in (Northern) Irish Cinema." *Irish University Review* 23, no. 1 (Spring/Summer 1996): 29–30.

———. 2001. *Shooting to Kill: Filmmaking and the "Troubles" in Northern Ireland.* Wiltshire, UK: Flicks Books.

———. 1988. *World Cinema 4: Ireland.* Trowbridge, UK: Flicks Books; also known as *Irish Cinema: An Illustrated History.* Dun Laoghaire, Ireland: Anna Livia Press, 1988.

McKay, Susan. 1984. "A Literature of Our Own: Recent Fiction by Irish Women." *Linen Hall Review* 1, no. 1 (Spring): 12–14.

———. 2000. *Northern Protestants: An Unsettled People.* Belfast: Blackstaff Press.

McKillen, Beth. 1982. "Irish Feminism and Nationalist Separation." *Eire-Ireland* 17, no. 3: 52–67.

McLoone, Martin. 2000. *Irish Film: The Emergence of a Contemporary Cinema.* London: British Film Institute.

McMahon, Sean. 1966. "Backgrounds for the Study of Irish Literature." *Eire-Ireland* 1: 77–88.

McMichael, Gary. 1999. *Ulster Voice: In Search of Common Ground in Northern Ireland.* Boulder, CO: Roberts Rinehart.

McMinn, Joanna, and Margaret Ward. 1985. "Belfast Women Against All Odds." In *Personally Speaking: Women's Thoughts on Women's Issues,* ed. Liz Steiner-Scott. Dublin: Attic Press.

McMinn, Joseph. 1980. "Contemporary Novels on the Troubles." *Etudes Irlandaises* 5: 113–21.

———, ed. 1992. *The Internationalism of Irish Literature and Drama.* Gerrards Cross: Colin Smythe.

McMullan, Anna. 1993. "Irish Women Playwrights since 1958." In *British and Irish*

Women Dramatists since 1958, ed. Trevor R. Griffiths and Margaret Lewellyn-Jones. Buckingham: Open Univ. Press.

McNab, Eilish. 1984. "Behind the Walls: Prison as a Feminist Issue . . . Strip-searching in Armagh Jail . . . the Supergrass System." *Irish Feminist Review '84*. Dublin: Women's Community Press.

McVeigh, Robbie. 1998. "Is Sectarianism Racism? Theorising the Racism/Sectarianism Interface." In *Rethinking Northern Ireland*, ed. David Miller. London: Addison, Wesley, Longman. 179–96.

McWilliams, Monica. 1993. "The Church, the State and the Women's Movement in Northern Ireland." In *Irish Women's Studies Reader*, ed. Ailbhe Smyth. Dublin: Attic Press.

———. 1995. "Struggling for Peace and Justice: Reflections on Women's Activism in Northern Ireland." In *Irish Women's Voices: Past and Present*, ed. Joan Hoff and Moureen Coulter. Bloomington: Indiana Univ. Press.

———. 1998. "Violence Against Women in Societies Under Stress." In *Re-thinking Violence Against Women*, ed. R. Emerson Dobash and Russell P. Dobash. London: Sage.

———, and Avila Kilmurray. 1997. "Athene on the Loose: The Origins of the Northern Ireland Women's Coalition." *Irish Journal of Feminist Studies* 2, no. 2: 1–21.

———, and J. McKernan. 1993. *Bringing It Out into the Open: Domestic Violence in Northern Ireland*. Belfast: HMSO.

Meehan, Paula. 1991. *The Man Who Was Marked by Winter*. Loughcrew, Co. Meath: Gallery Press.

Miller, David, ed. 1998. *Rethinking Northern Ireland: Culture, Ideology, and Colonialism*. London: Longman.

Miller, Nancy. 1988. *Subject to Change: Reading Feminist Writing*. New York: Columbia Univ. Press.

Miller, R. L. R. Wilford, and F. Donoghue. 1996. *Women and Political Participation in Northern Ireland*. Aldershot: Avebury.

Mitchell, Geraldine. 1991. *Escape to the West*. Dublin: Attic Press.

———. 1992. *Welcoming the French*. Dublin: Attic Press.

Mitchell, Juliet. *Psychoanalysis and Feminism*. Harmondsworth: Pelican Books, 1974.

———, and Ann Oakley, eds. *The Rights and Wrongs of Women*. Harmondsworth: Penguin, 1976.

———, and Ann Oakley. 1986. *What Is Feminism?* Oxford: Basil Blackwell.

Mitchell, Paul, and Rick Wilford, eds. 1999. *Politics in Northern Ireland*. Oxford: Westview Press.

Mohanty, Chandra Talpade. 1984. "Under Western Eyes: Feminist Scholarship and Colonial Discourses." *Boundary* 2, no. 12: 338–58.

Moi, Toril. 1985. *Sexual/Textual Politics: Feminist Literary Theory*. London: Methuen.

Molloy, Frances. 1998. *Women Are the Scourge of the Earth: Collected Short Stories*. London: White Row Press.

Moloney, Caitriona, and Helen Thompson, eds. 2003. *Irish Women Writers Speak Out: Voices From the Field*. Syracuse: Syracuse Univ. Press.

Monteith, Moira. 1986. *Women's Writing: A Challenge to Theory*. Brighton: Harvester Press.

Morash, Christopher. 2002. *A History of Irish Theatre, 1601–2000*. Cambridge: Cambridge Univ. Press.

Morley, Louise. 1992. "Women's Studies, Difference, and Internalised Oppression." *Women's Studies International Forum* 15, no. 4: 517–25.

Morrissey, Hazel. 1991. "Economic Change and the Position of Women in Northern Ireland." In *Culture and Politics in Northern Ireland 1960–1990*, ed. Eamonn Hughes. Milton Keynes: Open Univ. Press.

Morrissy, Mary. 1993. *A Lazy Eye*. London: Jonathan Cape.

———. 1995. *Mother of Pearl*. New York: Scribner.

Moynahan, Julian. 1995. *Anglo-Irish: The Literary Imagination in a Hyphenated Culture*. Princeton: Princeton Univ. Press.

Muinzer, Philomena. 1987. "Evacuating the Museum: The Crisis of Playwrighting in Ulster." *New Theatre Quarterly* 3, no. 9: 44–63.

Muldoon, Paul, ed. 1986. *Faber Book of Contemporary Irish Poetry*. London, Boston: Faber and Faber.

Mulholland, Marie, and Ailbhe Smyth. 1999. "A North-South Dialogue." *f/m* 3: 10–17.

Mulvey, Anne. 1992. "Irish Women's Studies and Community Activism: Reflections and Exemplars." *Women's Studies International Forum* 15, no. 4: 507–16.

Mulvey, Cris. 1992. *Changing the View: Summary of the Evaluation Report on the Allen Lane Foundation's Programme for Women's Groups in Ireland 1989–1991*. Dublin: Allen Lane Foundation.

Mulvihill, Margaret. 1987. *Low Overheads*. London: Pandora.

Murphy, Brenda. 1995. "A Social Call." In *The Hurt World: Short Stories of the Troubles*, ed. Michael Parker. Belfast: Blackstaff Press: 270–72.

Murphy, Clíona. 1989. *The Women's Suffrage Movement and Irish Society in the Early Twentieth Century.* Hemel Hempstead: Harvester Wheatsheaf.

———. 1992. "Women's History, Feminist History or Gender History?" *The Irish Review* 12: 21–26.

———. 1997. "A Problematic Relationship: European Women and Nationalism 1870–1915." In *Women and Irish History,* ed. Mary O'Dowd and Maryann Gialanella Valiulis. Dublin: Wolfhound: 144–58.

Murray, Christopher. 1997. *Twentieth-Century Irish Drama: Mirror Up to Nation.* Manchester: Manchester Univ. Press.

Nash, Catherine. 1993. "Remapping and Renaming: New Cartographies of Identity, Gender, and Landscape in Ireland." *Feminist Review* 44: 39–57.

National Geographic. 1994. Special Issue on Ireland. 186, no. 3 (Sept.).

National Women's Forum: Irish Women Speak Out. 1981. Dublin: Co-Op Books.

Nelson, Dorothy. 1982. *In Night's City.* Dublin: Wolfhound Press.

———. 1987. *Tar and Feathers.* Dublin: Wolfhound Press.

New Internationalist. Special Edition on Northern Ireland. May 1994.

Nicholson, Linda, ed. 1990. *Feminism/Postmodernism.* New York: Routledge.

Ní Dhuibhne, Éilís. 1988. *Blood and Water.* Dublin: Attic Press.

Ní Dhuibhne, Éilís. 1991. *Eating Women Is Not Recommended.* Dublin: Attic Press.

———. 1995. *Voices on the Wind: Women Poets of the Celtic Twilight.* Dublin: New Island Books.

———. 1997a. *The "Inland Ice" and Other Stories.* Belfast: Blackstaff Press.

———. 1997b. *Milseog an Tsamhraium.* Dublin: Cois Life Teoranta.

———. 1999. *The Dancers Dancing.* Belfast: Blackstaff Press.

———. 2000. *Dúnmharú sa Daingean.* Dublin: Cois Life Teoranta.

———. 2001. *The Pale Gold of Alaska.* Belfast: Blackstaff Press.

———. 2003. *Midwife to the Fairies.* Dublin: Attic.

Northern Ireland Women's Coalition. 1998. *Common Cause: The Story of the Northern Ireland Women's Coalition.* Belfast: NIWC.

O'Brien, Aine. 1992. "Situating Differences: Gender, Nation, and Everyday Life." *Irish Reporter* 8, no. 4: 29–31.

O'Brien, James H. 1982. "Three Irish Women Story Writers of the 1970s." In *Literature and the Changing Ireland,* ed. Peter Connolly, 199–205. Gerrards Cross: Colin Smythe.

O'Brien, Peggy, ed. 2000. *The Wake Forest Book of Irish Women's Poetry, 1967–2000.* Winston-Salem, NC: Wake Forest Univ. Press.

O'Carroll, Íde and E. Collins, eds. 1995. *Lesbian and Gay Visions of Ireland: Towards the Twenty-First Century*. London: Cassell.

O'Casey, Sean. 1963. *Juno and the Paycock*. In *Three Plays*. London: MacMillan.

O'Connor, Clairr. 1989. *When You Need Them*. Galway: Salmon Press.

———. 1991. *Belonging*. Dublin: Attic Press.

———. 1995. *Love in Another Room*. Dublin: Marino Books.

O'Connor, Pat. 1998. *Emerging Voices: Women in Contemporary Irish Society*. Dublin: Institute of Public Administration.

O'Connor, Theresa. 1997. *The Comic Tradition of Irish Women Writers*. Gainesville: Univ. Press of Florida.

ó Cuilleanáin, Cormac. 1984. "Irish Publishers: A Nation Once Too Often." *The Crane Bag* 8, no. 2: 115–23.

O'Donnell, Mary. 1992. *The Light-Makers*. Dublin: Poolbeg.

———. 1996. *Virgin and the Boy*. Dublin: Poolbeg.

O'Dowd, Liam. 1996. *On Intellectuals and Intellectual Life in Ireland*. Belfast: Institute of Irish Studies.

O'Dowd, Mary, and Sabine Wichert. 1995. *Chattel, Servant, or Citizen: Women's Status in Church, State and Society*. Belfast: Queen's Univ. of Belfast.

O'Dowd, Mary, and Maryann Valiulus. 1997. *Women and Irish History*. Dublin: Wolfhound.

O'Faolain, Nuala. 1999. *Are You Somebody? The Accidental Memoir of a Dublin Woman*. Dublin: Henry Holt.

———. 2001. *My Dream of You*. London: Michael Joseph.

———. 2003. *Almost There*. London: Michael Joseph.

O'Farrell, Kathleen. 1992. *Kilbroney*. Kerry: Brandon.

O'Glaisne, Risteard. 1981. "Irish and the Protestant Tradition." *The Crane Bag* 5, no. 2: 33–45.

O'Halloran, Clare. 1987. *Partition and the Limits of Irish Nationalism*. Dublin: Gill and Macmillan.

O'Hara, Elizabeth. 1993. *Singles*. Dublin: Attic Press.

O'Leary, Mary. 1997. "Lesbianism and Feminism: A Personal Reflection." *Irish Journal of Feminist Studies* 2, no. 1: 63–66.

O'Leary, Philip. 1994. *The Prose Literature of the Gaelic Revival, 1881–1921: Ideology and Innovation*. Univ. Park: Pennsylvania State Univ. Press.

O'Mahony, Patrick, and Gerard Delanty, eds. 1998. *Rethinking Irish History: Nationalism, Identity, and Ideology*. New York: St. Martin's Press.

ó Muirithe, Diarmaid. 1996. *The Words We Use.* Dublin: Four Courts.

———. 1999. *A Dictionary of Anglo-Irish.* Dublin: Four Courts.

O'Neill, Cathleen. 1992. *Telling It Like It Is.* Dublin: Combat Poverty Agency.

———. 1999. "Reclaiming and Transforming the (Irish) Women's Movement." *f/m* 3: 41–44.

O'Riordan, Kate. 1995. *Involved.* London: Flamingo.

———. 1997. *The Boy in the Moon.* London: Flamingo.

———. 2001. *The Angel in the House.* London: Flamingo.

———. 2003. *The Memory Stones.* London: Pocket Books.

Ormsby, Frank, ed. 1979. *Poets from the North of Ireland.* Belfast: Blackstaff.

———, ed. 1992. *Rage for Order, A: Poetry of the Northern Ireland Troubles.* Belfast: Blackstaff.

O'Toole, Fintan. 1990. *A Mass for Jesse James: A Journey Through 1980s Ireland.* Dublin: Raven Arts.

———. 1994. *Black Hole, Green Card: The Disappearance of Ireland.* Dublin: New Island Books.

———. 1997. *The Ex-Isle of Erin: Images of a Global Ireland.* Dublin: New Island Books.

———. 1998. *The Lie of the Land: Irish Identities.* Dublin: New Island Books.

———. 2003. *After the Ball: Ireland After the Boom.* Dublin: New Island.

ó Tuama, Seán. 1991. *Repossessions: Selected Essays on the Irish Literary Experience.* Cork: Cork Univ. Press.

Owens, Rosemary Cullen, ed. 1984. *Smashing Times. A History of the Irish Women's Suffrage Movement 1889–1922.* Dublin: Attic Press.

Palmer, Paulina. 1989. *Annotated Bibliography of Women's Fiction and Feminist Theory.* Brighton: Harvester Press.

———. 1993. *Contemporary Lesbian Writing: Dreams, Desires, Differences.* Milton Keynes: Open Univ. Press.

———. 1999. *Lesbian Gothic: Transgressive Fictions.* London: Continuum International Publishing.

Parker, Michael. 1995. *The Hurt World: Short Stories of the Troubles.* Belfast: Blackstaff Press.

———. 2000. "Shadows on a Glass: Self-Reflexivity in the Fiction of Deirdre Madden." *Irish University Review* 30, no. 1: 82–102.

Parker, Rozsika, and Griselda Pollock. 1987. *Framing Feminism Art and the Women's Movement 1970–1985.* London: Pandora.

Parry, Benita. 1987. "Problems in Current Theories of Colonial Discourse." *Oxford Literary Review* 9, no. 1–2: 27–58.

Patten, Eve, ed. 1995. *Returning to Ourselves: Papers from the John Hewitt Summer School.* Belfast: Lagan Press.

Peillon, Michel. 1984. "The Structure of Irish Ideology Revisited." In *Culture and Ideology in Ireland,* ed. Chris Curtin, Mary Kelly, and Liam O'Dowd. Galway: Galway Univ. Press.

Pelan, Rebecca. 1991. "Selling Yourself Abroad: Edna O'Brien's 'Stage-Irishness.' " In *Irish-Australian Studies,* ed. Philip Bull, Chris McConville, and Noel McLachlan. Melbourne: La Trobe Univ. Press. 247–58.

———. 1993. "Edna O'Brien's 'Irishness': An 'Act' of Resistance." *Canadian Journal of Irish Studies* 19, no. 1: 67–78.

Pelan, Rebecca. 1996. "Writing, Gender and Ideology in Contemporary Ireland." In *Irish-Australian Studies,* ed. Richard Davis, Jennifer Livett, Anne-Maree Whitaker, and Peter Moore. Sydney: Crossing Press. 327–36.

———. 1997. "Edna O'Brien's World of Nora Barnacle." *Canadian Journal of Irish Studies* 23, no. 2: 49–61.

———. 1999a. "In a Class of Their Own: Women in Theatre in Contemporary Ireland." In *(Post)Colonial Stages: Critical and Creative Views on Drama, Theatre, and Performance,* ed. Helen Gilbert, 243–52. Hebden Bridge: Dangaroo.

———. 1999b. "Undoing That 'Other' Conquest: Women's Writing from the Republic of Ireland.' *Canadian Journal of Irish Studies* Twenty-fifth Anniversary Double Issue. 25, no. 1 & 2: 126–46.

———. 2000a. "Antagonisms: Revisionism, Postcolonialism and Feminism in Ireland." *Journal of Commonwealth and Postcolonial Studies* (Special Issue: Ireland as Postcolonial): 119–37.

———. 2000b. "Interview with Evelyn Conlon." *Hecate* 26, no. 2: 62–73.

———. 2001. "Dramatic Tiers: Contemporary Women's Drama from Northern Ireland." *Australian Journal of Irish Studies* 1, no. 1: 267–75.

———. 2003. Introduction to *Divas: New Irish Women's Writing.* Galway: Arlen House.

Pelaschiar, Laura. 2000. "Transforming Belfast: The Evolving Rose of the City in Northern Irish Fiction." *Irish University Review* 30, no. 1: 117–31.

Penley, Constance. 1991. *Technoculture.* Minnesota: Univ. of Minnesota Press.

———. 1993. *Male Trouble (Camera Obscura).* Minnesota: Univ. of Minnesota Press.

———. 1997. *NASA/Trek: Popular Science and Sex in America.* London: Verso.

———. *Feminism and Film Theory.* London: British Film Institute.

Pettitt, Lance. 1998. *Screening Ireland: Film and Television Representation.* Manchester: Manchester Univ. Press.

Plowman, Gillian. n.d. *Me and My Friend.* Unpublished play. Performed 1988.

Porter, Elisabeth. 2000. "Risks and Responsibilities: Creating Dialogical Spaces in Northern Ireland." *International Feminist Journal of Politics* 2, no. 2: 163–84.

Pratt, Annis. 1982. *Archetypal Patterns in Women's Fiction.* Sussex: Harvester Press.

Prendiville, Patricia. 1988. "Divorce in Ireland: An Analysis of the Referendum to Amend the Constitution, June 1986." *Women's Studies International Forum* 11, no. 4: 355–63.

Prondzynski, Heather von. 1993. *The Quest.* Dublin: Attic Press.

Purcell, Deirdre. 1994. *Francey.* Dublin: Macmillan.

Rafroidi, Patrick, and Maurice Harmon, eds. 1976. *The Irish Novel in Our Time.* Lille: Université de Lille.

———, and Terence Brown, eds. 1979. *The Irish Short Story.* Gerrards Cross: Colin Smythe.

Rafroidi, Patrick, and Maurice Harmon. 1975. *The Irish Novel in Our Time.* Lille: Publications de L'Universite de Lille III.

———. 1977. "Bovarysm and the Irish Novel." *Irish University Review* 7, no. 2: 237–43.

———, and Terence Brown, eds. 1979. *The Irish Short Story.* Buckinghamshire: Colin Smythe.

Rajan, Rajeswari Sunder. 1992. *The Lie of the Land.* India: Oxford Univ. Press.

———. 2003. *The Scandal of the State.* Durham: Duke Univ. Press.

Randall, Vicky. 1992. "The Politics of Abortion: Ireland in Comparative Perspective." *Canadian Journal of Irish Studies* 18, no. 1: 121–28.

Reizbaum, Marilyn. 1992. "Canonical Double Cross: Scottish and Irish Women's Writing." In *Decolonizing Tradition: New Views of Twentieth-Century "British" Literary Canons,* ed. Karen R. Lawrence. Urbana: Univ. of Illinois Press, 2004.

Renza, Louis A. 1984. *"A White Heron" and the Question of Minor Literature.* Madison: Univ. of Wisconsin Press.

Richards, Maura. 1981. *Two to Tango.* Dublin: Ward River Press.

———. 1998. *Single Issue.* Dublin: Poolbeg.

Ridd, Rosemary, and Helen Calloway. 1985. *Caught Up in Conflict.* London: Macmillan.

Robinson, Lilian S. 1978. *Sex, Class, and Culture.* Bloomington: Indiana Univ. Press.

———. 1990. "Sometimes, Always, Never: Their Women's History and Ours." *New Literary History* 2: 377–93.

Robinson, Mary. 1978. "Women and the New Irish State." In *Women in Irish Society,* ed. Margaret MacCurtain and Donncha O'Corráin. Dublin: Arlen House.

———. 1988. "Women and the Law in Ireland." *Women's Studies International Forum* 11, no. 4: 351–54.

Roche, Anthony. 2000. "Introduction: Contemporary Irish Fiction." *Irish University Review* 30, no. 1: xii–xi.

Rockett, Kevin. 1995. *Still Irish: A Century of the Irish in Film.* Dublin: Red Mountain.

———. 1996. *The Irish Filmography: Fiction Films, 1896–1996.* Dublin: Red Mountain.

———. 2003. *Ten Years After: The Irish Film Board, 1993–2003.* Dublin: Irish Film Board.

Rockett, Kevin, Luke Gibbons, and John Hill. 1988. *Cinema and Ireland.* Beckenham: Croom Helm.

Rooney, Eddie. 1984. "From Republican Movement to Workers' Party: An Ideological Analysis." In *Culture and Ideology in Ireland,* ed. Curtin, Chris Curtin, Mary Kelly, and Liam O'Dowd. Galway: Galway Univ. Press: 79–91.

Rooney, Eilish. 1995. "Political Division, Practical Alliance: Problems for Women in Conflict." In *Irish Women's Voices: Past and Present,* ed. Joan Hoff and Moureen Coulter. Bloomington: Indiana Univ. Press.

———. 1999. "Critical Reflections and Situated Accounts." *Irish Journal of Feminist Studies* 3, no. 1: 97–106.

Rosaldo, Michelle Z., and L. Lamphére, eds. *Women, Culture, and Society.* Stanford, CA: Stanford Univ. Press, 1974.

Ronsley, Joseph, ed. *Myth and Reality in Irish Literature.* Ontario: Wilfred Laurier Univ. Press, 1977.

Rose, Kieran. 1994. *Diverse Communities: The Evolution of Lesbian and Gay Politics in Ireland.* Galway: Arlen House.

Ross, Stuart. 1994. "An Interview with Bernadette Devlin McAliskey." *Against the Current* 9, no. 1 (Mar.–Apr.): 38–41.

Rossiter, Ann. 1992. " 'Between the Devil and the Deep Blue Sea': Irish Women, Catholicism and Colonialism." In *Refusing Holy Orders: Women and Fundamentalism in Britain,* ed. Gita Sahgal and Nira Yuval-Davis. London: Virago.

Russ, Diana. 1989. *Essentially Speaking: Feminism, Nature, and Difference.* New York: Routledge.

Ryan, Louise. 1995. "Traditions and Double Moral Standards: The Irish Suffragists Critique of Nationalism." *Women's History Review* 4, no. 4: 487–503.

———. 1996. *Irish Feminism and the Vote: An Anthology of the Irish Citizen Newspaper 1912–1920.* Dublin: Folens.

———. 1997. "A Question of Loyalty: War, Nation, and Feminism in Early Twentieth Century Ireland." *Women's Studies International Forum* 20, no. 1: 21–32.

Sahgal, Gita, and Nira Yuval-Davis, eds. 1992. *Refusing Holy Orders: Women and Fundamentalism in Britain*. London: Virago.

Sailer, Susan Shaw, ed. 1997. *Representing Ireland: Gender, Class, Nationality*. Gainesville: Univ. Press of Florida.

Sales, Rosemary. 1997. *Women Divided: Gender, Religion, and Politics in Northern Ireland*. London: Routledge.

Sands, Bobby. 1983. *One Day in My Life*. London: Pluto.

———. 1981. *Skylark Sing Your Lonely Song: An Anthology of the Writings of Bobby Sands*. Cork: Mercier Press.

Scanlan, Patricia. 1990. *City Girl*. Dublin: Poolbeg Press.

———. 1991. *Apartment 3B*. Dublin: Poolbeg Press.

———. 1992. *Finishing Touches*. Dublin: Poolbeg Press.

———. 1994. *Foreign Affairs*. Dublin: Poolbeg Press.

———. 1996. *Promises*. Dublin: Poolbeg Press.

———. 1997. *Mirror, Mirror*. Dublin: Poolbeg Press.

The Second Blackstaff Book of Short Stories. 1991. Belfast: Blackstaff Press.

Segal, Lynne. 1999. *Why Feminism?* Oxford: Blackwell.

Sewell, Frank. 2000. *Modern Irish Poetry: A New Alhambra*. Oxford: Oxford Univ. Press.

Shannon, Catherine B. 1989. "Catholic Women and the Northern Irish Troubles." In *Ireland's Terrorist Trauma*, ed. Yonah Alexander and Alan O'Day. New York: Harvester Wheatsheaf.

———. 1992. "Recovering the Voices of the Women of the North." *Irish University Review* 12: 27–33.

———. 1995. "Women in Northern Ireland." In *Chattel, Servant, or Citizen: Women's Status in Church, State, and Society*, ed. Mary O'Dowd and Sabine Wichert. Historical Studies 19. Belfast: Institute of Irish Studies.

———. 1997. "The Woman Writer as Historical Witness: Northern Ireland, 1968–1994. An Interdisciplinary Perspective." In *Women and Irish History*, ed. Mary Ann Gialanella and Mary O'Dowd. Dublin: Wolfhound Press.

Sherry, Ruth. 1991. "How Is Irish Writing Reviewed?" *Cyphers* 31: 5–11.

Showalter, Elaine. 1984. *A Literature of their Own: British Women Novelists from Brontë to Lessing*. London: Virago.

———, ed. 1986. *The New Feminist Criticism: Essays on Women, Literature and Theory*. London: Virago.

———. 1987. *The Female Malady: Women, Madness and English Culture 1830–1980*. London: Virago.

————. 1989. *Speaking of Gender.* London: Routledge.

————. 1991. *Sister's Choice: Tradition and Change in American Women's Writing: The Clarendon Lectures, 1989.* Oxford: Clarendon Press.

————. 1993. *Daughters of Decadence: Women Writers of the Fin-de-Siecle.* London: Virago.

————. 1998. *Teaching Literature.* London: Picador.

Simons, Margaret A. 1979. "Racism and Feminism: A Schism in the Sisterhood." *Feminist Studies* 5, no. 2: 384–99.

Sinn Féin Policy Document. 1984. "Women in the New Ireland." (no pub. details.) Stamped 'Trinity College Library Dublin' 11 July.

Smith, Barbara. 1991. "The Truth That Never Hurts: Black Lesbians in Fiction in the 1980s." In *Feminism: An Anthology of Literary Theory and Criticism,* ed. Robyn Warhol and Diane Price Herndl. New Brunswick, NJ: Rutgers Univ. Press. 690–712.

Smyth, Ailbhe. 1985. "Women and Power in Ireland: Problems, Progress, Practice." *Women's Studies International Forum* 8, no. 4: 255–62.

————. 1987a. "Feminism in the South of Ireland: A Discussion." *H.U./The Honest Ulsterman* 83: 41–57.

————. 1987b. "Where the Women Are: Some Reflections on Women and Adult Education in Ireland." *Studies* 76, no. 302: 185–98.

————. 1991. "The Floozie in the Jacuzzi." *Feminist Studies* 17, no. 1:6–28.

————. 1992a. " 'A Great Day for the Women of Ireland': The Meaning of Mary Robinson's Presidency for Irish Women." *The Canadian Journal of Irish Studies* 8, no. 1: 61–75.

————. 1992b. "Sex Is Like Pitch: Feminism and Sexuality." *Irish Reporter* 8, no. 4: 13–15.

————. 1995. "States of Change: Reflections on Ireland in Several Uncertain Parts." *Feminist Review* 50: 24–43.

————. 1996. *Feminism, Community, Politics.* Dublin: WERRC Annual Conference Papers, UCD.

————, ed. 1992. *The Abortion Papers: Ireland.* Dublin: Attic Press.

————, ed. 1993a. *Irish/Women's Studies Reader.* Dublin: Attic Press.

————, ed. 1993b. *Wildish Things: An Anthology of New Irish Women's Writing.* Dublin: Attic Press.

Smyth, Gerry. 1997. *The Novel and the Nation.* London: Pluto.

————. 1998. *Decolonisation and Criticism: The Construction of Irish Literature.* London: Pluto.

————. 1999. "Irish Studies, Postcolonial Theory and the 'New' Essentialism." *Irish Studies Review* 7, no. 2: 211–20.

Speed, Anne. 1992. "Feminism and Republicanism." *Irish Reporter* 8, no. 4: 34–36.

Spelman, Elizabeth V. 1989. *Inessential Woman: The Problem of Exclusion in Feminist Theory.* Boston: Beacon.

Spivak, Gayatri Chakravorty. 1990. *The Post-Colonial Critic: Interviews, Strategies, Dialogues.* London: Routledge.

————. 1993a. *In Other Worlds: Essays in Cultural Politics.* New York: Routledge.

————. 1993b. *Outside in the Teaching Machine.* New York: Routledge.

————. 2003. *Death of a Discipline.* New York: Columbia Univ. Press.

Steiner Scott, Liz. 1985. *Personally Speaking: Women's Thoughts on Women's Issues.* Dublin: Attic Press.

Stevens, Lorna, Stephen Brown, and Pauline Maclaran. 2000. "Gender, Nationality and Cultural Representations of Ireland: An Irish Woman's Place?" *European Journal of Women's Studies* 7: 405–21.

Storey, Mark. 1988. *Poetry and Ireland Since 1800: A Source Book.* London: Routledge.

St. Peter, Christine. 1991. "Jennifer Johnston's Irish Troubles: A Materialist-Feminist Reading." In *Gender in Irish Writing,* ed. Toni O'Brien Johnson and David Cairns. Buckingham: Open Univ. Press. 112–18.

————, and Ron Marken. 1992. "Women and Irish Politics." *Canadian Journal of Irish Studies* 18, no. 1.

————. 2000. *Changing Ireland: Strategies in Contemporary Women's Fiction.* Basingstoke: Macmillan.

Stringer, Peter, and Gillian Robinson. 1991. *Social Attitudes in Northern Ireland.* Belfast: Blackstaff Press.

Strong, Eithne. *Degrees of Kindred.* Dublin: Tansy Books, 1979.

————. 1993. *The Love Riddle.* Dublin: Attic Press.

————. 1993. *Flesh: The Greatest Sin.* Dublin: Attic Press.

————. 1993. *Spatial Nosing: New and Selected Poems.* Dublin: Salmon Press.

Suleri, Sara. 1992. "Woman Skin Deep: Feminism and the Postcolonial Condition." *Critical Enquiry* 18, no. 4: 756–69.

Sullivan, Megan. 1999. *Women in Northern Ireland.* Gainesville: Univ. Press of Florida.

Swift, Todd, and Martin Mooney, eds. 1988. *Map-Makers Colours: New Poets of Northern Ireland.* Montreal: Nu-Age Editions.

Taillon, Ruth. 1992. Compiled on behalf of the Women's Support Network. *1993 Directory of Women's Voluntary Organisations in Northern Ireland.* Belfast: Trans-Act-Services.

Tallis, Raymond. 1988. *In Defence of Realism*. London: Edward Arnold.

Taylor, Alice. 1988a. *To School Through the Fields*. Kerry: Brandon Press.

———. 1988b. *An Irish Country Diary*. Kerry: Brandon Press.

———. 1989. *Close to the Earth*. Kerry: Brandon Press.

———. 1990. *Quench the Lamp*. Kerry: Brandon Press.

———. 1992. *The Village*. Kerry: Brandon Press.

———. 1995. *The Night Before Christmas*. Kerry: Brandon Press.

Thompson, Richard J. 1989. *Everlasting Voices: Aspects of the Modern Irish Short Story*. New York: Whitson Publishing.

Thompson, Spurgeon. 2001. "Introduction: Towards an Irish Cultural Studies." *Cultural Studies* 15, no. 1: 1–11.

Throne, Marilyn. 1991. "Irish Women Writers." *Colby Library Quarterly* 27, no. 1: 1–59.

Thuente, Mary Helen. 1994. *The Harp Restrung: The United Irishmen and the Rise of Irish Literary Nationalism*. Syracuse: Syracuse Univ. Press.

Todd, Janet. 1991. *Dictionary of British Women Writers*. London: Routledge.

———. 2001. *Mary Wollstonecraft*. London: Weidenfeld & Nicholson.

———. 2003a. *Rebel Daughters: Ireland in Conflict 1798*. New York: Viking.

———. 2003b. *Oroonoko, or the History of the Royal Slave (Aphra Behn)*. Harmondsworth; Middlesex: Penguin.

Todd, Loreto. 1989. *The Language of Irish Literature*. London: MacMillan Education.

———. 1999. *Green English: Ireland's Influence on the English Language*. Dublin: O'Brien Press.

Trotter, Mary. 2001. *Ireland's National Theaters: Political Performance and the Origins of the Irish Dramatic Movement*. Syracuse: Syracuse Univ. Press.

Tudor, Henry. 1972. *Political Myth*. New York: Praeger Publishers.

Tweedy, Hilda. 1992. *A Link in the Chain: The Story of the Irish Housewives Association 1942–1992*. Dublin: Attic Press.

Tyler, Carole-Anne. 1994. "Passing Narcissism, Identity, and Difference." *Differences* 6, no. 2 & 3: 212–48.

Tymoczko, Maria. 1999. *Translation in a Postcolonial Context: Early Irish Literature in English Translation*. Manchester: St. Jerome.

———, and Colin Ireland, eds. 2003. *Language and Tradition in Ireland: Continuities and Displacements*. Amherst: Univ. of Massachusetts Press.

Tynan, Jane. 1996. "Redefining Boundaries: Feminism, Women, and Nationalism in Ireland." *UCG Women's Studies Centre Review* 4: 21–30.

Urquhart, Diane. 1996. "In Defence of Ulster and the Empire: The Ulster Women's Unionist Council, 1911–1940." *UCG Women's Studies Centre Review* 4: 31–40.

———. 2000. *Women in Ulster Politics, 1890–1940*. Dublin: Irish Academic Press.

Valéra, Éamon de. 1943. "Speech to the Nation." Broadcast on Radio Éireann, 17 March.

Valiulis, Maryann Gialanella. 1992. "Defining Their Role in the New State: Irishwomen's Protest Against the Juries Act of 1927." *Canadian Journal of Irish Studies* 18, no. 1: 43–60.

———. 1995. "Power, Gender, and Identity in the Irish Free State." *Journal of Women's History* 6, no. 4/7, no. 1: 117–36.

Vance, Norman. 1990. *Irish Literature: A Social History. Tradition, Identity and Difference*. Oxford: Blackwell.

———. 2002. *Irish Literature Since 1800*. London, New York: Longman.

Viney, Ethna. 1989. *Ancient Wars: Sexuality and Oppression*. Dublin: Attic Press LIP Pamphlet.

Walshe, Dolores. 1992. *Moon Mad*. Dublin: Wolfhound Press.

Walshe, Éibhear. 1992. "Women in the Annex: Women Writers Talk to Eibhear Walshe about the Field Day Anthology." *Irish Studies Review* 2 (Winter): 13–14.

———. 1993. *Ordinary People Dancing: Essays on Kate O'Brien*. Cork: Cork Univ. Press.

———, ed. 1997. *Sex, Nation, and Dissent in Irish Writing*. Cork: Cork Univ. Press.

Ward, Margaret. 1981. " 'The Boldest and Most Unmanageable Revolutionaries.' Anna Parnell and the Ladies' Land League." *Hecate* 7, no. 2: 70–87.

———. 1986. *A Difficult, Dangerous Honesty: Ten Years of Feminism in Northern Ireland*. Belfast: Women's Book Collective.

———. 1993a. " 'Suffrage First—Above All Else!' ": An Account of the Irish Suffrage Movement." In *Irish Women's Studies Reader*, ed. Ailbhe Smyth. Dublin: Attic Press. 20–44.

———. 1993b. *Maud Gonne: A Life*. London: HarperCollins.

———. 1995. *In Their Own Voice: Women and Irish Nationalism*. Dublin: Attic Press.

———. 1997a. "Nationalism, Pacifism, Internationalism: Louie Bennett, Hanna Sheehy-Skeffington, and the Problems of 'Defining Feminism.' " In *Gender and Sexuality in Modern Ireland*, ed. Maryann Gialanella Valiulus and Anthony Bradley. Amherst: Univ. of Massachusetts Press. 60–84.

———. 1997b. *Hanna Sheehy Skeffington: A Life*. Dublin: Attic Press.

———. 1998. "National Liberation Movements and the Question of Women's Liberation: The Irish Experience." *Gender and Imperialism*. Ed. Clare Midgley. Manchester: Manchester Univ. Press.

————. n.d. "Women in Ireland 1968–1988: The Reality and the Illusion of Freedom." Unpublished paper. Queen's Univ. of Belfast. Offprint No. 8779.

Ward, Margaret, and Marie-Therese McGivern. 1980. "Images of Women in Northern Ireland." *The Crane Bag* 4, no. 1: 66–72.

Ward, Margaret, and Louise Ryan. 2002. *Gender, Identity, and the Irish Press, 1922–1937: Embodying the Nation.* Lampeter: Edwin Mellen Press.

Ware, Vron. 1992. *Beyond the Pale: White Women, Racism, and History.* London: Verso.

Warner, Marina. 1983. *Alone of All Her Sex: The Myth and Cult of the Virgin Mary.* New York: Vintage.

Watson, G. J. *Irish Identity and the Literary Identity.* London: Croom Helm, 1979.

Weedon, Chris. 1987. *Feminist Practice and Poststructuralist Theory.* Oxford: Basil Blackwell.

Weekes, Ann Owens. 1990. *Irish Women Writers: An Uncharted Tradition.* Lexington: Kentucky Univ. Press.

Welch, Robert. 1993. *Changing States: Transformations in Modern Irish Writing.* London: Routledge.

————. 1996. *The Oxford Companion to Irish Literature.* Oxford: Oxford Univ. Press.

Williams, J. E. Caerwyn, and Patrick K. Ford. 1992. *The Irish Literary Tradition.* Cardiff: Univ. of Wales Press.

Wills, Clair. 2001. "Women, Domesticity, and the Family: Recent Feminist Work in Irish Cultural Studies." *Cultural Studies* 15, no. 1: 33–57.

Wilmer, Steve. 1991. "Women's Theatre in Ireland." *New Theatre Quarterly* 7, no. 28: 353–60.

————. 1992. "Beyond National Theatre." *Irish Stage and Screen* 4, no. 3: 13–14.

Wilson, Elizabeth. 1992. *The Sphinx in the City: Urban Life, the Control of Disorder, and Women.* Berkeley: Univ. of California Press.

Women's Rights in Ireland. A Repsol Pamphlet. Dublin: National Women's Committee, Sinn Fein, 1975.

Women's Studies International Forum. 1988. Special Issue on Irish Feminism 11, no. 4.

Wondrich, Roberta Gefter. 2000. "Exilic Returns: Self and History Outside Ireland in Recent Irish Fiction." *Irish University Review* 30, no. 1: 1–16.

Wright, Elizabeth. 1984. *Psychoanalytic Criticism: Theory in Practice.* London: RKP.

————. 1998. *Psychoanalytic Criticism: A Reappraisal.* London: Polity.

————. 2000. *Postmodern Encounters: Lacan and Postfeminism.* London: Icon Books.

Wright, Nancy Means, and Dennis J. Hanna. 1990. "Irish Women Poets: Breaking the Silence." *Canadian Journal of Irish Studies* 16, no. 2: 57–65.

Write to the Core: Cregagh Writing Group. 1992. Belfast: Greenway Women's Press.

Yuval-Davis, Nira, and Floya Anthias, eds. 1993. *Racialized Boundaries: Race, Nation, Gender, Colour, and Class and the Anti-Racist Struggle.* London: Routledge.

———. 1997. *Gender and Nation.* London: Sage.

———, and Pnina Werbner, eds. 1999. *Women, Citizenship, and Difference.* London: Zed Books.

———, and Tijen Uguris, eds. 2004. *Space, Power, and Participation: Ethnic and Gender Divisions in Tenants' Participation in Public Housing.* London: Ashgate.

Index

abortion, 16n. 6, 20, 40, 100
Adams, Gerry, 113
"Adultery" and Other Stories and Poems, The, 4
Alice in Thunderland: Fairytales for Feminists (M. Kelly), 7
"All Fall Down" (Burke), 34
All of Us There (P. Devlin), 62; and time, 14–16, 118–20; 63
alternative revival, 21–22
Alyn, Marjory, 58
Anderson, Benedict, 50
Anderson, Linda, 83, 84–85, 92, 93
An End . . . and a Beginning, 5
Anglo-American feminism, xxxi–xxxii
Anglo-Irish literary tradition, 1–2
An Interlude with Seagulls: Memoirs of a Long Kesh Internee (B. Devlin), 68
"An Irish Fairy Tale" (Molloy), 56
Anti-Discrimination Act, 16n. 6
Anything School Can Do You Can Do Better (Mullarney), 4
Arlen House, 3, 4–5
Arnold, Matthew, 111
Ashby, Sue, 91
Aston, Elaine, 86
Attic Press, 3, 6–7, 12

Bambara, Toni Cade, 13–14
Barbara (fict.), 40–41
Bardwell, Leland, 6, 37–39, 40
Barr, Fiona, 80–82, 83
Barrett, Michèle, 106
Batsleer, Janet, xxx

Battersby, Eileen, xx–xxi
Beale, Jenny, 20
Beckett, Mary, 55–56, 85
Beckett, Samuel, 1, 126–27
Belfast Woman, A (M. Beckett), 55
Belle of the Belfast City, The (Reid), 86
Benstock, Shari, 57
Bergmann, Laurel, xv–xvi
Beth (fict.), 89
Between People, The (Manning), 58
Beyond Feminist Aesthetics (Felski), xxxi
Big House at Inver, The (Somerville/Ross), 2
Big House tradition, 1–2, 10, 59–60
Binchy, Maeve, 40
Binlids (B. Murphy et al.), 72
Biography of Desire (Dorcey), 9, 10, 11
"Birches" (Frost), 81
Blackstaff Press, 52, 53
Blackwood, Caroline, 59–60
Blind Fiddler of Glenadauch, The (Jones), 91
blood sacrifice myth, 66–68
Bloom (fict.), 11
Boland, Eavan, 4, 5
Bondagers (Glover), 90
Bork, Shirley, 58
Bowen, Elizabeth, 2
Boylan, Clare, 28, 32, 40, 42–43
Bray House, The (Ní Dhuibhne), 8
"Bride of Christ, The" (Strong), 42
Brophy, Catherine, 8, 32–33, 60
Burke, Helen Lucy, 5, 29–32, 34, 48
Butler-Cullingford, Elizabeth, 112
But Where Can I Go? Homeless Women in Dublin (S. Kennedy), 4

"Cage, The" (McEnaney), 55
Cairns, David, 19–20, 66–67
Cal (MacLaverty), 82
Callaghan, Louise C., 4
Callaghan, Mary Rose, 6, 42
"Calling of the Green, The" (M. Sands),
    61–62
Calvinist legacy, 96–97
capitalism, 50, 80
Captains and the King, The (Johnston), 56
Captive Voice, The/An Glór Gafa, 68
Cara (fict.), 10–11
Carleton, William, 127
Carr, Ruth Hooley, 52, 53–54
Castle Rackrent (Edgeworth), 2
Catherine (fict.), 40–41
Catholic Church: Conlon's interest in, 14;
    conservative alliance with state, xxiii,
    xxiv, 14–17; Daly's critique of, 33–34;
    freedom of women in, 100; as political
    agent, 94–95; separation from state,
    2–3; suffrage movement and, 24; as
    theme of women's literature, 3, 37–39,
    41–45, 51; view of Northern Ireland,
    70
Cauterised (Speers), 90
Cedric (fict.), 38
"Cedric Dear" (Bardwell), 38
Censorship of Publications Act of 1929,
    15
Charabanc Theatre Company, 86, 89–91
Charlotte (fict.), 48
"Cherubim" (Walker), 37
chick lit, xiii, xix, xxxii, 134
Cinderella on the Ball: Fairytales for Feminists,
    7
Civil Rights movement, 63, 73
Civil Services Act, 16n. 6
Civil War antagonisms, xxiii
Claffey, Anne, 7
Clancy, Tom, 82
Clark, Clara, 4
Clear, Caitríona, xxxiii
Cloud, Darrah, 90
Colette (fict.), 84
community-based women's groups,
    100–101

Conlon, Evelyn, 6, 13–14, 40, 43–47;
    "My Head Is Opening," 46–47
Connolly, James, 20, 21, 26
Constitution (1937), xxiv, 16–18, 26
Constitution (1972), 2
contraception, 15–16, 20, 100
Conversations with Palestinian Women
    (Lentin), 12
Coping Alone (Clark), 4
Coulter, Carol, xviii
Coward, Rosalind, 124, 130
creative production: connection to
    political movements, xxii–xxiii; effect
    of, xviii; influence of material
    conditions on, xxiv; political factors
    affecting, 14; women's movement and,
    xx
Criminal Law Act, 16
crisis of the subject, 104–5
Crone, Anne, 4
Crone, Joni, 8, 9
Crow Goddess, The (Finney), 8
Crying Game, The (Jordan), 83
Cú Chulainn, 65–66
Cuckoo (Anderson), 93
Cullen, Linda, 8
Cullen, Mary, xxxiii, 5, 23
Cullimore, Claudine, xi
cultural imperialism, 20–21, 50–51, 109,
    111
cultural issues, xi–xii, xxxii–xxxiii
Cummins, Mary, 9
"Curse, A" (B. Murphy), 72–73
"Custody Case, The" (Binchy), 40

Daisy Chain War (O'Neill), 13
Daly, Bishop Cahal, 70
Daly, Ita, 32, 33–34, 36, 48–49, 60
Dan (fict.), 84
Dangerous Fictions (Daly), 48–49
D'Arcy, Margaretta, 64
Dark Hole Days, The (Woods), 83–84
Dark Paradise (Brophy), 8
Davies, Tony, xxx
"Day of the Christening, The"
    (O'Carroll), 40

Deane, Seamus, 16, 21, 22, 65
Death Grows on You (Hill), 83
Devlin, Anne, 83, 85, 86–88
Devlin, Bobby, 68
Devlin, Polly, 62–63
Did You Hear the One About the Irishman (Reid), 86
Did Your Granny Have a Hammer? (Owens), 6
dirty protest, 64
divorce, 16n. 6, 17, 20, 70, 100
Dodds, Nigel, 98
domestic violence, 39–40, 56, 88, 90–91, 100
Donna (fict.), 86–88
Donoghue, Emma, 9, 10–11, 13, 117–18
Donovan, Katie, 127
Dora, or the Shifts of the Heart (P. Devlin), 63
Doran, Mary, 5
Dorcey, Mary, 7, 8–9, 22, 120
"Dove of Peace, The" (Bardwell), 39
Dowling, Clare, xiii
Down Town Women's Center, 65
Doyle, Roddy, 115
drama, xxiv, 85–92, 93–94
"Dream Recurring" and Other Stories and Poems, A, 4
Dubblejoint Productions, 72, 86n. 6
Dubliners (Joyce), 126
Duffy, Rita, xxii
Dunlop, Anne, xiii

Eagleton, Terry, 107, 118
Easter 1916 rebellion, 66, 67, 68
Edge, Sarah, 82
Edgeworth, Maria, 2
Edwards, Ruth Dudley, 8
Edwina (fict.), 60–61
Emigration Matters for Women, 7
employment, 16, 18, 94
Employment Equality Act, 16n. 6
"En Famille" (R. Kelly), 40–41
Enright, Anne, 13, 117, 118
Essential Guide for Women in Ireland, The (Martin), 4
essentialism, 121
ethnicity, 134

"Evils of Modern Dancing, The," 15
experimental fiction, 1, 13, 116–17, 126

Fairweather, Eileen, 71
family ideology: oppression of women and, xxiv; women's involvement in national struggles and, 82–83; women writers' engagement with, xiv–xv, 10, 48–49, 50
family law, 16n. 6, 17–18
"Family Picnic, A" (Daly), 36
family planning, 16n. 6
Farrell, Mairead, 64–65n. 3
Far Side of the Lough, The (P. Devlin), 63
Fast Forward (Dowling), xiii
"Fate of Aoife and the Children of Aobh, The" (Dorcey), 7
father figures, 10–11, 34–36, 60
Fean, Mary Ellen, 39–40
Felski, Rita, xxxi, 116–17, 130
Female Experience: The Story of the Women's Movement in Ireland, The (Rose), 4
Female Line, The, 52, 54–55, 58, 72, 75
feminism: accusations of exclusivity/ elitism, xxvii; as alternative political stance, xxvii; challenges to in Ireland, xxviii–xxix; complexities of term's use, xviii–xix; contemporary shift in emphasis, 102–3; contexts of in Ireland, xxii–xxiii; criticism of, xxxii–xxxiv; cross-border movement in Ireland, 114; current activity in Ireland, xxvii–xxix, 134; development of in Northern Ireland, 63–65, 71; development of new identity and, 50; diversification of, 102–3; facilitation of radicalism, xix–xx, xxvi–xxvii; foremost issues of, 104–5; formation of different consciousnesses in Ireland, xii; influence in Northern Ireland, xxiii, 52–53; interdisciplinary aspects of, xxi–xxii; lesbianism conjoining with, 9; nationalism and, 131–32; nature of literary criticism of, xxi–xxxi; postcolonialism and, 108–15; postmodernism and, xxxiii;

feminism (cont.)
    poststructuralists and, xxxi, 104–7;
    Protestant unionism and, 97–99;
    psychoanalytic approach to, 106;
    realist literature of, 119–20; recent
    changes in writings of, 134;
    representations of modern Ireland, 14;
    shift in discourses of, 124, 134;
    suffrage in Ireland and, 22–28;
    theoretical debates, xxxii–xxxiv, 130;
    theories of identity, 115–16; women's
    movement and, xiv; women's writings
    and, xxii. See also women's movement
Field Day Anthology of Irish Writing (Deane
    et al.), xx–xxi
Fields, Rona, 20
Finney, Patricia, 8
"Flights of Angels" (Murray), 40
Flitton, Sheila, 13
For All That I Found There (Blackwood),
    59–60
Forced Upon Us (B. Murphy), 72
Foster, R. F., 110n. 1
Freeman, Jo, xxxi
Free State. See Republic of Ireland
"Free Women in a Free Nation"
    (Markievicz), 23
French feminist theory, xxxi–xxxii, 105,
    107
Frieda (fict.), 86–88
Frost, Robert, 81

"Garden of Eden, The" (Ní Dhuibhne),
    40
Gardiner, Frances, 24
Gates, The (Johnston), 56
gender: current theory debates on, 130;
    national identity and, 44–45, 50, 132;
    realism and, 116–17
generational differences, 75–78, 88–89,
    93
genres: distinction of at Arlen House, 4;
    of Irish women writers, xxiiv, xxv, 133;
    of Northern Irish males, 82–85;
    stigmatization of realism, 116;
    thrillers, 8, 82–85; of women writer of

    the Republic of Ireland, 8–10; of
    women writers of Northern Ireland,
    82–92
Gibbons, Luke, 27
Girls Don't Do Honours (M. Cullen), 5
Girls in the Big Picture (Jones), 91
Give Them Stones (M. Beckett), 55
Glover, Sue, 90
"Goldilocks Finds a Home" (Russell), 7
Gold in the Streets (Jones), 91
Goldring, Maurice, 94, 96–97
Goodfellow, Mary Teresa, 73
government corruption, 73–75
Government of Ireland Act, 16
greatness, definition of, 125–27
Gregory, Augusta, 26

Haberstroh, Patricia Boyle, xxix, 127
Hamster Wheel, The (Jones), 91
Harding, Sandra, 115
Harry's Game (Seymour), 82
Hayes, Alan, 5n. 4
H Block/Armagh hunger strikes, 66–67n.
    4, 68
hegemonic ideologies: creation of
    Republic of Ireland as, 25; women's
    critique of, xiv–xv; women's writings
    as counter to, xxvii, 50–51
Hennessy, Rosemary, 104, 130
Henry John Shiels (fict.), 77, 79–80
He's Got to Go (O'Flanagan), xiii
Hidden Symptoms (D. Madden), 75, 83, 84
"Hi Ho, It's Off to Strike We Go!"
    (Maher), 7
Hill, Myrtle, xxxiii
Hill, Niki, 83
historical fiction, 13
history: feminist literature's engagement
    with, 105–6; formulations of, 112–13;
    fusion with myth in novels, 8; impact
    of women's writings on, xxii, 132; Irish
    feminist critics' work and, xxxii–xxxiii;
    of Irish males, xxii–xxiii;
    poststructuralist reluctance to engage,
    107; representation of women in,
    23–25, 26, 108; reproduction of

representations of, xxvi; revisionism
and, 110; role in Northern Ireland's
Troubles, 68–69; transformation of by
leaders, 27; women's emphasis on,
xxix–xxx
Holmes, Máire C., 8
Hood (Donoghue), 9, 10–12
Hooley, Ruth, 52, 53–54
Hopkins, Alannah, 13
Hoult, Norah, 4
House, The (Bardwell), 38
"Housekeeper's Cut" (Boylan), 28
housing, 73–82
How Many Miles to Babylon? (Johnston),
56
Hughes, Eamonn, 82–85
"Hyacinths" (C. O'Connor), 35, 60, 61

identity: challenge to binaries of, 88–89;
crisis of in Northern Ireland, 62;
feminist theories of, 115; Irish
feminists need of, xxxii–xxxiii. *See also*
national identity
ideologies: affect on writing, xxvii; blind
followers of, 79–80; effect on
individuals, 83; as enemy of women's
movement, 50; of nationalism, 69–70;
subversion of gender/class issues by,
80–81; women's involvement in
national struggles and, 82. *See also*
hegemonic ideologies
IFI. *See* Irish Feminist Information (IFI)
If You Can Talk You Can Write, 5
I Know My Own Heart (Donoghue), 9
Imagined Communities (Anderson), 50
imperialism, 14, 68–69, 80, 109, 114
independence struggle, 66–67, 68–69
industrialization, xxiii, 94
inequality, 63, 75
infanticide, 40
Innes, C. L., 26
"In Reply to Florence" (Conlon), 40
Interlude (M. Richards), 41–42
international feminism, 13–14, 50
international literature, 12–13
interpretive community, xiv

Ireland: demographics of, xiii; effects
of partitioning, 26; feminization
of, 19–20, 26–28, 111–13, 124;
globalization and, xii–xiii; as minority
culture, xxvix, xxxii; postcolonial
attempts at redefinition, 14–21. *See
also* Northern Ireland; Republic of
Ireland
Irish feminism, 107–8
Irish Feminist Information (IFI), 3, 5–6
Irish Feminist Review, 6
Irish language, 8, 11
Irish literary revival, 1
Irish Women: Image and Achievement (ed.
Chuilleanáin), 4
Irish Women's Guide Book and Diary, 5
Irish women writers: approach of,
131–32; Big House tradition and, 1–2;
change in focus after 1970, xii–xiii;
content of works of, xiii, xiv–xv;
contexts of writings, xii, xiv, xxii–xxiii,
131; counterhegemonic function of,
xxvii, 50–51; difficulties in discussion
of, xxxiii–xxxiv, 115–16, 130;
feminism of, xix–xx, 128–29; focus of,
xvi–xvii, xxii, xxiii–xxv, 3; freedom of,
2; image of women and, 26, 131, 133;
influence of, xiii–xiv, xxvi–xxvii; lack
of great representative of, 122–25;
literary freedom of, ix–x; major theory
debates and, 104, 130–31;
marginalization of, 104–5, 107–9;
modes of critique of, xxi–xxii, 122–26,
127–30; motivations of, xix; narrative
features of, xxvii; occlusion of,
xxix–xxxi, 53–55, 82; place in literary
world, xxxi–xxxii; polarization of
politics and, xxvii; politicization of,
xviii–xxiv; publication of works,
xvi–xvii, 53–55; ruminations
concerning, 122–23; shift in creative
focus, xxvii–xxviii; use of realism, xxv,
xxix–xxx, 116–24, 128–30, 133;
women's presses and, 3–7. *See also*
women writers of Northern Ireland;
women writers of the Republic of
Ireland

"Irish Women Writers, Marginalized by Whom?" (Donovan), 127
Irish writing, 1, 122–30. *See also* Irish women writers; women writers of Northern Ireland; women writers of the Republic of Ireland

Jayawardena, Kumari, 108
Jeffares, A. Norman, 118
Joe (fict.), 57–58, 84
Joe Best (fict.), 73–75
Johansson, Sheila Ryan, 23
John, Brian, 27
John, Mary, 115
Johnson, Barbara, 108
Johnston, Jennifer, 55, 56–58, 59–60, 85
Joke Goes a Long Way in the Country, A (Hopkins), 13
Jones, Marie, 85, 86, 90, 91, 92
Jordan, Neil, 83
Josie (fict.), 86–87
Joyce, James, 1, 11, 21, 126, 127, 129
Joyriders (Reid), 86
"June 23rd" (J. Kennedy), 60–61
Juries Act: of 1927, 15; of 1975, 16n. 6

Kate (fict.), 35–36
Kathleen (fict.), 56
Kavanagh, Patrick, 127
Keane, Mary Paul, 6, 12
Kearney, Richard, 68
Kelleher, Patricia, 5
Kelly, Maeve, 7, 13
Kelly, Rita, 5, 8, 40–41, 42
Kennedy, Jan, 60–61
Kennedy, Liam, 113
Kennedy, Stanislaus, 4
Kenny, Mary, 12
Keyes, Marian, xiii
Kiberd, Declan, 21, 25
Kiely, Benedict, 82
Killeen, The (Leland), 13
Kiss, The (L. Cullen), 8
Kissing the Frog (Dunlop), xiii

Kissing the Witch (Donoghue), 9
Kristeva, Julia, 105

Ladies and Gentlemen (Donoghue), 9
Landry, Donna, 106
language, 8, 10, 11, 18
"Last Confession, The" (Conlon), 43–45
"Last Infirmity, The" (Burke), 48
Last of a Dyin' Race, The (Reid), 86
Last September, The (Bowen), 2
Lavelle (fict.), 37
Lavin, Mary, 28
Lawrence, Karen, xxx
Lay Up Your Ends (Lynch/Jones), 90
"Leaving" (Reilly), 75–77
Leavis, Q. D., xxx
Leland, Mary, 13
Lentin, Ronit, 4, 6, 12
lesbian writing, 8–12, 41–42
"Letter, The" (Conlon), 40
Levine, June, 12
Levy, Bronwen, 109
Liberation of Margaret McCabe, The (Brophy), 8, 32–33, 60
Lies of Silence (Moore), 82
Life of Her Own, A (M. Kelly), 13
Lingard, Joan, 58
literature: connections to life, 46–48; contemplation of identity and, xi; feminist realism, 119–20; male literary tradition, 122–30; as means of expression on societal mores, 32; realism as ideology of, 118; reflect/interaction with ideology, xxvii; role in construction of nationalist mythology/identity, xxiv; significance of social function of, 117; as site of articulation of women's issues, xi; subjugation of women through, 19–21
"Little Madonna, The" (Boylan), 40
Llewelyn, Morgan, 8
Lloyd, David, 25, 126
Lola Comes Home (Cullimore), xiii
Long Kesh prison, 64, 66–67n. 4, 68
Long March, The (A. Devlin), 86

Lorcan Burke (fict.), 37
"Losing" (K. O'Brien), 28
Louise (fict.), 46–47
loyalism, 93, 98, 100
Lucy Sullivan Is Getting Married (Keyes), xiii
Luddy, Maria, xxxiii
Lyn (Levine/L. Madden), 12
Lynch, Martin, 90

MacBride, Maud Gonne, 23
MacCurtain, Margaret, xi, xxxiii, 4, 24
MacLaverty, Bernard, 82
MacLean, Gerald, 106
Mad and Bad Fairies: Fairytales for Feminists, 7
Mad Cyclist (Bardwell), 37–38
Madden, Deirdre, 75, 83, 84, 117
Madden, Lyn, 12
Madden-Simpson, Janet, 4, 122, 128
"Made in Heaven" (Treacy), 28
madness as escape, 38, 39, 40, 84
Maher, Mary, 7, 8
male literary tradition, 122–30
Manning, Kitty, 58
Marcus, Philip, 27
Margaret McCabe (fict.), 32–33
marital entrapment, 39, 55
Markievicz, Constance, 23, 26–27
Martha (fict.), 29–32, 51, 60–61
Martin, Janet, 4
Martina (fict.), 48–49
Mary (fict.), 36–37, 51
Matthews, Aiden, 117
Maxwell, D. E. S., 68
McAliskey, Bernadette Devlin, 69
McCabe, Patrick, 117
McCafferty, Nell, xxii
McCann, Eamonn, 68, 69
McDonough, Roisin, 71
McEnaney, Frances, 55
McFadyean, Melanie, 71
McKenna, Jill, 73–75
McManus, Liz, 40
McNeill, Janet, 4
McWilliams, Monica, xxiii
Meadbh Publishing, 52–53
Me and My Friend (Plowman), 90

Meaney, Gerardine, 112
men: decentering of, 51; father figures in
    women's literature, 10–11, 34–36, 60;
    feminization of Ireland and, 111–12;
    history centered on, xxii–xxiii; literary
    tradition of, 125–30; as narrators of
    women's stories, 43–45; portrayal of in
    Ourselves Alone, 87
"Mending Wall" (Frost), 81
Methven, Eleanor, 91
Michael Feeny (fict.), 61–62
"Midland Jihad" (McManus), 40
"Midwife to the Fairies" (Ní Dhuibhne),
    40
Minh-ha, Trinh T., 109
Missing Pieces: Women in Irish History, 5
Mitchell, Julie, 58
Mitchison, Amanda, 100
Modern Ireland (Foster), 110n. 1
modernist experimentalism, 1
Molloy, Frances, 55, 56, 85
Molly Bloom (fict.), 11
Moore, Brian, 82
Moore, Carole, 91
Moore, Ruth, 98
More Missing Pieces, 6
mother figures, 27–34, 36–37, 43–45, 60,
    75–77
"Moving" (Slattery), 39
Mrs. Mahon (fict.), 29–32
Mr. Wall (fict.), 10–11
Ms. Muffet and Others: Fairytales for Feminists,
    7
Mullarney, Máire, 4
Mullen, Molly, 18
Murphy, Brenda, 71–73
Murphy, Cliona, xxxiii
Murphy, Pat, xxii
Murray, Melissa, 40
"My Head Is Opening" (Conlon), 40,
    46–47
mythology, 8. *See also* nationalist
    mythology

"Naming the Names" (A. Devlin), 83
Nandy, Ashis, 112

national identity: affect on creative
production, 14; alliance of Catholic
Church/state and, xxiv; capitalism and
print technology and, 50; concept in
women's writing/politics, xxiii;
construction of, xxiv; cultural
imperialism and, 109; drama produced
by women concerning, 85–86;
feminization of Ireland and, 19;
gender and, 44–45, 50; influx of
refugees and, 70n. 5; interrogation of
fixed notions, 21; Irish feminism and,
108, 131; literature and, xi, 1; myth of
in Northern Ireland, 66–67;
postcolonial attempts at redefinition,
19, 66, 131; realistic re/presentation
of, 132; reexploitation of, xii–xiii; as
theme of women's literature, 38–39;
women's rejection of, 2–3
nationalism: development of feminism in
Northern Ireland and, 63–65; feminist
discourses and, 114, 132; feminization
of Ireland and, 111–12; formulation of
history and, 112–13; Irish feminism
and, xxviii–xxix, xxxii–xxxiii, 107–8;
as mobilizing ideology, 104;
subversion of issues of gender/class,
xxvii; unionism and, 94–95; views of
in Southern/Northern Ireland, 69–70
nationalist mythology: affect on creative
production, 14; alternative to, 21–22;
construction of, xxiv, 18–21; cultural
identity and, 1; debunking of, 51;
feminist struggle and, xxii–xxiii,
26–28, 131; incorporation of women,
23; in Northern Ireland, 65–73;
reexploitation of, xii–xiii; revisionism
and, 112–13; struggle of Gaels, 67–68;
women's writings' engagement with,
50–51, 56–57, 88, 93; Yeat's
contribution to, 18–19, 21–22
New Perspective, The (Price), 13, 117
Ní Chuilleanáin, Eiléan, 4, 17
NICRA, 68–69
Ní Dhuibhne, Éilís, 6, 8, 40
Night in November, A (Jones), 86n. 6
"Night Rider" (Bardwell), 38–39

Niland, Geraldine, 4
No Mate for the Magpie (Molloy), 56
No Regrets (Bardwell), 38
Northern Ireland: binary basis of politics
in, 54n. 1; construction of nationalist
mythology/identity, xxiv; cultural
imperialism in, 109; ideological
obscuring of issues, 79–80; influence
of women writers in, xxiii;
interpretation of revisionism/
postcolonialism dispute in, 111;
nature of women's writings in, xxiii,
xxiv–xxv; Republic's view of, 70–71;
sectarian divisions in, 68–69;
thematic emphasis, 131–32; view
of nationalism in, 69–70; women
activists in, 71; women's groups in,
100–101
Northern Ireland Civil Rights Association
(NICRA), 68–69
Northern Ireland Women's Movement,
65
Notions (Flitton), 13
Now You're Talkin' (Jones), 91

O'Brien, Edna, 1, 28, 42, 129
O'Brien, Flann, 127
O'Brien, Kate Cruise, 4, 28
O'Carroll, Harriett, 40
O'Casey, Sean, 19, 29, 129
O'Connor, Barbara, 118
O'Connor, Clairr, 35, 60, 61
ó Corráin, Donncha, 4
O'Donoghue, Noreen, 6
O'Dowd, Liam, 24, 66, 94
O'Dowd, Mary, xxxiii
O'Faolain, Julia, 1, 28, 122–23, 124–25n.
6
O'Faolain, Sean, 127
O'Flanagan, Sheila, xiii
Old Jest, The (Johnston), 57
O'Malley, Padraig, 94–95
ó Murchadha, Felix, 69–70
O'Neill, Joan, 13
"On the Inside of Cars" (Conlon), 46
O' Rourke, Rebecca, xxx

Oul Delf and False Teeth (Jones), 91
Ourselves Alone (A. Devlin), 86–88
Out for Ourselves: The Lives of Irish Lesbians and Gay Men, 6
Out-Haul, The (Hopkins), 13
Outlines: We Are Michael Field (Donoghue), 9
"Outpatients" (Bardwell), 39
Owens, Rosemary Cullen, xxxiii, 6

Paisley, Ian, 95, 97–98
Paisley, Rhonda, 98
Paley, Grace, 13–14
Palmer, Paulina, 103
"Palm House, The" (Bork), 58
parental control, 60–62
"Park, The" (Conlon), 45
"Park Going Days" (Conlon), 45–46
Parnell, Anna, 26
"Particular Calling, A" (Boylan), 42–43
partition, 26, 70–71, 95
Passages series, 55
Passions between Women: British Lesbian Culture, 1668-1801 (Donoghue), 9
paternalism, 109
Patricia Higgins (fict.), 42–43
Patrick Gallagher (fict.), 38–39
Patriot Games (Clancy), 82
Patten, Eve, 123
Pauline (fict.), 33
Pearce, Patrick, 66, 67–68, 88, 112
Pen (fict.), 11
Penley, Constance, 105
People and the Poor Law in Nineteenth-Century Ireland, The (Burke), 5
Plowman, Gillian, 90
Plummer, Ken, xiv
politics: absence of unionist women writers, 92–101; agenda of women's writings and, xi–xii; as Charabanc Theatre theme, 90; contemporary feminism and, 103–5; discussions of marginalization of Irish writers, 115; enabling nature of realism in, 121–22; as enemy of women's movement, 50; feminism as, xix; influence on women's

writing, xxiii; links to Irish writings, 1; polarization of, xxvii, 68–69; reflection of in women's writings, xxiii, 56–59; subversion of gender/class issues by, xxvii, 69, 80–81; view of women in, 23–25; women activists and, 71, 83; women in, 24, 25, 122; women on housing issues, 73–82; women's critiques of, xiv–xv, 7, 27; women writers of Northern Ireland on, xviii–xxii, 50, 63–65, 85–92. *See also specific ideology*
politics of difference framework, 115–16
Pollock, Ellen, 77–80
Poolbeg, xix
popular culture studies, xxx–xxxi
Portable Virgin, The (Enright), 13
postcolonialism: effect on feminist debate in Ireland, xxvi, 114; merging of minority/nonwhite, xxxiii; nonhegemonic Irish women writers and, 108–15; revisionism and, 110–13
postmodernism, xxxiii, 104
poststructuralism, xxxi, 104–7
Price, K. Arnold, 13, 117
Prone, Terry, 4, 5
protagonists: interrogation of hegemonic ideologies, xv; reader identification with, 120–21; women's use of central female, xxv; of women's writings of Northern Ireland, 63, 80–81, 83–84, 89, 93, 133; of women's writings of the Republic of Ireland, 29, 32–33, 35–37, 133
Protestantism, xxiv, 94–100
Proxopera (Kiely), 82
publishing: effect of political division among feminist groups, 65; increases in opportunities, 2; by Irish feminists, 3–7; in Northern Ireland, 52–55, 53–55; second wave of women's movement and, xv; shifts in after 1995, xix, 134; of women's works in Ireland/New Zealand, xv–xviii
Purcell, Deirdre, 12–13
Pure Murder: A Book about Drug Use (O'Donoghue/Richardson), 6

Queer Views, 7
"Quest, The" (Bardwell), 40

Rajan, Rajeswari, 104–5, 107, 119–20,
    121
Rapunzel's Revenge: Fairytales for Feminists, 6, 7
Real and Imagined Women (Rajan), 104–5
Real Charlotte, The (Somerville/Ross), 2
realism: as choice of Irish women writers,
    xxv, xxix–xxx, 116–24, 128–30, 133;
    complicity with patriarchal systems,
    116–17; criticisms of, 122–24; as main
    stream of literature, 1; political
    enablement of, 121;
    popularity/longevity of, 119; as tool of
    ideology of literature, 118
Reid, Christina, 85, 86, 88–89, 92, 97
Reilly, Anne-Marie, 75–77
Relatives Action Committee, 71
religion: Conlon's interest in, 14; Daly's
    critique of, 33–34; divisions in
    Northern Ireland and, 54n. 1; as
    theme of women's literature, 3, 37–39,
    41–45, 50, 51; troubles in Northern
    Ireland and, 68–69. See also Catholic
    Church; Protestantism
Remembering Light and Stone (D. Madden),
    117
Renan, Ernest, 111
"Reprisal, The" (McKenna), 73–75
Republic of Ireland: alliance with
    Catholic Church, xxiii, xxiv, 14–17;
    cultural imperialism in, 109;
    establishment of national identity,
    14–21; interpretation of
    revisionism/postcolonialism dispute
    in, 110–11; national identity in, 66;
    nature of women's writings in,
    xxiv–xxv; oppression of women in, 50;
    production of drama in, 85; revision of
    image of women, 131; separation of
    church and state, 2; view of
    nationalism in, 69; view of Northern
    Ireland, 70–71; women's groups in,
    100–101
revisionism, xviii, xxvi, 27, 110–14

Richards, Maura, 41–42
Richards, Shaun, 19–20, 66–67
Richardson, Sue, 6
Ride on Rapunzel: Fairytales for Feminists, 7
"Rita" (M. R. Callaghan), 42
Robert (fict.), 48–49
Robinson, Lilian, 127
Rockett, Kevin, 112–13
Róisín, Conroy, 5, 6
Rolston, Bill, 82
Rosaleen (fict.), 84
Rose, Catherine, 4
Rose McCusker (fict.), 77–79
Ross, Martin, 2
Rowbotham, Sheila, 23, 111–12
Russell, Sue, 7
Ryan, Mary, 13

Sands, Bobby, 66–67, 68, 88
Sands, Maggie, 61–62
Sarah (fict.), 88–89
Scattering of Mrs. Blake and Related Matters,
    The (Prone), 5
"Scene Around Six" (Pollock), 77–80
Scenes from a Country Wedding (Treacy), 13
"Season for Mothers, A" (Burke), 29–32
Season of Weddings, A (Levine), 12
sectarianism, 56–59, 68–69, 71, 90,
    91–93
Segal, Lynne, 106
Selected Poems (Boland), 5
sexual morality, 15–16, 97–98
Seymour, Gerald, 82
Shadow of Gulls, A (Finney), 8
Shadows on Our Skin (Johnston), 56, 57–58
"Shepherd's Bush" (Binchy), 40
Sheridan, F. D., 12–13
siege myths, 95–96
Singled Out: Single Mothers in Ireland, 5
Singular Attraction, A (Daly), 32, 33–34, 60
Sinn Féin, 23, 100
Sisters (Levine), 12
Sixpence in Her Shoe (Treacy), 13
Skeffington, Hanna Sheehy, 23, 26
Slattery, Catherine, 39
Sloan, Barry, 96

Smyth, Ailbhe, xxii, xxxiii, 7, 107
Snitow, Ann, 120
Socialist Women's Group, 65
Somerville, Edith, 2
Somewhere Over the Balcony (Jones), 91, 92
Sound of Anthems, The (Alyn), 58
"Space Invaders" (Murray), 40
Speed, Anne, xxviii
Speers, Neill, 90
Spivak, Gayatri Chakravorty, xxv, 108, 109
"Spring Cleaning" (Fean), 39–40
Stella (fict.), 56
stereotypes. *See* national identity
Stick Wife, The (Cloud), 90
Stir Fry (Donoghue), 9
Stones in His Pocket (Jones), 86n. 6
"Stopping by Woods" (Frost), 81
Stories by Contemporary Irish Women (Casey/Casey), xiii
Strong, Eithne, 6, 42
suffrage, 22–28, 73
suicide as escape, 39, 40, 81
Sunday Afternoons (Mitchell), 58
Surviving Sexual Abuse, 7
Sweeping Beauties: Fairytales for Feminists, 7
Synge, John M., 19, 129

Tain Bo Cuailgne (O'Grady), 27
Taking Scarlet as a Real Color (Conlon), 47
Tannehill, Ann, 53
Taylor, Alice, 13
Taylor, David, 96
Tea in a China Cup (Reid), 86, 88–89
"Technical Difficulties and the Plague" (Boylan), 40
Tell Them Everything: A Sojourn in the Prison of Her Majesty Queen Elizabeth II at Ard Macha (D'Arcy), 64
Territories of the Voice (De Salvo et al.), xiii, 72
Theresa Cassidy (fict.), 84
There We Have Been (Bardwell), 39
" 'This Novel Changes Lives': Are Women's Novels Feminist Novels?" (Coward), 124

thrillers, 8, 82–85
Timothy Sorohan (fict.), 47
Todd, Janet, 105–6
Toibin, Colm, 117–18
"Torture Mill-H Block, The" (B. Sands), 67
To Stay Alive (Anderson), 83, 84, 93
tradition, as instrument of present, 65
training courses, 5–6
Treacy, Maura, 13, 28
Treaty (1921), 16
Troubles, the: catalyst of, 73; as central theme of thrillers, 83–85; as context of Northern women's writing, 63, 92; criticism of Northern women's poetry and, 54; independence struggle and, 66–67; as part of unfinished revolution, 68; reenforcement of traditional family networks, 100; women's shaping of political material during, 71
"Trousseau" (R. Kelly), 42
Tuohy, Frank, 1–2

Ulysses (Joyce), 11, 126
"Under Control" (Beckett), 56
unionism: feminism and, 97–98, 133; lack of women writers, xxiv, 92–101; siege mentality of, 94–96; women's role in, 75
Unveiling Treasures (Weekes), xvii
Urquhart, Diane, xxxiii

Valéra, Éamon de, 14–15, 16, 19

Walker, Mary, 37
"Wall Reader, The" (Barr), 80–82, 83
"Wall Reader" and Other Stories, The, 4
Walshe, Dolores, 12–13
Ward, Margaret, xxii, xxxii–xxxiii, 24, 70, 113
Watermelon (Keyes), xiii
WCP. *See* Women's Community Press
WEB. *See* Women's Education Bureau

Weddins, Weeins, and Wakes (Jones), 91,
    92
Weedon, Chris, xxviii
Weekes, Ann Owens, xv, 60
Whelehan, Imelda, xxi–xxii
"Whispering Arch" and Other Stories, The
    (R. Kelly), 5
Whispers in the Wind (Ryan), 13
Who Owns Ireland, Who Owns You?
    (Owens), 6
Who's Minding the Children? (Lentin/Niland),
    4, 12
Whyte, J. H., 15
Wife, a Dog and a Maple Tree, A
    (Moore/Ashby), 91
Willis, Clair, xxxiii, 19
Wilson, Elizabeth, 102–3, 106
Woman Calling, A (A. Devlin), 86
Woman's Part: An Anthology of Short Fiction by
    and about Irishwomen, 1890-1960
    (Madden-Simpson), 4, 122, 128
women: accepted role of in Ireland, xxiv;
    dominant perception of, 23–25;
    effects of unification of Church/state
    on, 14–16; feminization of Ireland
    and, 111–13; formulations of history
    excluding, 112–14; images of in male
    literary tradition, 129; Irish image of,
    xxix, 26–28; marginalization of, 1, 19,
    115–16; mother figures in women's
    literature, 27–34, 36–37, 43, 60,
    75–78; in politics, 24, 25, 71, 83, 122;
    portrayal of by women of Northern
    Ireland, 77–78, 86–89; postcolonial
    legal limitations on, 15–18; Protestant
    view of role of, 97–98; realism as
    representative of, 120; reality for in
    Ireland, 20–21; revision of Irish image
    of, xviii, xxii, 3, 4–5, 26, 28–32, 131,
    133; role in thrillers, 82
Women Against Imperialism, 64
Women in Irish Society: The Historical
    Dimension (MacCurtain/Corráin), 4
Women on the Verge of HRT (Jones), 86n. 6
Women's Community Press (WCP), 3,
    6
Women's Education Bureau (WEB), 3, 5

women's groups, 100–101
women's movement: appearance of in
    Northern Ireland, 63; effects of
    second wave of, xi–xii, xv–xvii, xx,
    xxii, 133; facilitation of radicalism,
    xviii–xxii; feminism and, xiv, xix;
    founders of Irish organization, 12; as
    interpretive community for women's
    literature, xiv; Irish image of women
    and, 26–28; nationalist politics and,
    23–28; rise of women's groups and,
    100–101; suffrage in Ireland and,
    22–28; women's publishing as central
    component of, 3–4. See also feminism
Women's News, 53
women's presses, xvi, 2, 3–7, 50, 52–55
women's rights, 16–21, 22–28, 39
women's studies programs, 52–53
women writers of Ireland. See Irish women
    writers; women writers of Northern
    Ireland; women writers of the
    Republic of Ireland
women writers of New Zealand, xv–xvi
women writers of Northern Ireland: age
    of at first publication, 55, 57, 59;
    approach of, 131–32; context of works
    of, 63–65; drama production by,
    85–92; genre of, 82–92; major
    achievement of, 132–33; negotiation
    of line between art/politics and
    nationalism/gender, 71–73; occlusion
    of, 53–55, 82; portrayal of political
    divisions, 56–59; protagonists of
    stories of, 63, 80–81, 83–84, 89, 93,
    133; survey of writings, 55–63; themes
    of, 55–61, 73–82; thrillers and, 82–85;
    volume of works, 54–55; vs. women
    writers of the Republic of Ireland,
    xxiv–xxvii, 53–54, 60, 101, 133.
    See also Irish women writers; specific
    author
women writers of the Republic of Ireland:
    approach of, 28–29, 40, 131; Big
    House tradition, 1–2; challenge to
    political ideologies, 28–51, 132;
    challenge to women's image in Ireland,
    2–3, 28–51; changes in society

affecting, 2; drama production by, 85;
focus of, 3; freedom of, 2; genres of,
7–14; implied audience of, 10; interest
in international feminism, 13–14;
major achievement of, 50–51, 132;
political factors affecting, 14;
protagonists of stories of, 63; suffrage
and, 22–28; themes of, 38–50, 56,
72–82; use of existing traditions, 53;
use of language, 8, 10, 11, 18; women's
liberation movement and, 12–13;
women's presses and, 3–7; vs. women
writers of Northern Ireland,
xxiv–xxvii, 53–54, 60, 101, 133. *See
also* Irish women writers; *specific author*
Woods, Una, 83–84
Write Up Your Street, 6

Yeats, W. B.: assumption of Gregory's
plays, 26; characters of Irish heroism,
27; feminine characters of, 129;
greatness of, 126; principle of
continuity, 65; view of Ireland, 18–19,
21–22
Yuval-Davis, Nira, 108